W9-BKA-141

DATE DUE

DEALS
OF THE
CENTURY

DEALS
OF THE
CENTURY

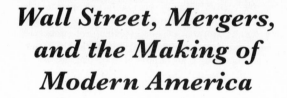

Wall Street, Mergers,
and the Making of
Modern America

CHARLES R. GEISST

WILEY

John Wiley & Sons, Inc.

Published by John Wiley & Sons, Inc., Hoboken, New Jersey
Published simultaneously in Canada

For general information on our other products and services, or technical support, please contact our Customer Care Department within the United States at 800-762-2974, outside the United States at 317-572-3993 or fax 317-572-4002.

Library of Congress Cataloging-in-Publication Data:
Geisst, Charles R.
   Deals of the century : Wall Street, mergers, and the making of modern America / Charles R. Geisst.
      p.   cm.
Includes bibliographical references.
ISBN 0-471-26397-4 (CLOTH)
1. Consolidation and merger of corporations—United States.   2. Consolidation and merger of corporations—Finance.   I. Title.
HG4023.M4G45   2004
338.8'3 0973—dc21   2003008868
Printed in the United States of America

10 9 8 7 6 5 4 3 2 1

For Meg

CONTENTS

INTRODUCTION

At the turn of the twentieth century, a New York writer
summed up a Wall Street deal that many thought marked the
twilight of capitalism. "The world, on the 3rd day of March
1901, ceased to be ruled by so-called statesmen," he wrote. They had
been replaced by the moneymen of Wall Street, the "world's real
rulers," who had helped fashion the largest merger deal ever
recorded. Wall Street struck its richest payday ever and the world
indeed changed.

Since that time, mergers and acquisitions (M&A) has been a specialty that many securities houses and banks view enviously. Many
would like to be in the business, but few actually achieve success in
this area. There is a reason for this envy, and its roots extend far
beyond the confines of Broad and Wall Streets. This esoteric side of
the securities business has been the major architect in changing the
face of American industry and society. The giant corporations that
emerged in the early twentieth century owe their origins to Wall
Street, the place where capital and business meet. Practitioners of
the M&A art have the unique distinction of being highly paid social
architects who can have more impact than a truckload of politicians,
academics, and social theorists. And yet very few members of the

public can name any of them. This has not always been the case, however.

The M&A business is as old as American industry, having gotten its start before the Civil War as companies in similar lines of business began to merge. During the 1880s and 1890s, the giant trusts were formed as strong companies often absorbed smaller, less powerful competitors to become modern corporations. But only with the dawn of the twentieth century did M&A gain serious momentum as influential Wall Street bankers became more heavily involved in the process. Some, like John Pierpont Morgan, the creator of U.S. Steel and a host of other huge companies, used their considerable influence to fashion mergers and maintain control over their creations by holding seats on the boards of the companies they created. Occasionally, others—like Clarence Dillon, the formative deal maker behind the Chrysler Corporation—actually tried running the businesses they created, with less success. In either case, most made sizable fortunes from their efforts, continuing the tradition of what was known as *finance capitalism*.

The term was originally used by socialist writers and critics to describe the role of financiers in the M&A process. According to the socialists, mergers were put together simply to benefit the bankers, who used other people's money to deal themselves into newly formed companies. Once in, they could then exercise control out of all proportion to their importance. Wall Street bankers had been exercising that sort of power for decades, but it was Morgan who was the epitome of the wheeling-and-dealing banker with his hands on the controls of money and credit. V. I. Lenin recognized Morgan's role at the center of American finance, although there sometimes was a strange awe in the manner in which he discussed the banker. Lenin had in mind Marx's idea about the redistribution of wealth, but it was Morgan who best practiced it. Unfortunately, wealth and power were not accruing to the people but only to those who sat at the pinnacle of Wall Street power.

What some critics found so insidious about Wall Street was that finance capital appeared to have taken precedence over entrepreneurs and innovators. Everyone knew that Thomas Edison had created the lightbulb and that Cyrus McCormick had invented the reaper and that both inventions had helped change society. But the changes had come under the auspices of Wall Street bankers who had financed the companies rather than the leadership of the inventors, who often were bewildered or just bored by finance itself. The key to the bankers' success was access to the large sums of capital necessary to help the companies expand. Since the capital depended upon a small group of financiers, the entire process smacked of crony capitalism. Money needed for expansion was concentrated in the hands of a few who were neither elected to their jobs nor accountable to anyone for the way they practiced them.

Since the middle of the nineteenth century, concentration of capital has been key to the merger movement. More than any other Wall Street activity, with the exception of corporate securities underwriting, concentration of capital is understood as a measure of an investment bank's prowess and influence in the market. Over the past 50 years, access to large amounts of capital and the ability to reorganize a company usually have been associated with the larger securities firms and banks. When smaller firms unknown outside of Wall Street exercise their prowess, it only adds to the general suspicion that crony capitalism is still rampant despite the bevy of banking and securities laws passed since the 1930s. How could a small investment bank have helped organize huge conglomerates in the 1960s? How could a few men unknown outside Wall Street have had so much power over American workers and the products they made? Lenin's answer to these questions would have been the same as that of the average person in the street—crony capitalism.

The M&A process is so pervasive in American life that probably most medium- and large-size companies have been affected by it at some time in their corporate histories. And for every notable deal there have been dozens of others that never made the press. The deals included here necessarily are confined to the largest, with the longest legs. They either helped shape an industry for a long period of time or were of such size that they cannot be ignored. Some clearly were not successful; in fact, there is considerable opinion that most did not accomplish their objectives but did nevertheless benefit bankers and executives. What is clear about the trend, however, is that it relies heavily upon a strong stock market and the small investor for its impetus. Without these two factors, the M&A train quickly becomes derailed because inflated stock prices, used to finance many acquisitions, are not present. In all merger binges—whether in the 1920s, 1960s, or 1990s—the market was necessary to bid up prices. Strong stock prices meant that companies could use their stock as currency, paying high premiums for their acquisitions, sometimes even surprising Wall Street by the amounts. When the urge to merge struck buying companies, no price was too high for a company they just had to have. The phenomenon is not new. In 1931, *The Magazine of Wall Street* remarked, "It is a peculiar fact that past history clearly shows that the merger movement is very much stimulated by good times, particularly a bull market in stocks, while there is a marked tendency for consolidations to decrease in number under the reverse conditions when one would think economy were most needed."

The history of deal making reveals two interesting themes repeated time and again over the past century. The first tends to agree with Lenin and critics of consolidation, especially when the only apparent beneficiaries are company executives and their bankers. The structure of investment banking in this specialty is unusually oligarchic, even by Wall Street standards. Deals are done by the influential and the powerful, often with far-reaching results in both finance and the society beyond. This oligarchic nature has been evident since the first significant deal of the century in 1901 and remains so today despite the fact that the business world has grown larger and securities firms have multiplied in number. The oil and airline industries in the 1970s and 1980s were severely shaken by several key figures and their bankers—to the point where it was legitimate to ask exactly who these people were and how they got to exercise so much influence over vital industries.

The other theme deals with an equally entrepreneurial part of human nature. In 1878, a group of clever businessmen built a railroad designed to link Chicago with the East Coast. The route was currently served by a line owned by William Vanderbilt, the son of "Commodore" Cornelius Vanderbilt. Afraid that the competition would cut into his profits, Vanderbilt begrudgingly bought out the Nickel Plate Railroad at a heavy price. Competition was thought to be ruinous in the nineteenth century, so buying out a competitor was seen as a necessary expense of doing business. It would not be the last time the practice was attempted successfully against Vanderbilt. The Nickel Plate strategy became a clever way of making money, especially in a boom market. The major company in the field had to be convinced that buying out the competition was cheaper than living with it. Soon, no shortage of "competitors" appeared in all sorts of industries.

Another significant piece of the M&A puzzle can be found in the widely used term *synergy*. The concept became popular in the 1960s as a means of describing the magic Wall Street and corporate America claim occurs when a suitable merger between two companies maximizes future value. Wags in the nineteenth century referred to the idea as alchemy. In nontechnical terms, synergy means that the new, combined entity is greater than the sum of its parts. More precisely, it means that synergy is equal to the value of a new, merged company plus the premium paid to create it by buying the acquired company. In the first significant deal in merger history, Pierpont Morgan brought the newly formed U.S. Steel to market for $1.4 billion in new stock. The premium over its asset value at the time was $700 million. The amount was astonishing at the time and many commentators could not fully grasp the amounts involved. The term *synergy* was not known, but another, more colorful term—*watered stock*—was used to describe expensive stock valued well above its asset value. In order for the U.S. Steel deal to work over the long run, it would have to produce profits that would justify its high premium. When it became clear that the profits were not what had originally been expected, Morgan turned to political pressures to keep steel in demand by advocating a strong navy to keep the peace. Ironically, he did not see the newfangled automobile as producing enough demand for steel and ignored Detroit in its early years. The influence of M&A was extending far beyond the confines of Wall Street, even with the first significant deal of the century. The U.S. Steel deal was only the most recent example of the close connection between finance and politics.

Almost a hundred years later, the premium Morgan paid for U.S. Steel would pale in comparison to the hefty premiums paid by aggressive suitors using M&A to add to their companies' infrastructures and operating capacities. In the 1990s, keenly aware that time was of the essence, many high-technology companies discarded all standard valuation techniques and began paying prices based upon multiples of sales or potential sales for acquisitions with little more to recommend themselves than an idea. By discarding traditional valuation techniques, they acknowledged that synergy had finally come of age. But the stock market bubble of the late 1990s could not be sustained because its traditional supporters—small investors—began to abandon the market as the excesses of the merger trend became clear. Synergy needed robust market support in order to succeed. When that evaporated, so too did the merger trend.

Since the late nineteenth century, Progressives had been criticizing large corporations for their negative effects on American life. Dozens of books and studies appeared indicating that American corporate wealth was more concentrated and inequitable than appeared on the surface. There obviously was a difference between a company's public relations and its true nature. Consolidated industries were destroying competition and the American sense of fair play by swallowing smaller competitors. Wall Street bankers grew rich off the trend, helping create large companies simply to reap fat investment banking fees while disregarding the implications for society at large. The lament was as old as the merger trend itself, but in the 1920s it began to assume a greater degree of credibility than ever before.

After World War I, modern American consumers appeared on the scene and catering to them became the main strategy of business. The automobile industry had also developed quickly and was revolutionizing modern life. Ironically, these two great forces of change in American life were viewed as highly pedestrian by influential New York bankers, at least in their formative years. Pierpont Morgan considered the automobile nothing more than a fad, like the bicycle, that would eventually pass into oblivion. Equally, the notion that people could shop in large department stores carrying many sorts of items was totally lost on bankers who were not in the habit of shopping for themselves. As a result, M&A bankers did not actively participate in financing many of these new ventures. That lack of faith opened the door for a new generation of small investment bankers only too happy to provide financing where their better-bred colleagues deigned not to tread.

The 1930s proved to be a watershed for Wall Street in more than one respect. Finance capitalism came to the forefront more than at any other time since the early days of the century. The empires of J.P. Morgan & Co., Kuhn Loeb, Dillon Read, and Lehman Brothers elicited criticism from many quarters. Populist agrarians in Congress thought these firms to be part of an international banking conspiracy destined to enslave the farmer and average citizen. Others saw them as a genuine threat to American democracy, agents of the corporate state that was growing in Europe. Their detractors feared that their influence was the back door to fascism without the accompanying European ideology.

By 1950, the social and political climate had changed markedly. Mergers again began transforming the American social and economic landscape. Although thousands of mergers had been accomplished since the beginning of the century, the effects of the largest could still be clearly felt. U.S. Steel was still the largest company in its industry, while International Harvester, General Motors, Commonwealth Edison, and AT&T retained dominant positions, much as they had before World War I. Technology and a growing population would help many fledgling industries break new ground, and Wall Street was quick to sign them up as companies that would propel the economy through the second half of the century.

Merger bankers became power brokers to companies whose grasp was international. Originally, many of the huge companies formed by Morgan in the earlier part of the century were mainly domestic. After World War II, corporations spread their tentacles much wider as American overseas investment expanded dramatically. Several became emblematic of American corporate power abroad. By dint of their size and economic muscle, they also became symbols of arrogance, interventionism, and self-aggrandizement.

Rather than employ gunboat diplomacy to foster its aims, the United States was now spreading its influence through multinational companies, many of which were stronger than their host countries.

The conglomerates developed during the 1950s and 1960s were actually older companies that became shell vehicles for a new type of expansion. Enterprising conglomerators used them as holding companies, which would then begin buying up others in what eventually became a frenzy of acquisition. Like the raiders, the conglomerators were as different from each other as could be imagined. What they shared in common was their belief that growth could best be achieved by buying profitable companies, adding them to the holding company stable, and watching the stock price rise rapidly as a result. Yet for all of the publicity attached to the mergers craze building in the 1960s, it was notable that the total number of mergers occurring in 1963 was still less than the number consummated during the heyday of the McKinley administration in 1898.

Despite their fame and fortune in the 1960s, none of the conglomerates were ever included in the Dow Jones Industrial Average, a measure of success for the largest corporations. Their flamboyant success and buccaneer tactics made them the nouveau riche of corporate America, causing a reaction in traditional executive suites around the country. Their investment bankers recognized the reaction and kept their heads down for fear of offending their old-line clients. And fear of conglomerate power eventually led to a congressional investigation. The hearings, which began in the summer of 1969, set off a string of adverse publicity for conglomerates even before the conglomerates' political problems surfaced. The top conglomerates and their chief executives were called to testify, reminiscent of hearings almost four decades earlier after the stock market crash of 1929. Conglomerators were called to testify about their organizations, as were their investment bankers. Although the hearings were a corporate affair, bankers played a central role in forming the corporation and found themselves front and center.

At the same time, high real rates of interest took hold and became part and parcel of the financial markets. Borrowing became more respectable as a result, and the amount of debt accumulated in the late 1970s and 1980s seemed to prove recently constructed academic theories about capital structure and portfolio diversification. Investors apparently did not worry about the amount of debt companies piled onto their balance sheets as long as their prospects seemed bright. Once-esoteric Wall Street practices came out of the closet and became new buzzwords. They all included heavy borrowing. Junk bonds, management buyouts, and leveraged buyouts (LBOs) all became accepted in corporate suites, while the public tried to figure out how a handful of executives could afford to buy out their own companies, often for billions of dollars. The traditional world of Wall Street was apparently turned upside down.

The early 1980s were primed for the merger movement to begin again after a hiatus during the later 1970s. Stock values were low and many acquisitions could be made at price/earnings (PE) multiples much lower than those of the previous decade. But values were also low for the acquiring companies, so these new financing techniques were not based on buyers issuing more stock to pay for their purchases but on borrowing money. Investing in debt from less-than-investment-grade borrowers was not practical unless the yield was high enough to compensate for the risk involved. In the case of junk bonds and LBOs, the potential compensation was high enough to entice many institutional investors to provide the necessary cash. Developing the market became the primary challenge.

The stock market collapse of October 1987 temporarily derailed the takeover trend. Deals already in progress were not as badly affected as new proposals. Within two years, deals diminished significantly. Like many other merger trends before it, the 1980s binge slowed considerably as investors were forced to the sidelines. Although the trend owed more to debt than to equity financing, it could not continue unabated in the wake of significant investor losses and the recession that followed. Many of the fears about the Decade of Greed came to fruition shortly after the market drop. The first recession experienced in eight years took its toll on corporate balance sheets, the labor market, and investor psychology. Everyone agreed that the 1980s had been a boom such as not seen for decades. Not everyone agreed that it was a good thing, however.

INTRODUCTION

Following the recession of 1991, merger activity proved that constant motion was becoming a hallmark of Wall Street. Never content to leave a stone unturned, merger specialists seized on a new series of events to further their goal of restructuring corporate America in the quest for even greater fees. A significant relaxing of antitrust actions during the Reagan and first Bush administrations left the field clear for many mergers that previously would not have been allowed. If the 1980s witnessed the siege of corporate Rome by the new tribes bent on creating new corporate values, the 1990s demonstrated that no sector of the economy was considered sacrosanct. There were no areas left unprotected from merger and consolidation.

As merger deals became larger in the 1990s, they became reflective of a trend that had begun during the Reagan administration. Fueled ideologically by the notion that government interference in business should be minimal, that administration began deregulating many enterprises that had witnessed the strong, visible hand of government since the New Deal. The argument that the marketplace could allocate resources efficiently without a set of guidelines imposed from above, with its virtues and its flaws, became the prevailing economic ideology of the decade, especially since many of the old Democratic ideas about regulation had proved messy and produced less than desirable results.

While the political debate raged over the advisability of continued deregulation, investment bankers quickly spied an opportunity to cash in on the trend. If the assumption about mergers and acquisitions being at the nexus of law and economics was correct, then that intersection would witness many traffic jams, crashes, and trips to the bank over the next decade. For the first time in the twentieth century, M&A activity was not being closely monitored and attacked by government. Now it was being tolerated as a natural part of the new economy, emerging after the inflation and high oil prices of the past subsided.

After the stock market recovered from the early 1990s recession, mergers again went on a binge not seen since the mid-1980s. In previous decades, mergers had often provoked congressional hearings. In the 1990s, the new type of corporate merger did not engender the same sorts of fear but criticisms rose to the surface nevertheless. The Clinton administration adopted a more benign attitude as long as prospective merger candidates convinced it that mergers did no harm to employment. The economic arguments for large mergers prevailed and only those that seriously were considered to undermine competition were investigated. Otherwise, the atmosphere of the 1990s was much like that of the 1980s, with the exception of a few large, well-publicized antitrust cases.

The 1990s were also the decade of the financial merger. Many of the most notable deals of the decade were among financial service companies once forbidden to operate under the same roof. Banks, investment banks, and insurance companies began merging in a frenzy to create the next financial powerhouse that would embrace all sorts of financial services under one roof. Furious activity of this sort had not been seen since the 1920s, in pre-Crash days when National City Bank and others fashioned themselves as financial department stores. In their rush to the altar, many of these companies were in direct conflict with the existing banking and securities laws, passed during the Depression, forbidding marriages between them.

An unknown factor entered the marketplace at the close of the century that changed the rules of the merger game. A new ruling by the Financial Accounting Standards Board (FASB) changed the method used for accounting for mergers, eclipsing decades of use. Even more mature, diversified international companies could not escape the new ruling. Not since the FASB changed its rules to account for overseas assets and liabilities of U.S. companies in the mid-1980s had such a potential mess hit the stock market. But one implication already was clear: Future M&A activity had to take the new rule into account because pool accounting was no longer permitted. And the notion that the problem was ephemeral because it was only an accounting technicality was no longer valid because the rule recognized that too many high prices paid for acquisitions were being ignored in the original pool accounting method, seeking to incorporate earnings immediately into the acquiring company while ignoring the goodwill problem. Goodwill was poised to usher in a bad period for the merger trend.

During the merger mania of the 1990s, deal makers on Wall Street scored their biggest victory. After thousands of deals that changed the face of many industries, finally they were able to change the structure of their own industry in the name of efficiency and improved competition. Although they were successful in the process, many questions began to be raised about the efficacy and intent of the changes. Were the deck chairs rearranged simply to charge more fees or would they prove to give a better view of the landscape?

The lateness of the trend in financial services attested to the importance that regulators attributed to the sector. Unlike airlines, public utilities, or oil companies, banks and savings institutions were considered to operate as a sort of public trust. Their purpose was to protect the savings of their depositors, not to assume risk that the depositors themselves would not have taken if left to their own devices. The original banking laws passed during the first year of the New Deal in 1933 recognized the principle and enshrined it in the Banking Act of 1933, universally known as the Glass-Steagall Act. The law proved remarkably resilient for over 50 years before finally being challenged on a wide front by bankers and the Fed itself. By the time it was challenged, the original intent had faded far into the background.

As financial institutions continued to merge, old criticisms began to surface about the efficacy of the mergers. The record comparing commercial banks before and after the first round of merger activity did not prove the argument, however. Most indicators that banks used to measure their success remained the same, and their operating results actually declined after many of the largest mergers. If they were successfully offering expanded services to customers at lower rates, the economies-of-scale argument employed at the time did not seem to be panning out. Many bankers argued that the drop in the stock market indices and a slowing economy made performance more difficult and that without the mergers their results would have been substantially better.

Times changed and deals got bigger and more sophisticated, but the original terms still have relevance. Unfortunately, many deals at the end of the century were in the same position. The emergence of the new accounting standard means that many deals probably will not be able to produce synergies because of the goodwill that looms over future earnings. But the emergence of a new, tougher accounting standard does not obscure the fact that many deals were done for their own sake—they produced wonderful results for the target company shareholders and executives in the deal as well as the investment bankers. Shareholders in the new company created by merger were less than thrilled, however, by many of their subsequent results. The historical record of the deals discussed here supports the conclusion that many deals were bad ideas to begin with and would not produce any decent results after being completed.

Having the twentieth century end on a note similar to that on which it began is ironic, especially in light of the securities and banking laws passed to regulate the financial system. Throughout its history, M&A has been the major game played on Wall Street: the grand chess game that dominates all others. The effects and by-products have had far-reaching consequences—more than most commentators or financiers are publicly willing to admit. Industries have been built, dismantled, and reorganized by nonelected, private-sector executives driven mostly by the profits extracted by the deal rather than any serious potential of growth for the future. Wall Street has had a profound impact on the nature of American society since the Civil War and has been able to operate in an environment remarkably free of serious restraint against mergers despite all of the banking and securities laws passed to keep it in check. After over 150 years of merger deals, M&A still clung to the new math of synergy. After the principals in a merger had been paid and the investment bankers and lawyers subtracted their fees, there might still be some value left for shareholders in the new merged company. To date, the record has not been strong in this respect.

CHAPTER 1

BUILDING THE INFRASTRUCTURE

God made the world in 4004 B.C. but it was reorganized in 1901 by James J. Hill, J. Pierpont Morgan, and John D. Rockefeller.

Life, *1902*

T he dawn of the twentieth century brought widespread prosperity in the United States. The economy recovered from a severe depression in the mid-1890s and business was growing again at a rapid pace. William McKinley was president and businessmen were welcome in the White House. Yet discontent with big business was more prevalent among working people and farmers, who saw themselves as mere pawns on the chessboard of business. The press and muckrakers provided a shadow conscience for the country through exposés of working conditions and corrupt labor practices.

The first decade of the twentieth century was characterized by strong antitrust sentiments culminating in several significant lawsuits that altered the American corporate landscape. Ironically, the century began by opening a window of opportunity that allowed several huge mergers to occur during what otherwise has become known as the Progressive Era. Once Theodore Roosevelt succeeded McKinley, a constant tug-of-war between big business and government began. Twenty years later, it was not clear who had won the struggle.

Prior to World War I, the tension between business, government, and other sectors of society did not prevent a strong drive toward mergers and acquisition. Although the Sherman Act was passed in 1890, its language was vague and did not prevent the formation of large trusts—the name first used to describe large holding company–style organizations that held the stock of many related companies, many of which were in the same business. The language of the act was purposely vague and many lawyers specializing in corporate affairs found simple ways to circumvent it. The first significant victory for the Justice Department came in 1911 when Standard Oil and American Tobacco were ordered dismantled. But in the intervening 20 years, big business emerged stronger than ever, aided by Wall Street bankers who recognized the enormous fees that could be earned by consolidating industries in the name of greater efficiencies.

At the turn of the century, Wall Street was dominated by several influential investment banking firms. Among them were Kuhn Loeb & Co., J. & S. Seligman & Co., Kidder Peabody, and Lee Higginson & Co. The most powerful by far was J.P. Morgan & Co., headed by the legendary and mercurial John Pierpont Morgan, the senior banker on the Street to whom the rest bowed in deference. Morgan learned the art of banking from his father, Junius Spencer Morgan, who spent the bulk of his banking career in London as senior partner at the firm of George Peabody & Co., which became J.S. Morgan & Co. upon Peabody's retirement in 1859. Pierpont spent some time at the firm before embarking on his own career in New York before the Civil War. By the mid-1870s, he had become a major Wall Street figure in his own right. The European influence weighed heavily on the Morgans and set the tone for American financing until 1929.

In the nineteenth century, extending into the early twentieth, investment banking was built upon carefully cultivated relationships between bankers and their clients. Europe's most powerful bankers, the Barings of London and the Rothschilds of Paris and London, dominated finance through an intricate network of relationships assiduously developed over decades of close contact with the crowned heads of Europe and their powerful ministers. The Rothschild alliance with the French crown, dating from the post-Napoleonic period, was close and paid handsome dividends. The Barings' relationship with the British crown was equally close and produced similar results, so much so that Talleyrand remarked that there were six great powers in post-Napoleonic Europe—Britain, France, Germany, Russia, Austria-Hungary, and the Barings. Against this background, the Morgans, especially Junius Spencer, learned their craft.

European banking styles also had a tangible effect on American financing in the nineteenth century. Since the United States relied heavily on foreign investment to develop its infrastructure, notably the railroads, the European bankers became central to the process of American development. The Rothschilds and Barings poured hundreds of millions into the country on behalf of their clients. The British crown was reported to be a heavy investor in the first Bank of the United States, even after the War of 1812. Many of the bonds that financed railroad expansion after the Civil War were purchased by British and continental investors, as were many municipal bonds of major cities on the East Coast. Until World War I, the United States remained heavily reliant upon foreign capital. Much of that capital was funneled into the country by Morgan after 1880 as Barings and the Rothschilds began to diminish in importance. Morgan continued in the grand tradition as banker to power brokers, politicos, and the newly emergent corporate ruling class in the United States. In his role as banker, he also became a consolidator of industry, a role that was a natural extension of the aggregation of capital that he already represented so well.

Between the Civil War and the end of the nineteenth century, some of the American infrastructure had already been put in place. The railroads had been laid coast to coast, the telegraph followed the rails, and the agricultural system was highly productive. Newer inventions like the telephone and electric power were showing signs of promise, although they needed large infusions of capital in order to become standardized. But the job of completing the infrastructure remained and Morgan and other bankers spied their opportunity. As long as the country remained short of capital, investment banking opportunities abounded.

By 1900, Morgan's achievements were already legendary. He formed the Edison General Electric Company from Thomas Edison's old interests and then enlarged it by merging it with the rival Thompson-Houston Electric Company to form General Electric in 1892. In the process, he defeated an effort by industrialist Henry Villard, an executive of Edison, who planned to have the company take over Thompson-Houston. After Morgan's victory, Villard and an Edison lieutenant, Samuel Insull, left the company to pursue their own ventures. Insull would appear again to do battle with the House of Morgan under Pierpont's son Jack. General Electric was known as a pioneering company, primarily for Edison's inventions and innovations, although it was actually a power producer.

Several years later, Morgan helped organize the bailout of the U.S. Treasury during the gold crisis of 1894. The operation earned him the distinction of being the unofficial central banker of the United States. Both operations brought notoriety but would come back to haunt him decades later. His activities clearly marked the high point for the age of the finance titans, but not everyone was pleased with the oligarchical links between government and Wall Street. Criticized in the press for their handling of many of these affairs, the House of Morgan and Wall Street in general would discover that antitrusters and Congress had long memories that would attribute many problems to events before and during World War I.

Before federal banking and securities laws were passed in the 1930s, American banking was a mosaic of traditional corporate banking and securities services. A client could obtain a loan, have securities issued, or merge with another company simply by whispering to his investment banker, who also was often a director of the company. Morgan and his partners practiced this form of discreet banking better than anyone else. By the turn of the century, he and his limited number of partners sat on the boards of dozens of major companies, controlling a large percentage of American corporate wealth. From that vantage point, they could see the strengths and weaknesses of American corporate structure and all of the possibilities that they provided. In the grand tradition inherited from the Europeans, the focus of their attention became companies rather than governments. The vast number of American companies competing in the marketplace meant that many were too small to survive but presented wonderful opportunities of scale. Their independent potential was limited, but when combined their possibilities were endless.

Although Wall Street helped consolidate industry, it was certainly not the brains behind business innovation, only the banker. Andrew Carnegie, Alexander Graham Bell, Thomas A. Edison, and Cyrus McCormick were the innovators in their respective industries. For sundry reasons, each was better at innovation than at finance and corporate governance and eventually allowed Morgan to replace him. While the trend toward consolidation and banker-dominated industries may have been a sign of the times, the repercussions of the growing oligopoly of financier-dominated industries set off those warning bells that reverberated for years to come. Crony capitalism Wall Street style was still in great force, although the influence of the major New York banking and securities houses did not extend west of the Hudson unless the deal makers could forge relationships with companies with national business. In the early twentieth century that was where most of the profitable business was to be found.

Brains alone did not create the large trusts around the turn of the century. A multitude of economic and political factors contributed to the growth of large corporations, often cobbled together by swallowing smaller competitors. Several equally compelling theories have been advanced to explain the rise of the trusts and consolidations. They usually have political undertones, helping to explain why, despite the trust-busting efforts of Theodore Roosevelt, trust formation continued during his administration and extended well beyond, into the administrations of Taft and Wilson as well. But when Wall Street was concerned, the underlying factors were simpler to understand. They revolved around money. Bankers who promoted and facilitated takeovers stood to profit handsomely from the fees they reaped as a result of a successful merger. Corporate officers employed a host of explanations for one company taking over another, from achieving economies of scale to integrating their various corporate functions. The bankers who assisted them had less efficient ambitions in mind. They simply eyed deals by the amount of fees that could be made from the transaction.

BUILDING THE INFRASTRUCTURE

While there is nothing new about the motives, the role bankers played in developing modern America is more complicated. When a banker and a corporate officer decided to merge two companies, there was little to stand in their way since they both stood to profit from the deal. Reasons could be found later. On the corporate side, the deals were put together by people seeking to profit from the merger rather than improve their respective businesses. While the motive cannot be faulted, the lack of looking beyond the deal often caused severe distortions for industry and society. J. P. Morgan and (later) Clarence Dillon were able financiers but were not interested in running a business, nor did they possess the expertise to do so. As a result, they are remembered for the deals themselves rather than the industries they sought to consolidate. When Morgan and his partners sought to extend their influence by expanding beyond the deals, they were often criticized for exerting political influence that came at the expense of other people's money. The businesses they created were often criticized for being less efficient than their predecessors.

Banking in the United States prior to World War I was somewhat different from the banking practiced later in the century. It was based upon cozy, informal relationships rather than simple credit evaluations and client history. Bankers granted loans and agreed to issue securities for corporate clients based upon the social and economic standing and general reputation of the client. Clients had to court bankers in order to get good terms for loans and negotiated securities deals rather than the other way around. The procedures were especially critical because the United States lacked a central bank prior to 1913 and many booms and busts in the business cycle were created by an inelastic supply of money. Without a central bank, it was difficult to add credit to or drain credit from the markets, as the case may have been. When times were particularly difficult, many companies failed because credit became too difficult to obtain and working capital became extraordinarily hard to find. If a customer was not on the best terms with a banker, then failure became a very real possibility.

Bankers similarly realized the power they wielded and used it for their own ends. In return for extending credit, many insisted upon board seats and soon came to dominate the boards. Top bankers sitting on the boards of major corporations were a matter of necessity in many cases. Bankers controlled the supply of funds and angering them was not in the client companies' best interests. The lack of a central bank created a money oligopoly at the very heart of American society, referred to as the *money trust*. After the Napoleonic wars, Barings was considered the sixth great European power. By the turn of the next century, Wall Street, and especially J.P. Morgan & Co., was the fourth, unofficial branch of government. The only problem was that the usual system of checks and balances did not apply to this unofficial branch.

The political will did not exist in the late nineteenth century to put a stop to the practice. American industry was progressing at a faster pace than savings and investment, so that when a company needed large sums of money, expediency had to be served. In 1901, when J. P. Morgan formed U.S. Steel, the new company alone represented 1.60 percent of the national wealth. Its initial capitalization represented 64 percent of the national savings for that year. Given numbers of that sort, an enormous financing was much more difficult than in later years and bankers actively had to seek foreign investors if their deals were to be successes. At the turn of the twentieth century, British investors provided about 80 percent of the total of $3.15 billion in long-term foreign investments in the United States.[1] A year later, when Morgan formed the company, over $700 million was raised from investors in the company, a sizable amount by any counting. Foreign connections were extremely important for bankers: Without them, many of the new securities offerings would never have been sold.

The money trust was not impenetrable, so it technically could not be called a monopoly. However, a concentration of capital was definitely a barrier to entry to the exclusive group. But brains also counted on Wall Street, and after World War I new firms entered the investment banking business, in a sense replicating the entry of many other new firms into many sectors of the economy. When the established money trust firms ignored new businesses such as automobiles and retailing, these new entrants were more than happy to oblige by underwriting their securities and providing short-term lines of credit by selling commercial paper. But at the turn of the century, the money trust temporarily ruled supreme. No significant mergers could be done without employing at least one of the money trust firms. Most often that meant employing the others, since many of the banks never did a deal exclusively without the aid of others.

As long as the power was applied to helping the country in times of crisis, criticism seemed inappropriate. The gold crisis of 1894 was perhaps the best example. When the gold supply of the Treasury began to run dangerously low because of the severe recession of 1893 and a loss of confidence by foreign investors, Morgan teamed with the Treasury and the Cleveland administration to stabilize Treasury reserves, ensuring that the federal government would not default on its outstanding debt. Without the services of Morgan and his ally August Belmont, default would have occurred, seriously impairing the ability of the United States to continue attracting foreign investment. Knowing how to allocate scarce resources in times of crisis was a skill the United States sorely needed. But practicing it from a self-assumed imperial vantage point was a different matter. Critics of the American ad hoc banking system became more vociferous as time passed. In the meantime, the money trust used its position to its own advantage by reshaping American industry in its own image. For the next 30 years, complaints were heard but never seriously considered, despite the establishment of the Federal Reserve in 1913. As long as the reshaping was in keeping with American dreams and aspirations, the benefits appeared to outweigh the disadvantages.

In practical terms, the move toward consolidation at the dawn of the twentieth century was made easier by a lax attitude toward antitrust for several crucial years. Although the Sherman Act was passed in 1890, a window of opportunity opened during the McKinley administration, especially after a pivotal Supreme Court decision. After the court handed down its decision in the *United States v. E.C. Knight Co.* in 1895, absolving a member of the sugar trust of restraining trade in Pennsylvania, many consolidations began and antitrust actions temporarily ceased. The window was not open long, but long enough to allow the creation of the world's largest company.

The sheer size of the deal and the audacity with which it was brought to market served notice that American business was intent on becoming a world-beater.

One common corporate notion of the times has been forgotten but explains much about the consolidation movement that was roaring at the turn of the twentieth century. Railroad baron James J. Hill said it best when he described trusts having formed "as the result of an effort to obviate ruinous competition." Many small and medium-sized companies vied for markets in the late nineteenth century and many of the larger, more successful corporate heads believed that too much competition led to economic ruin. Unlike economic theories that see competition as the engine of free markets, the corporate ideology of a hundred years ago was exactly the opposite. Competition was chaos, while consolidation meant higher profits and less internecine battling within an industry. As soon as bankers learned the theory, they put it to good use. They helped lead the way out of this supposed chaos—for a price.

The price was an overabundance of common stock issued on behalf of the new merged entity. Accounting practices at the time considered any stock issued above and beyond the asset value of a company as "watered." Simply, it was overcapitalization of a company's value. The excess was a dubious asset for investors but a bonanza for the investment bankers who helped issue it because they could charge underwriting fees on the total issue amount that easily could climb into the hundreds of millions of dollars. Since those fees were relatively high at the time, investment bankers realized it was in their interest to promote mergers and growth as a way to earn fat fees. The term *promoter* was applied to investment bankers, company insiders, or brokers who actively preached mergers as a way to achieve economic growth. The promoter did not necessarily have to be a banker or in the securities business, and if he was not, then he would arrange to have a syndicate sell his portion of the deal. Cynics claimed the only growth they were promoting was their own.

Financiers were providing a new concept to Wall Street that would later be called *synergy*. By fashioning a new company out of smaller ones and valuing it beyond simple asset value, Morgan and others created a whole that was greater than the sum of its parts. The intangible part of the whole—"water" as the critics maintained— was the goodwill and potential earnings of the company in the fore-seeable future. Both were difficult to value. In some cases the value was overstated, while at other times it was more closely related to tan-gible assets. Regardless, synergy was often elusive. Investors who bought stocks of the new consolidated entities had to determine the prospects for the new, enlarged industry. In a simpler era, lacking sophisticated evaluation tools, they relied more on the reputation of the financiers bringing the deal to market. Morgan deals may not have always been on the mark but they certainly attracted large amounts of money from the faithful.

WIND AND AIR

Trusts had been forming for almost 20 years when a group of steel men and bankers met at the University Club in New York in Decem-ber 1900. The main speaker was Charles M. Schwab, representing Andrew Carnegie. For the previous two years, Carnegie Steel had been in a state of constant turmoil and a rift had developed between Carnegie and Henry Clay Frick, his most significant lieutenant. Desiring to remove himself from the industry, Carnegie sent Schwab to test the waters for a merger. In his speech, Schwab alluded to the potential of a larger industry. In the audience was Pierpont Morgan. Schwab only had to hint at the idea to tweak the banker's interest. Negotiations between Morgan and Carnegie began quickly and were settled in a matter of months.

There was much at stake. The steel industry as a whole was the nation's premier industry. By 1900, American output was $1\frac{1}{2}$ times that of the United Kingdom, its nearest competitor. The market for steel appeared to be bright since railroads were the major source of demand. Morgan was keenly interested in railroads, holding many positions, including a major shareholding in the Northern Pacific, and saw the steel industry as a natural way of supplying the rails in a tidy scheme to profit from both industries. But the grand design had sev-eral flaws that would prove costly in the years ahead. The railroads' major routes already had been built, for the most part, and the era of constant expansion was nearing an end. If steel was to prosper as in the past, a new source of demand needed to be found.

Schwab was Carnegie's heir apparent. Thirty-eight years of age when he made the speech, he had joined Carnegie 20 years before, employed originally as a laborer. By the end of the nineteenth century, he was widely seen as Carnegie's successor, displacing Henry Clay Frick, with whom Carnegie had many increasingly unpleasant encounters. Frick was the manager of the Homestead steel plant in Pennsylvania, presiding over the breaking of the famous strike that became infamous in American labor history. During the 1890s, he and Carnegie failed to agree on many strategies for the steel company. Finally, in 1900 Frick was discovered to be involved in a land deal that had the potential to defraud Carnegie. The two had their final encounter in Frick's office in Pittsburgh in 1900 after Carnegie attempted to buy out Frick's interest in the company. Frick screamed at Carnegie, "For years I have been convinced that there is not an honest bone in your body. Now I know you are a goddamned thief!"[2] With that, he chased Carnegie from his office, with the older steel man running to avoid a physical confrontation.

Carnegie's empire was the crown jewel of the steel industry. The industry itself had many competitors and, despite some consolidation, was still quite diverse. Morgan entered the business in 1898 by forming the Federal Steel Corporation, one of the largest companies of the time, but still had significant competitors, notably John W. Gates at the American Steel & Wire Co. and the Moore brothers at the American Can and National Steel companies, among others. The banker's dislike of Carnegie and Gates was no secret since both represented what the imperious banker disdained—common men who would stoop to any level to win a deal. While Carnegie was known to be particularly shifty, Gates was clearly the more reprehensible of the two.

Gates's American Steel & Wire was the successor to the original company that made barbed wire, the popular form of fencing in the American West. After consolidating several smaller wire companies, Gates made his fortune and pursued his avocation, gambling. His nickname was "Bet a Million Gates," reflecting one of his favorite phrases, which he used on more than one occasion. The speculative side of Gates displeased Morgan, who personally abhorred speculation of any type. Gates's other famous habit, of spitting profusely (even indoors at the Waldorf-Astoria in New York, where he lived), did much to enhance his reputation as an uncouth gambler and womanizer.

Carnegie still was the bête noire of the industry, in Morgan's view, for attempting to break an informal cartel arrangement among the major producers by threatening to open his own tube company in Ohio, bringing him directly into a confrontation with Morgan's National Tube Co. Carnegie's tactics were brutally efficient and cutthroat. Elbert Gary, a lawyer working for Illinois Steel in the 1890s, remembered one incident when Carnegie was selling steel rails in Illinois for prices that Illinois Steel could not match. Gary stated at the time of the threat to the cartel, "The Carnegie Co. could do what it came very near to doing at one time, namely force the Illinois Steel Company into the hands of a receiver." Gates put it more succinctly: Carnegie's plans would "tear the National Tube, that Morgan had just put together, all to pieces."[3] The threat of new and potentially destructive competition in the industry finally forced Morgan's hand. Then Carnegie applied the coup de grâce by announcing plans that he intended to build a railroad to ship his products to market, competing directly with the Pennsylvania Railroad, in which Morgan held a substantial interest. Publicly displaying his plans to build a railroad to ship his products from the Great Lakes to the East Coast via Pittsburgh, Carnegie upset Morgan badly and in the process set up the purchase of his company.

Muckraking journalist Gustavus Myers wrote in 1911 that "the effect upon Morgan was galvanic. . . . Carnegie might carry out his threats; there was the danger. Had Morgan been dealing with the United States government he would have felt no great concern at threats he knew he could safely ignore; but in contesting with Carnegie, he was opposed by a magnate of whose power he had reason to be grimly apprehensive. How could Carnegie be placated, or dissuaded, or prevented from carrying out his ominous plans? One heroic way there was—to buy him out, and organize a trust."[4] The only way to succeed and preserve the investment was to absorb the Carnegie operation, ending what clearly was understood to be ruinous competition.

When Schwab made his indirect suggestion to the assemblage in New York, Morgan was quick to recognize a golden opportunity. Within two months, his buyout of Carnegie was complete and the United States Steel Corporation was born. With Carnegie out of the picture, Morgan's new empire emerged. Competition could still be found from smaller competitors and, contrary to popular opinion, the new monolith did not entirely dominate the industry. Cries of monopoly domination began almost immediately. Much of the fuss was created by the structure of the deal itself in addition to the potential power of the new company, the largest in the world. Carnegie's ploy enticed Morgan to buy him out. And it worked magnificently. After the deal was complete, Morgan told Carnegie that the price was worth it just to have him out of the business. More efficient motives such as economies of scale were not heard. The deal was the largest amount of going-away money ever paid to a competitor.

The consolidation made Carnegie the world's wealthiest man. Morgan paid him $420 million in securities for Carnegie Steel. The speed with which the deal was consummated amply illustrated that access to large amounts of capital was not a problem, for the amount of time between Schwab's speech and the official public announcement was only eight weeks. In addition to Carnegie, 30 others became rich by the deal, all employees of Carnegie or associated with his steel company in some way. But the nature of the deal and the speed with which it was accomplished proved troublesome for years to come.

Ten years after the deal, Charles Schwab testified before a House committee investigating the formation of U.S. Steel. Congressmen clearly saw the original buyout agreement as a blatant attempt to reduce competition. As Schwab was being questioned, a member of the committee read a passage aloud, quoting a highly regarded New York accountant who served as adviser to the committee: "It is well known the tendency, lately so conspicuous, to establish a community of ownership or a unified control over great industries as the only means of restraining destructive competition, leading to the incorporation of various great companies."[5] Schwab was then asked if that indeed was the motive for creating U.S. Steel. His response was measured. "It was not my understanding of the motive," he replied. The steel man was not about to make such an admission, especially 10 years after the deal, when the trustbusters were in their heyday.

Carnegie was paid $420 million for his properties, although estimates of the amount differ.[6] The entire amount was paid in 5 percent bonds of the company. The amount assigned to Carnegie was higher since existing bonds sold at 115 rather than par, so his amount was worth 15 percent more. Only at the hearings 10 years later did he supposedly discover that Morgan had issued more than $420 million to cover the payout. A member of the same committee asked Carnegie whether he was "aware that the United States Steel Corporation issued against the Carnegie Co. $492,000,000 worth of securities. . . . To be accurate, $492,006,160 was the amount of securities of the United States Steel Corporation which were put out to purchase the Carnegie Co."[7] For his part, Carnegie seemed surprised. "I have never heard of it," he replied.

What rapidly became clear was that the first significant deal of the century was overcapitalized using accounting standards of the time. The assets of the company amounted to an estimated $700 million, but the huge deal was syndicated and raised $1.4 billion, roughly twice the amount. At the time, the capitalization alone was equal to 8 percent of the country's gross national product. The $700 million excess was widely considered to be pure water, meaning that the value of the securities was already diluted when issued. However, viewing the price as the present value of the discounted estimated earnings stream presented a different picture. The total market capitalization of the company was 14 times the company's first-year consolidated earnings. On a price/earnings basis, the multiple was only about 14 times earnings, suggesting that the $1.4 billion figure was not unreasonable. Perhaps that was why Morgan told Carnegie some years later that if he had asked for $100 million more, he would have received it easily. When the wily Scot heard the remark, he became disconsolate for weeks afterward.

Morgan mounted a massive campaign on Wall Street in order to sell the new securities, employing over 300 dealers and banks. Of the total, $304 million was raised through bonds and the balance through stock, evenly split between common and preferred. The common stock was the most difficult to sell since it was still the least popular form of financing at the time. Investors aware of the travails of the common stock of the railroads in particular usually insisted on preferred stock or bonds, both of which paid a fixed rate of return. Sensitive to the problem, Morgan employed a noted stock manipulator and speculator, James Keene, to make a market in the stock by constantly trading it at higher and higher prices. Keene initially was successful and the stock sales went smoothly. Using Keene's services was an indication of how serious the sale was to Morgan since his reputation for being a sharp-edged manipulator was well known.

In percentage terms, the up-front fees earned from the deal were on the low side, about 2 percent of its total value. The syndicate put together by Morgan obviously could have taken more, but the outcry would have been more shrill than it was and the bankers were aware of the criticism. Underwriting the deals became one part of the bankers' profits—the visible part. The invisible side, not seen immediately by the public, was the stock that the bankers kept for themselves, cutting themselves in as shareholders and board members. But the underwriting part was reason enough to participate. The *New York Times* wrote that "many banks of considerable reputation in Wall Street rely almost entirely upon such profits for their income, letting the conventional banking business entirely alone."[8]

Wall Street and the rest of the country gasped at the size of the deal. The creation of U.S. Steel was not the only merger of the day, but nothing matched its size. In 1899, more than 1,200 mergers were recorded, representing a capitalization of $2.263 billion.[9] That represented an average deal of less than $2 million, so the steel merger two years later was monumental by any calculation—the largest deal ever done. The amount of new common shares was also staggering.

In 1901, the turnover of the New York Stock Exchange (NYSE) was 265 million shares and the sheer weight of the additional U.S. Steel shares caused a great overhang on the market that eventually brought about a postissue panic on Wall Street. Stock trading in the next two years actually declined because of the sheer size, although the promoters and underwriters did not mind. The deal generated around $50 million in gross fees for the underwriters, also a record sum. James Keene alone made almost $1 million for his efforts in organizing the support operation. At times, Big Steel accounted for 40 percent of the NYSE's turnover, a number suggesting that the market was well saturated. The deal would soon be criticized both for its sheer size and for the amount of fees generated by water.

Everyone touched by the deal prospered. Millionaires sprang up in Pittsburgh and New York and lavish homes were built in both cities to celebrate the windfall. Big Steel, as the company became known, was the world's largest corporation and the first to be capitalized over $1 billion, supplanting Standard Oil as the world's largest company. In the same year—also a bonanza for smaller mergers—422 other mergers took place, representing a total capitalization of $2.053 billion including Big Steel. When the $1.4 billion is subtracted, it can easily be seen that the average merger was still small compared to Morgan's behemoth. The amount of investment banking fees generated by the deal was about 7 percent on the amount of securities in excess of the asset value. Critics characterized the amount as nothing short of a bonanza for Wall Street and Morgan, who was widely suspected of sealing the deal in order to generate fees for his own bank. His activities demonstrated a whole new area of fat profits for Wall Street banks—advising and arranging mergers. While this activity had been around for years and made bankers and their clients rich, the sheer size of the deal introduced the world to the megadeal. Bankers who decided to enter the business also had to be able to sell the securities generated in order to pay for the deals, in many cases a task more difficult than simply putting a merger together on paper. If they could, was it worth $50 million, equivalent to the amount needed to employ 208,000 farmworkers for one year's labor? Soon it became apparent that investment banking certainly was more profitable than working for a living. Big Steel was admitted to the Dow Jones Industrial Average in April 1901. It joined the General Electric Company, which was one of the original stocks included in 1896. That gave Morgan 2 of the original 12 stocks comprising the index. Other Morgan-inspired companies would be added over the next several decades.

Despite all the publicity surrounding the deal and the commentary accompanying it, Big Steel still was not quite the dominant market force that critics first thought. The first annual report of the company became a milestone in finance, for billions of dollars never before had been printed under a corporate logo. The company reported long-term assets of $1.325 billion, current assets of $214.80 million, and total liabilities of $1.546 billion, of which $1.018 billion was in capital stock (shareholders' equity), split almost evenly between common and preferred stock. The stock was held by 25,000 preferred shareholders and 17,000 common shareholders. Net earnings for the first year of operation were $108 million, of which $56 million was paid in dividends. The company employed 168,000 people in its vast enterprises.[10] Its operations included 170 subsidiary companies, and, in addition to the steelmaking plant and iron ore, it held title to more than 100 steamships. By any calculation, the new company was a leviathan.

Morgan and his allies dominated the board. Directors included Morgan; Francis Peabody of Kidder Peabody, a firm that did much of its investment banking business through Morgan's auspices; Elbert Gary; John D. Rockefeller; Schwab; and Morgan partner George W. Perkins. Rockefeller was not in Morgan's camp, preferring to do much of the financing for his own Standard Oil through internally generated funds whenever possible. His vast enterprises also included sizable iron ore reserves, something that Morgan needed in the steel industry, and he could not afford to alienate the oil baron. After somewhat tortuous negotiations, Morgan, through Frick, bought the Rockefeller interest in the Mesaba mining range in Minnesota from John D. Rockefeller Jr., acting for his father. Part of the purchase price included $40 million in U.S. Steel stock, giving Rockefeller and his son seats on Big Steel's board.[11] The total purchase price was

$80 million, a decent sum considering that Rockefeller paid only about $500,000 for his mining interest originally.

The merger had little effect on the price of steel rails, which remained constant for the rest of the decade after the merger at $28 per 100 pounds.[12] The new giant company did not appear more efficient than its components were before the consolidation, and, other than having a new holding company structure, little appeared to have changed. Prices certainly did not fall as antitrusters wished. Perhaps as a result of the Rockefeller purchases, Big Steel remained committed to using ore in its steelmaking process rather than using scrap or adopting new production processes. As a result, it became known as a conservatively run business and actually began to lose market share over the next two decades. From 1901 to 1905, the company held 63 percent of the market for domestically produced steel. The amount slipped to 52 percent by World War I and continued to decline to 46 percent in the 1920s. During the same period, little was done to consolidate the operations of the giant company and its loose management structure did little to help it retain its market share or capture new markets.[13] The new monopoly was not working as well as intended.

The influence of financiers on the new company was not lost on Schwab, a steel man throughout his career. He became the first president of the new giant company but soon clashed with others closely allied to Morgan, including Judge Elbert Gary, chairman of the executive committee. After complaining that the financiers were not conversant with the industry, he finally resigned in 1903 and went on to purchase a floundering company—Bethlehem Steel, nicknamed "Bessie"—and reinvigorate it so that it would become a major competitor of Big Steel by the time war broke out in Europe. Part of Big Steel's loss in market share would be Bessie's gain.

The heavy overhang of Big Steel plus an unanticipated stock market drop in May 1901 brought a panic on Wall Street. While the Big Steel issue was not the only cause, the market drop showed the underlying weaknesses of stocks that would lead to two more panics within several years. The 1901 affair was precipitated by a corner in the stock of the Northern Pacific Railroad. Two warring factions, one led by Morgan and James J. Hill, the railroad baron, and the other by Edward H. Harriman, the majority shareholder in the railroad, bid up the price of the stock to over $1,000 per share in an attempt to gain control. The rapidly rising price proved inviting and many short sellers joined the fray. The corner consumed all the available stock and none was left to cover the shorts. As a result, the market dropped precipitously since the price could not be maintained, and many small investors were left battered along with professional traders. Morgan won the battle, but the overall market was the loser. The stock price dropped to $325 and the panic came to a conclusion, but not without scores of angry investors and speculators having lost their savings and fortunes. The panic was followed by another in 1903, dubbed the "rich man's panic." Small investors again suffered sizable losses in the several-month-long market drop that ended by late August. Now a noticeable problem was developing: Without an army of investors to buy new issues, the market was limited in the amounts it could raise for further consolidations.

Despite a grandiose genius for forging enormous deals, Morgan was not a steel man. His interests in various industries such as railroads stemmed from the structural problems he saw within the industries and the ability to profit from them. Steel was no different. Organizationally, the new company obviously was larger, but it still employed traditional ways of manufacturing its various products. Time was proving that innovation was necessary. And innovation cost money. Finance was the master art of the age, superseding the innovations it financed. Thomas Edison once lamented, "My electric light inventions have brought me no profits, only forty years of litigation." With enough capital, many of his problems could have been avoided and the Wall Street bankers knew it well. When the railroads were first developed, it was recognized that they would be capital intensive, although many small competitors still tried their hand at providing services. Inventions were somewhat different since no one was certain that they would be met with universal success when perfected. Astute Wall Street bankers knew that innovation was lost without them and moved to capitalize on the fact quickly.

Another Morgan-inspired deal in the wake of U.S. Steel was an unequivocal flop, demonstrating that everything Morgan touched did not turn to gold. When he formed International Mercantile Marine just months after Big Steel, the public was decidedly less interested in purchasing new securities. The new trust was intended to be a combination of shipping companies that dominated the North Atlantic shipping lanes, notably American, British, and German interests. Morgan formed the company, fusing together the various individual companies, but was unable to sell the shares necessary to make it work. The New York Stock Exchange assumed that it had so much water on its books that it was denied a listing—a rare event. In 1906, four years after the initial offering of stock, the underwriters still had 80 percent of the unsold shares on their own books.[14] The failure led Morgan to keep his hand in shipping, although indirectly. He would see the U.S. Navy as a source of demand for his products, although in 1902 the fighting force was very limited.

While Big Steel was slowly losing market share because of internal factors, its directors and bankers sought to find new markets using their political influence. At this juncture, monopoly-like consolidation again began to take on sinister connotations that would indirectly haunt Morgan and his heir for decades. Ironically, Morgan and his partners failed to detect the coming revolution in automobiles. If they had, their fears for new markets would have been quickly assuaged since the auto industry in Detroit became the steel mills' largest customer and would remain so for decades. Instead, acting more like nineteenth-century men than those of the twentieth, Morgan and his allies put pressure on the government to build a bigger and better navy, hoping that the increased demand for their product would keep their investments afloat. When bankers became involved in national defense and wars, criticism was certain to be heard.

SPARE SOME CHANGE?

Almost immediately after the formation of Big Steel, another organization was founded that initially appeared to be unrelated to heavy industry. The Navy League was organized in 1902, originally to lobby for a stronger American naval presence. Patterned after a similarly named British organization, the league was dedicated to maintaining a strong navy in the face of international military overtures by European powers and Japan. The membership excluded active navy personnel but included many former officers and politicians. Among the league's small group of officers was Herbert L. Satterlee, Morgan's son-in-law. The group also chose seven honorary vice presidents, including Morgan and Perry Belmont of the Belmont banking family and a close ally of Morgan on Wall Street.

Although its members and officers were enthusiastic about the league's purpose, the public did not take much notice of the new organization. The league began a public education campaign to show how the country's navy was woefully underequipped to meet the rigors of the late imperialistic era. The navy had 307 ships commissioned at the time, but only 10 battleships and 16 cruisers were capable of battle.[15] Despite words of encouragement from Theodore Roosevelt, the league remained behind the scenes and made no impact upon the public. The navy had undertaken a building program under Roosevelt to increase its strength, but the league did not appear to have been a cause of the buildup. The organization initially appeared to be little more than a club, popular only among navy enthusiasts.

Although it got off to a slow start, the Navy League picked up considerable momentum as World War I approached. It was also criticized for being a special interest organization supported by big business. At a peace conference held in New York in 1909, Oswald Garrison Villard, the son of industrialist Henry Villard, spoke out forcibly against the league, questioning its intentions. "Who is really behind the advocacy of an increased army and navy," he asked an audience at a New York church, "a combination of wicked persons who stand to profit by a big navy . . . it has a treasurer and counsel who are close relatives of the man who organized the shipbuilding trust and the International Mercantile Marine and who themselves are interested in many companies that make a profit out of the building of ships and armor plate and on its board of directors [sits] the man who owns all the nickel mines in the United States."[16] Villard's reference clearly was to Morgan and his allies, no friends of his father in past dealings. The International Mercantile Marine was one of the few Morgan failures but to nonfinanciers was still seen as a source of conspiracy and corruption.

Within a few years, the attack on the Navy League became more vociferous. Although it failed to attract a major benefactor, it did have many contributors, mostly in the steel industry. Henry Clay Frick, Charles Schwab, Elbert Gary, and Morgan all made small contributions, eventually drawing the ire of pacifists and those who wanted no part of a war in Europe. Henry Ford, no friend of Morgan, printed a copy of a speech made by Representative Clyde Tavenner in the House, in which Tavenner called out the name of every steelmaker who had ever contributed to the Navy League. Under the title "The Navy League Unmasked," Ford repeated Tavenner's charge that the league was nothing more than a front for the manufacturing interests, meaning steel and shipbuilding.[17]

The Navy League finally produced results for its contributors and supporters in August 1916 when a large naval bill passed Congress and was signed into law by Woodrow Wilson. Though Wilson was initially opposed to American war preparations, his mind was changed by the sinking of the *Lusitania* in the North Atlantic. After years of lobbying for an expanded navy, the league finally got satisfaction when the largest naval buildup in the country's history was finally authorized. Over 150 ships were to be built by 1919 so that the United States would become the greatest naval power on earth. The cost for the buildup exceeded $600 million. The league also was among the first to suggest how it could be paid for: It issued a resolution stating that a huge bond issue for $500 million should be issued to help pay the costs. "A large bond issue of, if necessary, $500 million should be authorized at once," the league stated. "These bonds would be rapidly absorbed by the American people for such a purpose."[18] The league undoubtedly derived the large number from a loan that was being organized by Morgan and other New York bankers on behalf of Britain and France, which was issued in the fall of 1915. The Anglo-French loan for $500 million was the largest of its type ever raised and selling it proved to be a difficult task. Financing for the navy buildup was provided by Liberty Loans sold directly by the Treasury to investors and savers. The Treasury did not pay a commission to Wall Street houses for helping sell them.

The war helped Big Steel and the other manufacturers. Steel production jumped 30 percent during the war years and then remained flat through most of the 1930s. Charles Schwab did particularly well at Bethlehem Steel. Ten years after Schwab left U.S. Steel to strike out on his own, his Bethlehem Steel was growing steadily. In 1914, he made a trip to London to meet with Lord Kitchener, the British Secretary of War. The two men negotiated for Bethlehem to supply the British with ordnance and ships. Aware of the trend of consolidation in American industry, Kitchener exacted a pledge from Schwab not to sell his company as long as he was under contract. "I want you to pledge that the control of the Bethlehem Steel Corporation will not be sold by you or your associates under five years from now," the cabinet minister requested. After Schwab agreed, he returned home with over $50 million in contracts.[19]

Bethlehem was not quite the competitor to U.S. Steel that events suggested, however. There was a substantial Morgan interest in the number two producer after Big Steel was created, and only the turn of events created by the war stopped a merger. Three steel producers shared the market for steel plate when war broke out, and it was feared that merging two of them—the Carnegie Works of U.S. Steel and Bethlehem—might bring unwanted attention from the antitrust division of the Justice Department. Secretary of the Navy Josephus Daniels remarked that some form of divine providence kept these three manufacturers from being investigated and that "it became even plainer than last year that the government is at the mercy of the three manufacturers of armor plate whose policy is to make the government pay prices much beyond a fair profit."[20]

Big Steel had little reason to complain during the early years of the war. Income rose from $23 million in 1914 to $271 million two years later. Even by 1920, when the war was over, it still remained at $110 million.[21] The war years were the best that the company would experience for decades. Except for a few odd years, income remained

24

mostly flat for the 1920s and losses were incurred during the Depression years. Pierpont's son Jack became chairman of Big Steel in 1927 and was responsible for trying to prop up the price of the stock during the market crash of 1929.

The Navy League proved so successful that the model, and a few personnel, would reappear in the future as other pressure groups attempted to influence American social policy. During Prohibition, one of the league's key personnel, William Stayton, would lead the Association Against the Prohibition Amendment (AAPA) in its battle to have the Volstead Act repealed. After the law was repealed, Stayton went on to head the American Liberty League, an association dedicated to opposing the New Deal. All three organizations employed similar tactics as they went to war against their opponents, namely public education programs and pamphleteering.

SWORDS AND PLOWSHARES

Of the many consolidations organized by Morgan, combining major farm equipment companies into the International Harvester Company in 1902 was by far the least likely. Railroads, shipping, electric power production, and (later) telecommunications all were the sort of industries that fit the grand design of finance—sprawling companies that were capital intensive, requiring massive new doses of money in order to expand and thrive. Manufacturing harvesting equipment was much more mundane. The revolution brought by the automated reaper had already had its effect on American agriculture.

The reaper was invented by Cyrus McCormick in 1831, when he was only 22. Although demand for the new product initially was slow, refinements and publicity helped establish the concept among farmers who could afford to buy one. For the rest of the century, the McCormick Company dominated the industry. The increase in agricultural production brought about by the invention created a true revolution in agriculture. After McCormick moved his base of operations to the Midwest from his native Virginia before the Civil War, the mechanical reaper he perfected became extremely popular. Both the dramatic increase in grain production and the rise of Chicago as an agricultural and railroad center were attributed to McCormick's invention.

After McCormick's death in 1884, the company continued under his son Cyrus Jr. Ruinously competitive, the industry was dominated by two family-run firms. Its major competitor was the Deering Co., another family-owned operation. Between them, the two companies shared almost 70 percent of the industry. In 1890, an attempt at consolidation with McCormick under the name of the American Harvester Co. failed after a short period, mainly because of a lack of financing. The severe economic downturn of the mid-1890s put further pressure on the two companies, which were fighting each other fiercely for market share when they were not discussing merger. Capital for expansion was desperately needed, but the industry was traditionally Midwestern and did not trust bankers, especially those from Wall Street. But all the principals involved realized that without fresh capital increased competition would only continue. As a result, they put out feelers to interested parties and friends looking for potential investors. The Deerings approached Elbert Gary at U.S. Steel, while the McCormicks approached George W. Perkins, a partner of J. P. Morgan. The deal would be the first major coup for Perkins, who had joined Morgan several years before while still keeping his old job at New York Life, an insurance company. A deal would be imminent because they had approached the same banker through slightly different paths.

Perkins worked out merger plans that consolidated the two companies into the International Harvester Co. Three smaller competitors also joined the new company, which officially was born in July 1902. It controlled 85 percent of the production of harvesting machines and had assets of around $110 million.[22] Compared to U.S. Steel, the company was a minnow, but it did provide useful demand for Big Steel's products. Its new board included Perkins and several other Morgan allies. But its financing was the biggest surprise.

Unlike the situation of Big Steel, the new stock issued in International Harvester did not contain much water. The assets of the

26

combined company were valued at $105 million and the value of the stock issue was only $120 million, suggesting that the amount of water was only 15 percent above asset value. Perkins explained the extra capital to McCormick, stating that "the House of Morgan would estimate the working capital necessary to organize the new concern, and form a syndicate to raise the money. If $10 million were needed, the syndicate would issue $15 million in stock, the extra millions representing the syndicate's 'bonus.' . . . Morgan would also insist upon choosing all the officers and directors of the new company."[23] Half of the capitalization was represented by common stock and the other half was in the form of preferred stock. In contemporary terms, the deal was more properly priced than many other Morgan creations. But its market already appeared to be stagnant. The individual companies sold more harvesting machines in the 1890s than the new combination did 10 years later. The reapers had relatively long life spans and did not require quick replacement. Harvester's profit margin was relatively thin and did not exceed 4 percent.[24]

Morgan himself appeared only mildly enthusiastic about the new combination. When informed about the terms of the deal by Perkins, he replied, "Plan seems satisfactory and safe. Approve signing preliminary contract if you agree."[25] Although the new company indeed held a monopoly in the industry, it was no bonanza. As a result, the payout for the merger was small when compared to Big Steel. The bank earned a $3 million fee from the offering. Morgan's imprint loomed over the board of directors and the finance committee especially. Included were Perkins, George F. Baker, and Elbert Gary along with McCormick and Charles Deering. The deal proved lucrative for the McCormicks and Deerings. In the 1930s, they were reported to be among America's 60 wealthiest families, with fortunes estimated at $212 million and $50 million, respectively.[26]

Harvester served another purpose for Morgan and Wall Street even if it did not create a fee-generating bonanza. Its public relations value was worth millions by itself. The name McCormick, like Edison and Bell, was a mainstay in American life and the product was a true American original. Morgan had an affinity for taking over companies of famous inventors, and the consolidation of the harvester industry seemed a natural if a bit off the beaten path for the bank. In the wake of the Sherman Antitrust Act, it seemed good insurance to forge trusts based upon solid inventions that undisputedly were the mainstays of the American economy. How long that attitude would hold up under pressure was another matter.

Perkins set out to portray the new company as a good trust. As trusts were pursued by the Roosevelt administration, a distinction was made between good and bad trusts. Acknowledging that a company was a trust, or monopoly, supporters claimed that as long as it did not harm the public by restraining competition or rigging prices, it should be allowed to continue as a good trust. Originally, Theodore Roosevelt went along with the idea, although the tide began to turn by the time his successor, William Howard Taft, took office.

An unlikely figure also made a killing on the Harvester deal. A New York businessman, Frank Munsey, was invited into the initial offering and turned over his initial allocation of shares very quickly. He then was invited into other Morgan deals, where his fortune appreciated considerably. Between 1907 and 1911, he became the largest shareholder in U.S. Steel, holding between $30 million and $50 million worth of stock. He owed this phenomenal amount to his friendship with Perkins, whom he first met in 1895.[27] But Munsey was not an industrialist or banker. He was a newspaperman closely allied with Morgan interests.

Munsey operated newspapers in New York before the turn of the century and acquired a reputation for buying and then closing papers without any apparent reason. He originally purchased the New York *Star*, the *Daily News*, and the Washington *Times*, among others, before either closing them or selling them to other interests. He continued after he was no longer involved with Big Steel, using his $40 million fortune to finance his operations. While his method was not clear, muckrakers interpreted his actions more clearly. He was allied with the House of Morgan and acted as its henchman in the press. If a paper was hostile to Morgan, Munsey would buy it and close it. The papers he kept open were favorable to the bank, extolling its virtues at every opportunity. His magazine, *Munsey's Magazine*, was especially kind to U.S. Steel when he happened to be its largest shareholder.[28] Paying off friends in this manner was a standard operation by Morgan and other bankers and would come to light in Senate investigations nearly 30 years later.

Munsey's Magazine attributed prosperity to the development of a new attitude on Wall Street that had strong moralistic overtones— just the sort needed to convince politicians and the public that the country and the Street were on the right path. The year preceding the U.S. Steel deal was a good one for stocks, and the magazine knew the reasons. "The good times now electrifying security markets are not at all a sudden outburst," it stated in 1899. "Though small heed attended their development, these good times have been growing and extending and strengthening every day since when, two Novembers ago, the integrity of our financial purpose was certified at the ballot box," (referring to McKinley's election). The author of the article, H. Allaway, was certain that the McKinley years would be a "new and eventual chapter in the history of the financial center of America," adding a sugar-coated optimism to the period that would also characterize many of the same strong merger periods in the following century.[29]

War was also good for International Harvester. Even before the United States officially entered the fray, results for harvesting equipment were encouraging. The value of farm equipment used doubled between 1915 and 1920. Agricultural production increased sharply as exports to Europe grew substantially. Putting the nation on a war footing proved profitable for the United States, especially after the loans to the Allies and the navy buildup in 1916. The American aid program to the European Allies, providing food and other staples, caused sharply higher food and commodity prices, forcing several of the commodity futures exchanges to suspend trading. J.P. Morgan & Co. served as the official procurement agent for the British government and took in $30 million as a result. When combined with the success of U.S. Steel, a picture emerged that proved unflattering to Morgan and other financiers in the years to come. They would be accused of profiteering at the expense of the government in times of national crisis. What made the charge remarkable was not that it was made but when it was made—in 1936.

The two deals made Morgan $53 million and, when combined with the General Electric deal, made him the most influential banker of his generation. In the 10-year period from 1902 to 1912, Morgan underwrote $1.95 billion of new securities of interstate corporations. Although the bank did not make its profit-and-loss statements public, that would represent underwriting fees of around $60 million in addition to the $50 million made from the U.S. Steel deal.[30] The money trust was now in full bloom and no one at the time denied that it existed. Trying to pinpoint its abuses was another matter since many of the Morgan deals appeared to be in the interest of progress, although charges of watering continued. And while U.S. Steel may have been the most powerful and wide-ranging Morgan company, another deal sealed before Pierpont's death in 1913 proved to be the longest lasting of any Morgan company. Again, technological ability and skill gave way to finance as the telephone industry consolidated early in the twentieth century.

LONG DISTANCE

Several years after the formation of Big Steel and International Harvester, Morgan's financial skills once again were brought to bear on another company originally founded by a Scots-American. Unlike steel and harvesting equipment, this new industry was capable of explosive growth. Like many other industries born after the Civil War, it was begging to be consolidated.

Alexander Graham Bell's telephone became one of the most sought-after inventions of the nineteenth century, mainly because it was one of the few technological innovations that could be purchased by the general public. Demand for the product far outstripped the supply of available telephones and transmission lines, and Bell found himself in the traditional conumdrum of many inventors-turned-businessmen. Technology could carry his telephone company only so far on its merit. Large amounts of capital were needed if the invention were to reach its full potential.

Bell's original company was organized as the Bell Telephone Co. in 1878. Its first general manager, Theodore Vail, was hired away from the U.S. Post Office by Thomas Watson, one of Bell's early colleagues. From that point, the company developed quickly owing to Vail's management expertise and farsightedness. When Vail took the reins, fewer than 26,000 telephones were in service. Over the course of the next 10 years, he imposed his own design on the company, transforming it into a system rather than just a telephone company. Of its several original components, the American Telephone & Telegraph Company proved to be the most functional. Other parts of the company, namely the New England Telephone Company, sold licenses to smaller companies operating under the Bell name. Equipment was purchased from a subsidiary, the Western Electric Co. In order to strengthen the parent company's position, Western Electric was forbidden to sell equipment to rival companies. Vail fused these operations together under AT&T so that the parts would operate as a system, enabling users to make calls on standard equipment over standard transmission lines. Within two years, the number of telephones in use had doubled. Western Electric was fully added to the Bell companies in 1882.

Not being a banker, Vail was unsympathetic to those who wanted to create financial synergies out of his more efficient and expanded company. To him, consolidation was necessary to provide better service, not print more stock shares. Like many industrialists of the day, he preferred to use retained earnings to drive expansion rather than pay high dividend yields to investors. After repeated clashes with others in the company and its bankers, he resigned in 1887. His departure left the company short of energy and vision. Most important, Bell's original patents were due to expire in 1893 and 1894. Without a clear strategy, the company would be in a difficult position. Smaller competitors were lining up, anticipating the expiration. Prior to the patents' expiration, Bell held a monopoly over the fledging industry, but that was soon to change. Nevertheless, the number of phones continued to expand exponentially. By 1892, over 260,000 sets were in use.[31] Entrepreneurs viewed the industry as a cash generator. By the end of the century, over 6,000 new, mostly local, companies entered the field after the patents expired. Chaos clearly reigned.

The popularity of the telephone exploded in the early twentieth century. In 1900, 1 million telephones were in use; by 1907, the number jumped to over 6 million. The number of telephone poles in existence quadrupled, as did the total number of miles of phone wire. But the number of daily calls made only doubled, held down by the relative expense of making a call. Toll (long distance) calls especially were expensive. The cost of a call between New York City and Philadelphia rose slightly during the seven-year period, while calls to Chicago and Denver remained about the same. Three minutes from New York to Philadelphia cost 75 cents, while one minute to Chicago was about $5.00 and Denver around $11.00.[32] A call to Denver was about 1 percent of the average family's income at the time, although the price did tumble when regular nationwide service was established after World War I.

In many respects, conditions in the telephone industry were similar to those in the steel industry. The major difference was that they were far worse. Competition after 1894 was ruinous and customers were purchasing incompatible equipment from local companies that made the old Bell companies look efficient by comparison. AT&T's bankers, led by Kidder Peabody & Co., invited Vail back to run the company in 1900, but he turned them down. Until the turn of the century, AT&T's main bankers were in Boston, where the original Bell was located. But raising additional capital for AT&T was a job beyond the reach of Kidder Peabody. Earlier Bell issues were sold to investors first in Boston and then on Wall Street, but the capital infusions that AT&T required were too large for the Boston stock market to absorb. If telephone service was to expand, the industry and its investors would have to recognize that, like the railroads, it was capital intensive and would need large infusions of money in order to improve equipment and services. In 1902, Morgan and other New York bankers stepped in and reorganized financing for the company. Kidder Peabody remained in Morgan syndicates for new issues, but Morgan was now clearly in the driver's seat. True to form, he needed strong leadership for the company and again turned to Vail in 1906. This time the former chief executive accepted the job. Bankers did not relinquish their role in the company, but they did bow to Vail's superior management skills. The new company was stacked with Morgan men and allies. Included were George F. Baker, Henry P. Davison, Henry L. Higginson of Lee Higginson in Boston, and Robert Winsor of Kidder Peabody. Finally, the bankers and investors accepted Vail's ideas for expansion, and the modern Bell system was reborn.

The company acquired the Western Union Co. in 1909 in a deal that did not please the Justice Department because it gave the phone company control of the telegraphs as well. Within four years, AT&T reached an accommodation with the government through which it divested of Western Union, reverting solely to the telephone business. The business continued to grow exponentially. By 1923, there were 15 million telephone sets in use, of which 10 million were connected to the Bell system.[33] The *American Review of Reviews* commented in the same year, "It would be a commonplace remark to say that when wireless telephoning became practical, about the year 1914, no one dreamed that its use would ever be general or popular . . . the rapidity with which the thing has spread has possibly not been equaled in all the centuries of human progress."

At the time, the refinancing and reorganization of AT&T was not considered one of the major Morgan deals. Yet it would prove to be one of the most long lasting. The first deal for the company was a $100 million bond underwritten by the New York group along with Kidder Peabody. The deal became the first of many that Morgan underwrote for AT&T, both in bonds and common stock. The relationships between the two became one of the longer-lasting client-investment banking relationships in the twentieth century. When Morgan divested its investment banking operations to Morgan Stanley in 1934, the new firm assumed the mantle as major investment banker to AT&T.

The Morgan deals created the mergers and acquisitions business on Wall Street that became a staple for the rest of the twentieth century. Wielding his influential access to investment funds both at home and from abroad, Morgan and other bankers like Jacob Schiff of Kuhn Loeb & Co. were able to insinuate themselves into deals using other people's money, to use a phrase common at the time. The circle of influence that developed was substantial. Bankers began to sit on company boards, lending advice and money. The top New York bankers held so many board seats that the annual meetings of many companies became little more than fraternity parties. The implications of this concentration of industrial and financial power set off many alarms in state capitals and Washington.

Interlocking directorships became the buzzword of the day. Bankers who congregated on boards of companies supposedly competing with each other were seen blocking free competition between the companies, seeking to line their own pockets with monopolistic interference in the marketplace. Although the period prior to World War I witnessed many antitrust actions by the Justice Department and saw the publication of several well-known muckraking books, on balance the period was still favorable to big business. The most egregious industrial combinations were challenged in the courts but the record remained on the side of business. Even when Standard Oil and American Tobacco were ordered broken up by the Supreme Court in 1911, critics demonstrated that John D. Rockefeller and James B. Duke still held power over their respective industries despite the creation of new, supposedly competitive companies. Summarizing a brief history of Standard Oil, the *New York Times* concluded that "John D. Rockefeller grew wealthier after Standard Oil was broken up in 1911."[34]

LOOKING FOR LAMBS

After two Wall Street panics within a six-year period, finding fresh cash for merger deals was becoming a difficult task. Small investors were never a significant force in the market at the time because the amount of personal wealth was not great. If huge deals were to continue, a source of funds needed to be found. Bankers argued that national pride and power were at stake, while critics viewed the process as simply another way for the bankers to line their own pockets while waving the flag.

During the first decade of the twentieth century, national savings did not make much progress. By 1908, they had reverted to their

1901 level. Most of the national wealth was concentrated in cities; the wealth in agricultural states formed a very small part of the total. Individuals used commercial banks and savings and loan associations to deposit their savings. The big New York bankers did very little business with them, however. The money trust banks were mostly wholesale institutions, taking deposits from businesses. But small investors would have to contribute some cash to the process so that underwriting big deals would continue. The other place cash could be found was in the life insurance companies. If they were avid buyers of money trust underwritings, deals could continue unabated.

Life insurance was a perfect target for the money trust. Sales of life policies topped the $2 billion level for the first time in 1902.[35] If bankers could take control of life insurance companies, they could sell them many of the new issues they used to finance mergers. In Wall Street parlance, this was known as *stuffing* a captive portfolio. It was also one of the major reasons that commercial banking, investment banking, and life insurance were separated in the Banking (Glass-Steagall) Act passed in 1933 following congressional hearings in the wake of the 1929 Crash.

The life insurance industry was rife with scandal during the early 1900s. It was also one of the few institutional investors in the country, so controversy was to be expected. Investing funds on a fiduciary basis was limited at the time and trust companies, along with the insurers, were the only major sources of funds for new securities issues. In the three years after the U.S. Steel deal, the securities assets of the insurers rose sharply while their capital and surplus remained flat, suggesting that they had been buying more than the usual amount of new issues. They had the market mainly to themselves because pension funds were not yet a significant force in the market and mutual funds had not been developed. Naturally, Wall Street bankers coveted the insurers and the trust companies as outlets for their newly minted securities. The cozy relationship was made worse by the antics of some of the insurance company executives at the time.

The New York–based insurance companies were the largest in the country and were most susceptible to abuse. Life insurance in particular was dominated by New York Life, the Equitable Life Assurance Society, and the Mutual Life Insurance Company. These companies were prime candidates for outside influence because life insurance, by its very nature, required long-term assets to match up against its long-term liabilities. Other forms of insurance, such as fire or casualty, required shorter-term assets and could often survive better by simply paying claims out of current premium income. The life insurance companies traditionally required less liquidity than other types and therefore could also be stuffed with more questionable securities that could escape notice until a much later date. They were perfect repositories for securities that required a home.

Trust companies filled the same prescription. The companies administered the wills and estates of the wealthy and viewed their clients' funds as captive. Morgan purchased the Guaranty Trust Company in 1910 and was on friendly terms with the Bankers Trust Company, originally founded in 1903 by Henry P. Davidson and Thomas Lamont. Bankers Trust originally intended to draw referrals from Morgan, who was not yet in the trust business but soon entered after realizing the trust's potential. Davison and Lamont eventually joined J.P. Morgan & Co. as partners, adding to the interlocking nature of the money trust. The trusts were relatively well behaved compared to some of the insurers.

The insurer with the worst reputation in New York circles was the Equitable. The company founded by Henry Baldwin Hyde passed to his 23-year-old son James in 1899. The young president delighted the New York press by throwing a large party at an exclusive New York restaurant decorated like the palace at Versailles for the occasion. The cost for the gala reportedly exceeded $200,000, and the New York *World*, owned by Joseph Pulitzer, made the affair front-page news. The unwanted publicity alarmed the usually puritanical Wall Street bankers, who formed an investigating committee headed by Henry Clay Frick, one of the Equitable's directors. The result was predictable. The inquiry suggested that the top directors of the company be sacked, but before any action could be taken an official state inquiry was begun in New York.

BUILDING THE INFRASTRUCTURE

The investigation was known as the Armstrong committee hearings, named after state senator William W. Armstrong. He was assisted by his chief counsel, Charles Evans Hughes, at the time a little-known lawyer. Beginning in the fall of 1905, the committee delved into the affairs of the Equitable and the activities of bankers and their relations with insurers. The board members of Equitable had all since departed and the company had been sold, but the alleged ties between the insurers and Wall Street were becoming well recognized. Over a four-month period, the Armstrong committee probed the relationships. Wall Street banks emerged looking particularly ravenous. The Equitable alone was sitting on a hoard of around $500 million in cash and liquid assets, mostly returns on investments and premium income. With a lure like that, bankers would not be far behind.

Politicians also enjoyed the insurers' largesse. The insurers reportedly kept a slush fund to bribe politicians in Albany, including cash payments and maintaining a house of ill repute in which to entertain legislators. But the most revealing part of the hearings centered on the matter of purchasing securities from bankers. George W. Perkins, a partner at Morgan and an executive at New York Life at the same time, became one of Hughes's favorite witnesses because he detailed the relationships with an insouciance suggesting that bankers knew best. He described how his company regularly bought securities from Morgan and how it had been a major buyer of U.S. Steel shares and bonds in particular. About $39 million had been invested in Big Steel since its original issue. Many of the common shares were purchased at relatively high prices and subsequently tumbled in the ensuing panics.

More damning was Perkins's testimony relating how New York Life also bought around $4 million worth of shares in International Mercantile Marine. When the issue subsequently floundered, the investment was sold back to Morgan after losing $80,000. Morgan apparently had second thoughts about the soundness of the investment and absorbed half the loss personally, but his largesse did not appease his inquisitors. When combined with the admissions of other Wall Streeters, the overall record was not particularly flattering. But it did reveal how Wall Street worked and also showed how many partners at top banks got their jobs in the first place.

For his part, Perkins was investigated by the district attorney in New York but was never prosecuted for malfeasance since no evidence of criminal intent could be found. A grand jury in New York City heard testimony about Perkins's actions but failed to return an indictment. The inaction led Gustavus Myers to remark sarcastically that "for a rich and powerful man to commit any fraud with *criminal intent* was a principle unknown to practical jurisprudence. The farce dragged out for a while; not one of the participants of great wealth was even incommoded by the formality of a trial."[36]

The Armstrong hearings caused many of the states to consider measures to control insurance companies within their individual borders. The matter became particularly urgent because legislation had been introduced into Congress seeking a federal law to control insurance companies, something many of the states opposed. As far as they were concerned, insurance remained a local matter that should be controlled at the state level. Accordingly, over 100 governors, attorneys general, and insurance commissioners met in 1906 in Chicago to discuss a uniform insurance law that they could all agree upon. It was doubtful whether insurance regulation could be constitutionally justified in Congress, so many of the states then adopted their own insurance laws, including New York in 1906.

Morgan officially invested in Equitable in 1909 when he, George Baker, and James Stillman of the National City Bank of New York purchased its stock. The price was in excess of what even a prudent investor would have paid since the Equitable's dividend yield at the price was negligible and its value far exceeded the market. The only plausible explanation was that it allowed the bankers access to the company's assets, still a sizable pile of cash at the time. Insurance company investments also became an integral part of the Pujo hearings in Congress in 1912, in which all senior bankers, including Pierpont Morgan, were invited to testify. The hearings were prompted in part by the revelations of the Armstrong committee seven years before and were much better publicized, much to Wall Street's chagrin.

After the Armstrong hearings and the Panic of 1907, when Morgan again assisted the Treasury in averting a collapse of several financial institutions on Wall Street, sentiment was building against the bank and its power. Discussions had begun unofficially on the feasibility of a new central bank for the United States, which would finally see the light of day in 1912 when the Federal Reserve Act was passed. But Morgan's power was beginning to be seen in a more sinister light. The idea that the New York banker was the unofficial central banker of the country did not sit well with many Democrats and Progressives. In May 1908, Congress passed a resolution that the motto "In God We Trust," should be used on all coins issued by the Treasury. The unofficial motto "In Morgan We Trust" was no longer a laughing matter as the political climate began to change.

IN THE CROSS HAIRS

The mergers and acquisitions drive and the revelations of the Armstrong committee brought criticism of Wall Street and industry in general. The close relationship between financiers and their industrial clients drew fire as many Progressives worried that the very fiber of American democracy was being threatened. Fuel was added to the fire by Senator Robert LaFollette of Wisconsin, who made a memorable speech in the Senate in March 1908. He had made other long rambling speeches before, but this one, in which he described interlocking directorships, was full of information not generally known. In it, he described how just 100 men from finance and industry controlled American industry through interlocking board seats on major corporations.

The Pujo hearings made LaFollette's fears abundantly clear in 1912. The hearings were called by Representative Arsenee Pujo of Louisiana. Chief counsel for the committee was Samuel Untermyer, a New York lawyer who became the bête noire of the investment banking community for years to come. Untermyer's attitude toward the long list of bankers called to testify was probing and direct. Never a friend of the banking coterie, he had the distinction of being the first congressionally approved inquisitor of the money trust. Among those interviewed by the committee were most of the senior bankers in New York, including Pierpont Morgan himself. Morgan was not accustomed to being questioned, and his answers to Untermyer were direct but revealed almost nothing specific about his business other than some generalizations about his methods of dealing with banking clients. Despite the bland testimony, the committee was nevertheless able to construct a picture of the power of the money trust that would endure long after the hearings themselves had been forgotten.

It was revealed that Morgan men directly or indirectly held over 340 directorships in 118 corporations, representing over $22 billion in capitalization. The Pujo committee discovered that J.P. Morgan & Co. held directorships in four other insurance companies besides the Equitable. That paled in comparison with the other banks' influence. Of the 14 banks mentioned by the committee, the senior partners held 103 board seats in 60 insurance companies, many of which were overlaps.[37] The evidence became more damning when the committee demonstrated the overlap among the banks themselves because of the interlocking directorships, where each bank had at least one director on the board of another.

Exactly how Morgan had come to gain control of the Equitable was a central part of the hearings. James Hyde had sold his holdings in the company to Thomas Fortune Ryan, a self-made New York millionaire, from whom Morgan had purchased them. Ryan had a reputation of being very astute, and although Morgan paid an inflated price it was questionable why Ryan would have relinquished control. In a classic bit of repartee between Morgan and Untermyer, the financier let very little about the sale slip from his lips.

Q. Did Mr. Ryan offer this stock to you?
A. I asked him to sell it to me.
Q. You asked him to sell it to you?
A. Yes.
Q. Did you tell him why you wanted it?
A. No; I told him it was a good thing for me to have.
Q. Did he tell you that he wanted to sell it?
A. No; but he sold it.

Q. He did not want to sell it; but when you said you wanted it, he sold it?

A. He did not say that he did not want to sell it.

Q. What did he say when you told him you would like to have it and thought you ought to have it?

A. He hesitated about it, and finally sold it.[38]

The Pujo Committee was not fooled by Morgan's close-to-the-vest attitude. In its final report it stated flatly, "Mr. Morgan's conception of what constitutes power and control in the financial world is so peculiar as to invalidate all his conclusions based upon it."[39] Pierpont's aloofness from the outside world, especially regarding the nascent automobile industry, would cost his bank heavily in lost opportunities in the years ahead.

ENTER THE INTANGIBLE

The Antitrust Division of the Justice Department actively sought to restrain many of the trusts and combinations forming during the first decade of the twentieth century, alleging violations of the Sherman Act. Morgan's consolidations were no exception. He was involved in all of the notable cases except those against Standard Oil and American Tobacco. The period was one of consolidation by bankers and counterpunching by the government to determine the course of American industry and finance.

Throughout the two decades before World War I, it appeared that the government held the upper hand. With the exception of the *E.C. Knight* decision, which opened the window to dozens if not hundreds of mergers, the government had won more cases than it had lost in the federal courts. The most notable was the epic *United States v. Northern Securities Co.* case. Northern Securities was a holding company controlled by Morgan, Harriman, and Hill interests. Henry Villard had previously had a controlling interest in the company but lost it to Morgan. The court ruled that Northern's monopoly on rail traffic west of the Mississippi was illegal. When the decision was announced, Theodore Roosevelt, whose Justice Department initiated the suit, stated, "Without this success the National Government must have remained in the impotence to which it had been reduced in the Knight decision."

Adding to Wall Street's woes were suits filed against Standard Oil, American Tobacco, U.S. Steel, and International Harvester. Roosevelt initiated the suits against Standard Oil and American Tobacco. Finally, in 1911 both were deemed to be in violation of the Sherman Act and ordered broken up by the Supreme Court in the two most momentous decisions under the 20-year old law. Mergers and acquisitions specialists later acknowledged that one of the serious threats to a deal, and to the arbitrageurs who often sought to play the stocks of two companies against each other, was regulatory interference from either the Antitrust Division of the Justice Department or the Federal Trade Commission. Any deal-killing pronouncements from either regulatory body could upset the delicate balance on which many deals hinged. After the Standard Oil and American Tobacco decisions, the issue emerged for the first time. Now federal regulators had to be considered a worthy opponent of Wall Street in its effort to forge merger deals.

The Justice Department began investigating U.S. Steel in 1905, looking for signs of horizontal monopoly. The new company quickly became known as the "steel trust" and Theodore Roosevelt's administration began to actively investigate its activities. It took over two years of testimony before suit was filed. Little did anyone realize that the case would become the longest-lasting antitrust case to date. Further damage to the company was done by hearings in Congress in 1912 when George W. Perkins made a case for the company being a good trust. In evidence presented before a Senate committee called by Senator Moses Clapp, a member of the Interstate Commerce Committee, Perkins claimed that the company essentially was a good trust because it provided increased efficiency in the industry, a conclusion that was highly suspect at the time. Since efficiency was in the country's best interests, Perkins argued, the company should be allowed to continue without government tampering.

Louis Brandeis, crusading against Morgan, the railroads, and investment banking for decades, took the opposite position. Rather than argue against the steel combination, he focused his testimony on the money trust. Morgan's fat fees for floating Big Steel securities had not been forgotten. Brandeis claimed that the only reason bankers were interested in industry was the fees they could charge for a consolidation. His point was political, but a hard economic analysis of the company would have done more to support it. Responding to Perkins's contention, Brandeis added, "I am so convinced of the economic fallacy in a huge unit that if we make competition possible, if we create conditions where there could be reasonable competition that these monsters would fall to the ground."[40]

The investigations did not stop with Big Steel. International Harvester also was charged with violations of the Sherman Act in 1912. The huge market share it held in its industry was too conspicuous to go unnoticed. The good and bad trust ideas were again being floated. International Harvester had its share of antitrust troubles. With an acknowledged monopoly in its industry, the company was susceptible to antitrust action since its 80 percent market share had not changed. After the antitrust suit was filed against the company, seeking its dissolution, a lower court found in favor of the government and Harvester appealed to the Supreme Court. Then, inexplicably, it suddenly withdrew its appeal and consented to be broken into two parts. The case was the first in which a major company agreed to the government's contentions and went peaceably.

Continuing the string of bad luck for Morgan-inspired companies, the Supreme Court issued a decree in 1911 forbidding General Electric and several of its competitors from engaging in unlawful practices in producing light bulbs. While not in the same league as some of the other momentous court decisions of the period, it nevertheless helped prove Brandeis's point to detractors of Morgan and the consolidation movement. Jack Morgan had better luck with AT&T. Despite its clear monopoly in the telephone business, AT&T was the one Morgan creation that would continue in business with the blessing of Congress, allowed to operate as a monopoly. Despite the Wall Street influence, which became anathema to many in the Justice Department and Congress, AT&T became one of the few government-sanctioned private monopolies in the country. After complaints by smaller phone companies during World War I that AT&T was stifling competition, the government reached an accommodation with the phone giant in 1921, allowing it to purchase smaller rivals subject to regulatory approval. The service provided by AT&T during the war was of high quality and the government did not want to see it decline simply in the name of increased competition. As a result of the Willis-Graham law, AT&T assumed a virtual monopoly over American telephone service that would last for 60 years.

Another Morgan victory emerged with the U.S. Steel decision in 1920, reached after almost 15 years of investigation, suits, and appeals. The Supreme Court ruled by a 4-to-3 margin that the company did not abuse its position in the marketplace and should not be broken up. The court effectively conceded that it was a good trust after all. The victory was a bitter pill for Brandeis on more than one count. After years of writing, lecturing, and commenting in the press about the evils of the money trust, he was appointed to the Supreme Court by Woodrow Wilson. Because of his previous connections, he recused himself from the decision. The other justice abstaining was James McReynolds, who served as attorney general under Wilson. As a result, the case was resolved in Big Steel's favor. Clearly, the decision would have gone against the company if the two had voted.

The decision paved the way for a decade of mergers and acquisitions on an even larger scale. Although Big Steel benefited from the diminished court decision, three consecutive Republican administrations proved friendly to big business and provided little opposition to consolidations. New growth industries were emerging quickly as the American infrastructure developed and matured. The country now had its telephones, steel mills, and food on its table. The new industries about to emerge would prove even more profitable to their investment bankers because they would cater to consumer tastes, the true engine of growth after World War I.

NOTES

1. United States Department of Commerce, *Historical Statistics of the United States: Colonial Times to 1957* (Washington: U.S. Government Printing Office, 1957), pp. 151, 155.

2. George Wheeler, *Pierpont Morgan & Friends: The Anatomy of a Myth* (Engle-wood Cliffs, NJ: Prentice Hall, 1973), p. 222.

3. Kenneth Warren, *Big Steel: The First Century of the United States Steel Corporation, 1901–2001* (Pittsburgh: University of Pittsburgh Press, 2001), p. 11.

4. Gustavus Myers, *History of the Great American Fortunes* (Chicago: Charles H. Kerr & Co., 1911), vol. III, p. 257.

5. *Hearings before the Committee Investigating the United States Steel Corporation*, 62nd Congress, 2nd Session, 1911–1912, pp. 1278–1314.

6. Estimates at the time and since assumed Carnegie received $480 million, including $80 million representing two years' profits of the company. See Jean Strouse, *Morgan: American Financier* (New York: Random House, 1999), pp. 403–404.

7. *U.S. Steel Hearings*, p. 1301.

8. *New York Times*, March 4, 1902.

9. *Historical Statistics*, p. 572.

10. United States Steel Corporation, Annual Report, December 31, 1902.

11. Ron Chernow, *Titan: The Life of John D. Rockefeller, Sr.* (New York: Random House, 1998), p. 393.

12. *Historical Statistics*, p. 123.

13. Gabriel Kolko, *The Triumph of Conservatism: A Reinterpretation of American History, 1900–1916* (Chicago: Quadrangle Books, 1963), p. 37. Lester D. Chandler Jr., *The Visible Hand: The Managerial Revolution in American Business* (Cambridge, MA: Harvard University Press, 1977), p. 361.

14. Ron Chernow, *The House of Morgan: An American Banking Dynasty & the Rise of Modern Finance* (New York: Simon & Schuster, 1990), p. 103.

15. Armin Rappaport, *The Navy League of the United States* (Detroit: Wayne State University Press, 1962), p. 41.

16. Ibid., p. 22.

17. Melvin I. Urofsky, *Big Steel & the Wilson Administration* (Columbus: Ohio State University Press, 1969), p. 112.

18. *New York Times*, May 12, 1915.

19. Urofsky, p. 90.

20. Quoted in Anna Rochester, *Rulers of America: A Study of Finance Capital* (New York: International Publishers, 1936), p. 210.

21. Warren, p. 363.

22. Barbara Marsh, *A Corporate Tragedy: The Agony of International Harvester Company* (Garden City, NY: Doubleday, 1985), p. 41.

23. Bernard Weisberger, *The Dream Maker: William C. Durant, Founder of General Motors* (Boston: Little, Brown, 1979), p. 128.

24. Marsh, p. 42.
25. Strouse, p. 470.
26. Ferdinand Lundberg, *America's 60 Families* (New York: Citadel Press, 1937), pp. 26–27.
27. Ibid., pp. 106–107.
28. Ibid., pp. 252–254.
29. H. Allaway, "The New Wall Street," *Munsey's Magazine*, April 1899.
30. House Report, 62nd Congress, 3rd session. Numbers were reported by the Pujo committee studying the money trust and represent only those public deals of an interstate nature.
31. *Historical Statistics*, p. 481.
32. Ibid., pp. 480–481.
33. Ibid., p. 472.
34. *New York Times*, May 16, 1911.
35. *Historical Statistics*, p. 673.
36. Myers, p. 612.
37. House Report, 62nd Congress, 3rd session, p. 2 ff.
38. Ibid.
39. Ibid.
40. Alpheus T. Mason, *Brandeis: A Free Man's Life* (New York: Viking Press, 1946), p. 355.

CHAPTER 2

DRIVING TO THE STORE

It is a peculiar fact that past history clearly shows that the merger movement is very much stimulated by good times, particularly a bull market in stocks, while there is a marked tendency for consolidations to decrease in number under the reverse conditions when one would think economy were most needed.

The Magazine of Wall Street, *1931*

In the first decade of the twentieth century, the American infrastructure was expanding rapidly. In addition to steel and telephone consolidation, great strides were made in fashioning a large, efficient automobile manufacturing base that would rapidly become the centerpiece of American industry. While the U.S. Navy became a great source of demand for steel during World War I as bankers had hoped, the automobile industry would far outstrip it over the years, becoming the country's best-known industry. Like many other large industries, auto manufacturing would draw the attention of bankers. As with the telephone, steel, and harvesting equipment businesses, the bankers would only become interested once the industry proved itself. In the early years, bankers were extremely wary of the newfangled automobile, viewing its financing as too risky.

Once the automobile became established, other new industries began to appear. Component manufacturers sprang up along with finance companies and insurance companies. Distances became less problematic and people began to use the car for everyday tasks and leisure travel. The drive was not always easy, however. Many of the country's roads were in poor shape and quickly wreaked havoc on the new contraptions. The automobile's popularity demonstrated that the U.S. was on the verge of a revolution in the way it traveled and did business. Visionaries in retailing quickly spied an opportunity.

The already popular method of mail order selling was about to be joined by large retailing chains. Critics in rural areas would characterize these chains as a direct attack on the American way of life. Small-town stores and suppliers owned by local merchants were invaded and often replaced by large chain stores that aroused suspicion in rural areas because of their purported ties to Wall Street. The large stores proved to be an ineluctable force, however. Once entrenched, they became a staple of small-town living as well as well-known icons in the cities.

Ironically, influential New York bankers viewed these two great revolutions in American life as highly pedestrian, at least in their formative years. Pierpont Morgan considered the automobile nothing more than a fad, like the bicycle, that would eventually pass into oblivion. Equally, the notion that people could shop in large department stores carrying many sorts of items was totally lost on bankers who were not in the habit of shopping for themselves. As a result, the money trust did not actively participate in financing many of these new ventures. That lack of faith opened the door for a new generation of investment bankers only too happy to provide financing where their better-bred colleagues did not deign to tread. The rise of Goldman Sachs, Charles E. Merrill, Lehman Brothers, and Dillon Read demonstrated that the ranks of investment banking could be cracked by small firms as long as they specialized in small, up-and-coming companies rather than the established pillars of American industry. Morgan did begin to realize that retailers were the wave of the future. The board of Montgomery Ward became dominated by Morgan allies, although not partners of the bank. The same was true of Marshall Field, which was dominated by the large Chicago banks having a direct tie with Morgan since the days of the money trust investigation.

The automobile industry in particular produced a breed of self-made industrialist who had little time for New York bankers. William C. Durant and Henry Ford both avoided, and were avoided by, Wall

Street bankers accustomed to cutting themselves into deals and companies' board seats as a condition of financing. Ford turned down more than one lucrative proposal to take his company public. Walter Chrysler kept investment banker Clarence Dillon at arm's length before finally agreeing to purchase Dodge Brothers from him. The automakers were self-made and self-educated men who felt uncomfortable in the presence of supercilious bankers, especially those at J.P. Morgan & Co., who viewed them as uncouth tinkerers. The same uneasy relationship would also be seen in the dealings between Wall Street and the utilities industry later in the 1920s.

Deal making took a very sophisticated turn after the Big Steel consolidation. The new giant corporations took on the aura of states within a state and bankers became the statesmen in the process. Pierpont Morgan became arguably the most powerful man in the country—more powerful than even Teddy Roosevelt—and his partners and lawyers were widely viewed as the equivalents of cabinet ministers. This aura did not sit well with the automakers. Henry Ford, the embodiment of the self-made man, viewed financiers with extreme distrust, once labeling Jay Gould and Morgan "Jews," despite the fact that they both were Protestants. To Ford, anyone who loaned money was a Jew and a Jew was one who loaned money because he was precluded from doing anything else.[1] Ford's extreme anti-Semitic, anti-Wall Street views and his loathing of Morgan would have profound consequences for his company, especially after it was overtaken by General Motors in the mid-1920s.

Ford and the automakers in general were not alone in this view. Thomas Edison and Theodore Vail also had little time for bankers, but both eventually succumbed to financial pressures and let the wolves in the door. Their alternative to bank financing was to use retained earnings as much as possible to finance expansion. Using retained earnings demonstrated that the companies were successful and that the stock would appreciate as a result. Bankers, in contrast, favored paying dividends to shareholders in order to make the stock as attractive as possible to investors. The major benefit of using retained earnings was that the companies could maintain their independence from predatory bankers who exacted too high a price for their services. How long they were able to do so often depended upon the tightness of managerial controls over the companies. Those with tight controls, such as Ford, remained aloof from Wall Street for decades. Those who often had trouble compiling sensible financial statements, such as Durant's General Motors, had short futures as independents.

GRAND DREAMS

During the early 1900s, dozens of manufacturers were producing automobiles. The popularity of automobiles was never in doubt: The public avidly began buying them as soon as they were made. Often, purchasing a car took a great leap of faith because the early models were unreliable, uncomfortable, and sometimes dangerous. People suffered fatal injuries when the crankshaft recoiled and struck them as they were attempting to start the motor. Nevertheless, even before 1910 the auto industry had clear leaders among the dozens of competitors.

The General Motors Corporation was the brainchild of William Crapo Durant, better known as Billy. Born in 1861 in Flint, Michigan, he was raised by his mother. He left high school at 17 eagerly seeking business experience. Then came a series of odd jobs: he became a traveling cigar salesman and a bookkeeper. After riding in a horse-drawn carriage fitted with coil cushioned seats, he became so enamored of the design that he borrowed $1,500 from a local bank and bought the company. He and his partner, J. Dallas Dort, moved the company to Flint and set up shop as the Flint Road Cart Company. Durant became the salesman for the operation. By the beginning of the twentieth century, it was producing more than 75,000 carriages and wagons per year and employed 1,500 men. Durant became a mainstay of Flint because of the economic benefits he brought to the town as well as his never-ending sense of optimism. He was a salesman's salesman, and became a millionaire as well.

But the life of the horse-drawn carriage was about to wane as the new automobile showed signs of promise. Durant had taken a few rides in early automobiles but was not interested in them until he rode in a Buick Roadster, which so impressed him that he became treasurer and chief executive officer of the company at the behest of its president, James Whiting. The company had been founded by David Buick, a transplanted Scot. One of Durant's first official actions was to increase its capital four times. Yet all was not clear sailing in the industry. The early years of Buick and Ford were troubled as an automobile trade association called the Selden group sued Ford and Durant for using an internal combustion engine that was patented and licensed by the group. Initially, Ford and Durant refused to pay their licensing fees, although Durant eventually capitulated. Ford won the battle when the New York Court of Appeals ruled that all internal combustion engines were not the same. The cartel was defeated. Free of legal proceedings, Durant's company began to grow.

Durant clearly had bigger and better things in mind than a single car manufacturer. He wanted to consolidate the industry into one huge company that would be able to employ economies of scale in order to turn a profit. Unlike harvesters, however, automobiles were still fairly new and did not have a proven track record. In many respects, the industry was in much the same shape as steel, telephones, and harvesting equipment had been at the turn of the century. It suffered from excessive competition, lack of standards, unreliable products, and larger-than-life executives who ran their companies like personal fiefdoms. Durant was no different. He too wanted to expand on a grand scale.

Durant began talks with J.P. Morgan & Co. in 1907 about creating a giant company to be called the United Motors Corporation. His original idea was to combine his Buick with the Maxwell-Briscoe Company and then add the Ford and Reo companies to the fold. If that could have been accomplished, the company clearly would have dominated the young industry. Herbert Satterlee represented Morgan in the talks. They came at a propitious time, because Henry Ford was on the verge of announcing the introduction of his new Model T. Then the talks bogged down quickly. Durant's idea was to combine the companies in an exchange of stock, but his potential partners had other ideas. Ford wanted cash, not stock in the new company. His price was $3 million. If the deal had gone through, the price would have been a pittance compared to what Carnegie had been paid for his steel company. But Ford's success was still in front of him and the amount was highly speculative at the moment.

Durant persisted in forging ahead although some of the Morgan partners were not impressed as he avidly promoted his company's stock. Morgan's senior attorney, Francis L. Stetson, was less than enthusiastic after meeting Durant in New York. Stetson suspected that Durant was pushing ahead with the deal simply to boost the price of his own Buick stock, which was listed on the Detroit Stock Exchange rather than the New York Stock Exchange. It was not the first or the last time that Durant would arouse suspicions about his motives in a deal. Nevertheless, he met with Pierpont Morgan and made his case for the consolidation, but his pleas fell upon deaf ears. Morgan was not impressed with him and did not believe that the automobile would make a lasting impression on American life. Durant wrote to his lawyer after the meeting, "If you think it is an easy matter to get money from New York capitalists to finance a motor car proposition in Michigan, you have another guess coming . . . money is hard to get owing to a somewhat uncomfortable feeling of uneasiness and a general distrust of the automobile proposition."[2]

Refusing to concede defeat, Durant pushed ahead with his plan although the merger was now minuscule in comparison with the original plan. Buick was merged with another company, the Olds Motor Works, and the new General Motors Company was finally born in September 1908. Ford, Maxwell-Briscoe, and Reo went their separate ways. GM became the major challenger to Ford, whose Model T proved to be a resounding success. Originally, Ford produced cars relatively cheaply, aimed at the average citizen who could not afford more expensive models. Buick still made more expensive touring cars and before 1910 was producing more cars annually than Ford. The new company was smaller than Durant had originally hoped, but he went on a buying spree that would quickly enlarge it.

Within two years, Durant's new empire totaled 28 companies. He acquired the Cadillac Motor Company and the Champion Ignition Company, a manufacturer of spark plugs, along with many smaller car and truck manufacturers. By 1910, a persistent problem arose: He was running out of money. General Motors could only issue so much stock to pay for these acquisitions before the dilution became so great that the company would be worthless, so Durant turned to the banks again. After approaching two Morgan allies, Lee Higginson and Kuhn Loeb, Durant turned to a Chicago bank, the Continental Savings and Trust, which agreed to loan almost $10 million. It then backed away after discovering that GM lacked a central bookkeeping system.[3] Apparently, General Motors' borrowings were not recorded with any accuracy so the banks could not determine how much debt the company had accumulated.

Long, hard negotiations produced a rescue package of $15 million that was put together by Lee Higginson and J. & W. Seligman, a New York investment bank. As a condition, bankers got three of the five newly created trustee seats in the company. Durant remained as a vice president of the company but now had to submit to standard financial controls. The recapitalization, small by Wall Street standards, took the form of five-year notes yielding 6 percent interest. These were immediately bought by financial institutions, illustrating that the automobile industry in general had gained an enormous amount of respect among institutional investors.[4] Billy Durant had the cash needed to continue his operations but he was now on a short leash. He was also the first vice president of the company—a clear demotion. His bankers would not tolerate any sloppy bookkeeping or overly ambitious expansion plans. Lee Higginson & Co. officially stated after the deal was done, "Here is a concern which got into trouble, not from lack of earnings but from lack of management. We now take the business up, put in an able board of directors and an able finance committee and become part of the management during the life of these notes."[5]

Bankers effectively ruled GM for the next several years. Overall, the automobile industry grew at a strong pace during this period, with the number of cars produced nationwide increasing almost 500 percent between 1910 and 1915. General Motors contributed about 20 percent of the total in 1910, but the number slipped to around 8 percent in 1915. The popularity of the Model T was partly responsible, but the bankers' basic conservatism was also to blame. One of GM's operating vice presidents summed up the situation by stating, "The bankers were too skeptical about the future of the automobile industry. They were chiefly interested in trying to realize savings, so they closed down some plants, concentrating in others . . . under Durant the company might have had a little financial difficulty now and then, but it would have grown much faster and its earnings would have been much greater."[6]

While General Motors was under the watchful eye of bankers, a significant development in automobile history occurred when the Lincoln Highway was announced. In 1912, highways in the country were poor—in some cases perilous. Graded and paved roads existed only in urban areas, while the rest of the country suffered dirt roads, many of which were not graded properly. The popularity of the automobile prompted the development of a coast-to-coast highway that was named after Abraham Lincoln. The road was funded locally, linking and improving existing roads. When eventually completed, it stretched from New York City to San Francisco through such places as South Bend, Indiana; Omaha, Nebraska; Cheyenne, Wyoming; and Reno, Nevada. Rather than a grand building project, as the Interstate Highway System would be in the 1950s, it was the logical linking of roads and places that provided direct access between the two coasts. When the road was officially announced in 1913, a huge celebration was held in San Francisco at the opera house. The gala spared no expense and was attended by Ruggerio Leoncavallo, the composer of *Pagliacci*. Naturally, it was funded by a local car dealers' association that recognized the opportunity. The *San Francisco Examiner* proudly announced, "The celebration is in honor of the greatest highway project that was ever undertaken . . . we want to start the project with a boom."[7]

The boom almost did not occur. Henry Ford refused to lend his support to the project. Local farmers in the prairie states often tried to sabotage it, considering it an invasion of their livelihoods. The road was supported by Carl Fisher, the real estate developer of Miami Beach and the Indianapolis Motor Speedway. Ford believed that the roads should be funded from the public purse rather than organized by private citizens. Eventually, the roads were supported by many state funds and cost only $10 million to complete. The highway would prove invaluable during World War I, when convoys of trucks were used to carry goods and equipment between states. The link, which covered almost 3,400 miles, was not complete until 1925, but its completion did coincide with one of the great auto manufacturing booms of the century. Pierpont Morgan died in 1913. He never lived to see the new "fad" become the country's premier industry.

New entrants to the auto industry were also finding financing that would make auto production even more competitive. In 1911, Lehman Brothers and Goldman Sachs, at the time second-tier Wall Street firms, brought the Studebaker Corporation to market. Previously, Studebaker had made carriages and wagons, similar to Durant's company. Within a year, it was the third largest automaker but subsequently slipped to fifth place during World War I. Studebaker was a major auto manufacturer in its day and became one of the components of the Dow Jones Industrial Average, being included in 1916. It was dropped from the index in 1924.

The auto companies all had a common thread that made bankers wary. One of the bankers' main problems with the auto industry was the matter of strong one-man control. In 1916, Thomas Lamont, a Morgan partner, tried to persuade Henry Ford to take his company public. Not realizing that Ford did not believe in public ownership—or bankers, for that matter—Lamont pitched the virtues of going public to the automaker and managed to offend him in the process. Writing to Ford, Lamont stated somewhat bluntly, "The present makeup of your company is your only weakness. So long as the control of your company rests absolutely in your hands, just so long is the future of the business dependent upon the life of one man."[8] Lamont was not telling Ford anything he did not already know. The automaker just liked personal control, as did Durant. Ford ignored the pleas, and his company did not go public until 1957, when Goldman Sachs led its first public offering. Ford remained the one big deal that got away in the 1920s' consolidation boom.

Capital for expansion was not a problem for Ford as it constantly was for General Motors. Henry Ford had good reason to be suspicious of Lamont and Morgan because they were preaching the virtues of a process he did not need at the time. Years before product differentiation became the norm in manufacturing, his Model T was the simple staple of his company. Constantly reducing the price, he made the car affordable for the average worker, something GM could not claim for its models. In 1913, Ford reported profits of $25 million on capital of only $2 million. The percentage return was thought to be the highest ever recorded and prompted Ford to raise his workers' wages and shorten their working hours. He announced that the company would retain half of the profit and distribute the other half to the workers, in proportion to their wages at the time. Bankers were aghast at the idea of distributing profits to workers, but Ford ruled his company with an iron fist. "Our capital," he stated, "is $2 million but our assets now are about $35 million. We have no stock in the market. There are only seven stockholders in the company, and of those Mr. James Couzens and I hold the majority. My holdings are 58½ percent."[9] Naturally, Lamont's pleas were to fall upon deaf ears.

Ford's unusual methods were producing strong results. Realizing that his reliance on internally generated funds and his dislike of bankers made him especially reliant on his workers' productivity, Ford announced his revolutionary scheme unheard of in American labor practice. After Ford distributed half of his company's earnings to his workers, the *New York Times* remarked, "The theory of the management of the Ford Company is distinctly utopian and runs dead against all experience. The movement for the bettering of society need not be universal; in their opinion, 'we think that one concern can make a start and create an example for other employers.' "[10] In other words, the company was treading on new ground and so far had been successful. The other shareholders had a different view, however. Two years later, they filed suit against Henry Ford for cutting the price of his cars. A court ruled in their favor, claiming that, regardless of his intentions, they had a right to decent payouts, not to be treated simply as secondaries behind the workers and Ford himself.

After Ford announced to his workers his payoff, which he called a "dividend," GM also announced a cash dividend to its stockholders. When the period of banker control was about to expire, the company announced a 50 percent dividend on the stock, which was trading at $50 per share. Paying out such a large amount indicated that the banker trustees were concerned about Ford's largesse. The company and Durant would have been happier if they had retained more of the earnings since it would have alleviated the need for some future financings.

Other than using retained earnings, Ford had a distinct distaste for indebtedness. His company never borrowed a penny, either in the short or long term, with one exception. Its treasurer stated emphatically, "We have no banking connections that could furnish us money . . . we never borrowed money but one season. If our production should be shut off for 30 days, we would have to borrow money."[11] But sitting on a large cash hoard was risky since it attracted investment bankers and potential takeovers. By 1926, after recovering from the recession that began the decade, Ford was valued at $1 billion, which put it in privileged company. Although Ford was private, a Wall Street firm, Hornblower & Weeks, made a bid for the company, which was naturally rejected. The firm estimated that Ford's assets were about $715 million and that its market value would be $1 billion. The firm intended to underwrite it for about $1.25 billion.

Durant had plans to take GM back from the bankers. He was not happy playing someone else's tune. The fiscal austerity the bankers placed on the company could be replaced by expansion plans once again if Durant held a majority of the stock. Using his recently founded Chevrolet Motor Company as a holding company, Durant quietly acquired a majority control of GM stock. The stock climbed as high as $550 per share as a result, indicating that the program was purchasing stock at inflated prices. This would become catastrophic later when it lost most of its value. But at the time, the sizable accumulations had the intended effect. Durant then announced his majority position to the GM board and stated that he was back in control. The shocked bankers could do little but acquiesce. One condition placed upon Durant was that John Raskob would become one of the new board members. Until that time, Raskob had been treasurer of the DuPont company and was a close ally of Pierre S. DuPont, who was also a Durant ally. The Delaware family was a major investor in GM and the choice of Raskob and others for the board was their method of keeping tabs on Durant.

The DuPonts' interest in General Motors was one of the wiser investments made by the gunpowder, paints, and varnishes firm. Recognizing automobiles as a potential source of demand for its products, DuPont made a $49 million investment in GM so that it could supply the automaker with the materials necessary to produce cars and parts. The link between the two companies suggested a vertical monopoly to the Justice Department, which charged DuPont with antitrust violations 40 years later in 1957. At the time, it was a stroke of genius because the returns from the GM investment helped propel DuPont forward. This was especially true since the enormous gains DuPont made selling munitions to the government during World War I were hard to duplicate in peacetime.

After regaining GM, Durant again began expansion plans with the full approval of the DuPonts, who owned about one-third of GM's stock. He engaged in a few new securities offerings, but the need for expansion capital was relentless. While desperately trying to prop up the company stock by using syndicates organized to purchase shares if they fell too low, Durant finally had to turn again to J.P. Morgan & Co. Pierpont had died and his son Jack was in charge at 23 Wall Street. Durant probably anticipated that he was about to sell his soul to the devil in return for capital. Agreeing to help, Morgan raised a total of $64 million. The bank subscribed to a new stock offering by buying up 1.4 million new shares of stock at $20 each for its own account, raising $28 million of the total in the process. The bank and its partners took $2 million for themselves as a fee. In addition, they kept rights for themselves to take an additional 200,000 common shares at $10 each, putting in the proverbial green shoe.

But the rub for Durant was the normal Morgan practice of dictating board seats. In 1920, several new members were added to the GM board, including Edward R. Stettinius, a Morgan partner; George Baker of the First National Bank; and Owen Young of the General Electric Company, another Morgan ally. The handwriting was on the wall for Durant.

An important part of the deal for Durant was holding up the price of the stock as he had in the past. He learned shortly afterward that Stettinius was actively selling 100,000 shares of the stock short and had profited by several hundred thousand dollars.[12] He confronted the banker, who in turn accused him of dealing on the side for himself, an old criticism of Durant. The automaker began to realize that he was no longer fully in control of the situation surrounding GM. Matters would be made worse when Morgan partners, including Dwight Morrow, concluded that Durant was speculating in the stock and decided to oust him from the company.

Durant's bubbling optimism about General Motors became his undoing. He was often in the habit of buying GM stock from friends and acquaintances, bailing them out of a declining market while recording the loss himself. The sale of the 100,000 shares became the straw that broke the camel's back, however. A commentator summed up the sale by stating, "Finally the odds became too great even for Durant's great courage and greater faith. His friends had been extricated without loss. But his entire personal fortune had been sacrificed. In a few short months he had turned himself from a man worth $90,000,000 to one owing $2,000,000."[13] His own personal fortune rode entirely on the back of his beloved but poorly run company.

Durant's management style was at the heart of his problems. The loose management techniques, ad hoc decisions, and relentless expansion frustrated even his closer colleagues and alienated his bankers twice within a 10-year period. Durant was also the opposite of Ford in another respect: His concern for the average person centered on the investor, not his workers. The basis for the Morgan partners' consternation was the Durant Corporation, set up in 1920 by Billy for the alleged purpose of promoting the shares to small investors. The company was advising them to hold the stock for the long run, suggesting to many critics that it was nothing more than a way to prop up shares in a flagging market. Naturally, the Morgan partners saw it differently, viewing the hastily constructed company as simply another of Durant's manipulations of the stock price for his own ends. Making matters worse, Durant did not bother to inform them of his new investment company before announcing it publicly. Automobile production nationwide had slowed because of the recession of 1920 and inventories had swollen as economic conditions forced stocks lower. Stocks were under pressure, and some wondered whether Durant had devised a scheme to stabilize GM. Small investors were likely to hold stock longer than professionals, hopefully maintaining its price or at least putting no further downward pressure on it. Whatever Durant's motives, the strategy backfired as he finally lost control of GM forever.

In 1916, Henry Ford made his often-quoted remark about history and the past. "History is more or less bunk," he growled. "It's tradition. We don't want tradition. We want to live in the present, and the only history that's worth a tinker's damn is the history we make today." Taken in the context of the automobile industry at the time, his point was not totally unfounded. Clearly in the driver's seat in his industry, Ford made sure that bankers were effectively kept at arm's length from his company, enabling Detroit to remain at least partially free from Wall Street influences until after World War II. Ford had learned from history that banker influence spelled slow growth and eventual loss of control of companies by their founders.

General Motors shares continued to decline in a poor market, and it was revealed that Durant was short cash because he had been buying shares in one of his support accounts on margin. He was faced with a margin call when the stock hit $12 per share. Morgan bankers were asked to intervene and found debts much greater than simply the $1 million that Durant claimed was the problem. Fearing a stock market panic if the news leaked out, they arranged to buy Durant's shares at $9.50 each, putting up $20 million of their own funds. The DuPonts put in an additional $7 million.[14] General Motors was saved but Durant was not. His resignation was part of the deal, and in November 1920 he lost his company for the second time.

After losing the company, Durant was poor in 1920 but not quite penniless. His personal bank account was only worth a few thousand dollars before the legal proceedings rearranging GM were completed. When asked if he was on the verge of ruin, he responded, "Am I broke? Well I'll tell you. I'm the richest man in America . . . in friends." After his ouster, he went on to found a small company called Durant Motors and became one of the largest stock market operators of the 1920s, lending credence to all of the rumors that had circulated about him for years. Using borrowed (margin) money, he would make a purported $100 million in the market bubble leading up to 1929 only to lose it all again after the Crash. He eventually returned to his hometown of Flint, Michigan, where he managed a bowling alley in his later years. His one memento of all his years in business was his original bankbook that he had kept since he was a boy. The several hundred dollars deposited originally had compounded to $7,000 over the years.

Regardless of Durant's personal misfortune, the creation of General Motors was the greatest series of deals made in the early twentieth century, eclipsing U.S. Steel in importance and longevity. The Morgan partnership's eventual entry into the company's affairs was inevitable given Durant's inability to keep his hands off the company stock. By the time GM required rescue for the second time, it had grown so large that only a money trust bank was capable of putting it on the proper course. General Motors eventually would overtake Ford by the mid-1920s as the largest automaker. Being so successful would also attract a host of imitators, some of which would be highly successful.

UNLIKELY COMPETITION

By the early 1920s, it was more than apparent that the automobile industry was one of the country's most significant businesses. Ford and General Motors were the two largest manufacturers, and a host of smaller carmakers also vied for consumers' attention. Between 1902 and 1926, 12 manufacturers expanded to 44. More astonishing was the number of companies that folded during the same period.

Over 125 manufacturers tried their hand at producing cars before throwing in the towel.[15] Pierpont Morgan's notion that the auto was just another passing fad could not have proved more incorrect, although if he had been examining the number of failed firms alone his conclusion would have appeared somewhat realistic. The circumstances surrounding Henry Ford's snubbing of the bank's offer to take his company public proved that the House of Morgan was falling slowly out of tune with twentieth-century industry.

The coup at General Motors helped stem that tide, but the House of Morgan clearly had lost some significant opportunities in the industry between 1907 and 1920. Being allied with GM put the bank in the catbird seat as it looked out over the industry. Henry Ford may not have held bankers in much esteem, but Morgan's influence at GM suggested that the bank could still help structure the industry for the future, earning fat fees in the process. The DuPonts installed Alfred Sloan as the head of GM in 1923, ushering in a new period of professional management and product innovation. The auto industry now required all the professional management available. The business was no longer an innovator's delight. By 1923, car registrations totaled 13.2 million, almost equal to the number of telephone sets in use.[16]

At the same time, the investment banking business was admitting new members to its ranks. The number of Wall Street securities firms was increasing as many of the smaller, up-and-coming businesses needed someone to help find capital for expansion. The dominant banks such as Morgan, Kuhn Loeb, Kidder Peabody, and Lee Higginson maintained their close ties with established, large companies, but smaller firms such as Charles E. Merrill & Co., Salomon Brothers, Lehman Brothers, and Goldman Sachs were gaining underwriting and trading business from the less established but potentially growth-oriented industries such as retail stores and auto component manufacturers. The big banks would not be bothered with these firms. They either did not understand their businesses or found them too mundane to deal with.

One of the smaller investment banks doing solid but not spectacular business on Wall Street during World War I was William

Read & Company, a small bond house that vied for the occasional underwriting job. Founded in 1905 by Read, the firm was the successor to the older Vermilye & Co., founded in the nineteenth century, at which Read had worked for years. The new firm established a reputation by developing bond valuation techniques that would come into general use in the decades ahead. Read made one of his most astute hires when he convinced a young Harvard graduate named Clarence Dillon to work for him in 1913. Although Read did not realize it at the time, hiring Dillon was equivalent to hiring J.P. Morgan & Co. It would change his firm forever.

Dillon began working for Read as a bond salesman in the firm's Chicago office but soon began branching out into other fields of endeavor. Visibility on Wall Street was gained by arranging deals, not selling them, and Dillon quickly developed a taste for battle early in his career. After a year in Chicago, he moved to New York, where he gained considerable influence with more senior Wall Street figures like Bernard Baruch. Becoming a close colleague to Baruch after serving as an assistant to the already legendary investor on the War Industries Board, Dillon found himself in the limelight after the war ended. The recession of 1920 hit the automobile industry particularly hard. The same slowdown that led to Billy Durant's fall also caused severe problems for a well-known tire manufacturer, the Goodyear Tire and Rubber Company. With sales falling and inventories mounting, even Goldman Sachs, Goodyear's investment banker, thought it was headed for bankruptcy. The company's lawyers suggested that it contact Dillon about the possibility of finding cash so that it could stay in business. That proved to be a propitious but costly choice.

Dillon agreed to help finance a bailout package. He put together a deal consisting of stock, bonds, and preferred stock. The bonds were unsecured, something of an innovation at the time since debt was usually secured by assets. Dillon also created a class of special stock that he could cash in once the deal proved successful. And, in keeping with the spirit of more accomplished deal makers, he assigned a consulting company, which he controlled, to advise Goodyear on strategy at the cost of $250,000 per year. Many on Wall

Street considered the deal outrageous, but a reluctant Goodyear board accepted it and the company survived. Dillon found himself in the league of major deal makers of the day. Now he would have to repeat the coup in order to be considered more than just a flash in the pan. As a result of the deals, William Read & Co. became known as Dillon Read & Co.

Dillon's career began to blossom at about the same time a young executive, dismayed by Billy Durant's loose management techniques, left General Motors to strike out on his own. Walter Chrysler founded Chrysler Motors in 1923, after working as chief of operations at General Motors. An inveterate tinkerer, Chrysler had worked for a railroad before joining GM. He purchased his first car in 1905, then disassembled it and reassembled it so that he could learn as much about automobiles as possible. His cars became very popular and within a short time his company was considered one of the respected minor manufacturers after Ford and GM.

Although known as an investment banker, Dillon was presented with the opportunity of a lifetime in 1925. The Dodge Brothers Motor Company was put up for sale after the death of the two brothers, John and Horace. The surviving members of the family decided to sell and sought the aid of bankers. Dodge was the third major manufacturer and the company was considered a plum despite the recent recession. A broker representing the family approached Dillon to see whether the young banker could find a potential buyer and signed a letter of intent with him, effectively awarding him the mandate. But the competition was also in the hunt. Jack Morgan also approached the family, assuming that Dodge would make a good acquisition for GM. It appeared that Dillon had little chance of consummating the deal.

Dillon was neither intimidated by Morgan nor afraid of offering aggressive terms in order to win the company. In a deal that astounded Wall Street, he offered the Dodge family $146 million, all in cash. Another $20 million was offered as incentives to the family, bringing the total purchase price to $166 million. The offer beat Morgan by a considerable margin since the venerable bank offered $155 million, of which only $65 million was in cash. Dillon did not base his offer on the value of the company's assets but estimated its future earnings and discounted them to arrive at his purchase price, exceeding Morgan's offer in the process. The Dodge family recognized a good deal and accepted Dillon's offer.

Dillon used a similar technique to the one in the Goodyear deal to gain control of Dodge. He sold a package of securities, keeping enough common stock to ensure the company remained in his hands. The issue also made his firm and the Wall Street underwriters a considerable fee. The underwriting syndicate for the deal included 380 investment banks, which split underwriting fees of $14.5 million. It sold $75 million worth of bonds, and $85 million of preferred stock, while Dillon kept the common stock. The public provided $160 million of the purchase price, while the balance was provided by Dillon Read. The securities sale took place on April 1, 1925, no doubt bringing a smile to the partners of Dillon Read since the public securities were oversubscribed several times. Dillon's holdings were valued at about $34.5 million at the time of the sale, putting him in the same league as Pierpont Morgan. Wall Street had found a new deal maker.

The Dodge deal unleashed a speculative wave on the stock exchange in much the same way that the U.S. Steel deal had done over 20 years before. After the deal was concluded, the *New York Times* commented, "The speculation in motor-car shares, which has been the focus of this particular Stock Exchange speculation, was really started when $146,000,000 was paid by a bankers' syndicate for the Dodge Brothers automobile property. That appealed to the speculative imagination last April; the excitement reached its climax when some of the companies reported earnings almost double those of the same period a year ago. It was further stimulated by the familiar Wall Street rumors of 'amalgamation,' 'mergers,' 'buying for control.' "[17]

In 1925, Clarence Dillon became the head of Dodge Brothers, even though he had no experience in the auto business. The coup was a classic example of a financier seizing control of a business in which he had no experience. Time would tell whether Dillon would make a good automobile man. Initially, the company's prospects seemed bright. In 1926, Dodge was the third-largest manufacturer, producing about one-quarter of Ford's output.[18] But the competition remained very stiff. In 1924, Henry Ford celebrated the 10 millionth Ford to come off his assembly lines. Dozens of smaller manufacturers were producing specialty cars of all sorts. Within three years of his purchase, Dillon had the evidence he needed. He did not prove to be a good automobile executive and wanted to sell the company. The management he installed was not successful and it was clear that his investment was in danger. The best-selling Dodge was priced at $895, $400 more than the Ford Model T. A price-conscious buying public began to abandon Dodge and its sales fell dramatically. Selling the company would not be an easy matter since competition in the industry was still extremely strong and Ford and General Motors were not likely buyers. Dillon needed to replicate earlier deals by arranging a merger with another midsize company that would produce a stronger company as a result. By 1928, Walter Chrysler was in such a position since his cars had become very popular. But would he consider buying Dodge?

Chrysler knew that Dillon wanted out of Dodge. Alfred Sloan at General Motors originally put Dillon in touch with Chrysler, thinking the two might make a good match. General Motors was no longer interested in Dodge, perhaps because of their recent adversarial history. And Billy Durant consistently was mentioned as a potential buyer of Dodge since he hoped to again compete with GM through his small Durant Motors. Dealing with Durant was not a prospect that excited automakers or financiers. Dillon was less than enamored of Durant. "I knew Clarence Dillon was worried," Walter Chrysler said, "I believe he realized that the momentum given to the business by John and Horace Dodge was lessening. We had some talks about the Dodge business," but nothing materialized.[19] Although Dillon pressed Chrysler on more than one occasion, the carmaker maintained that the prospective purchase price was always too high. Finally he paid Dillon $170 million, all in securities.

Shareholders had much to cheer about, at least initially. Chrysler stock rose from $60 per share before the deal to over $140 three months after it was announced. Then reality and the post-1929 market took over. By early 1931, Chrysler traded at $15. Earnings were responsible for the sharp decline. The company earned $7 per share in 1928 but only 56 cents at the end of 1930.

Those integrally involved with the automobile industry naturally saw the opportunities the new industry offered. Bankers were a bit slower, needing to be convinced. By the mid-1920s no more convincing was needed. The money Clarence Dillon made on Dodge and Hornblower & Weeks' bid for Ford were ample proof. In 1927, Goldman Sachs partner Waddill Catchings wrote that the industry was the greatest source of American prosperity since 1910. It also created a new industry—installment credit—which blossomed to more than $4 billion outstanding by the mid-1920s. The market value of automobile companies listed on the NYSE appreciated more than $1 billion during 1925 alone, and a year later the net profits of GM exceeded $186 million, greater than those in any other business.[20] The car was powering America in more ways than one. Mergers and acquisitions were quickly powering Wall Street.

Dillon's deal was responsible for the modern phenomenon of mergers fueling a stock market rally. Now it was becoming clear that the finances of consolidated companies were stronger than those of the previous independent companies and that investors were drawn to what appeared to be strong earnings based upon the merged entity. One of the major causes of the 1929 crash was now in place. The pattern would be repeated in varying degrees throughout the history of the markets.

Clarence Dillon celebrated his successes by building a series of homes, the grandest of which was located on East 80th Street in Manhattan. There he built a townhouse with 30 rooms that required a staff of 14. His next-door neighbor was William Vincent Astor, a great-great grandson of John Jacob Astor. Like many Wall Street partners, Dillon was very conscious about security and also hired guards to protect the residence. There were also ex-Marines on the payroll of Dillon Read to guard its downtown offices.

Dillon created the modern M&A business for smaller firms on Wall Street, refining techniques first put into play by the original money trust banks. His successful bid for Dodge and subsequent sale to Chrysler demonstrated that the mergers and acquisitions business was certainly capital intensive but that the money did not necessarily have to come from a money trust bank. Brains and agility were enough to win a mandate that could then be financed later if the deal had market appeal. This formula would be used time and again in the M&A business throughout the twentieth century as both small and large firms competed for fees. Dillon's investment bank was perfect proof and continued to be a major player in the field until the 1990s.

The auto industry introduced another revolution in American life—installment purchases. Because of the price of new cars, the only way most buyers could afford them was by paying for them on credit. Most of the manufacturers quickly developed finance arms such as General Motors Acceptance Corp., which provided financing for both dealers and customers. The phenomenon was not only American: European manufacturers also adopted the concept. Citroen used installment credit extensively in France at about the same time the Americans adopted it. The plans were crucial to the success of many manufacturers, especially Ford, since bank credit was not used and the company relied upon a constant stream of sales to provide its liquidity. By the mid-1920s, several hundred firms provided automobile installment credit in the United States in addition to the manufacturers.

Buying on time was also encouraged in many other industries. The 1920s witnessed one of the great consumer booms, and many companies extended credit for purchases of radios and kitchen appliances in addition to autos and home mortgages. At heart, consumer credit was created because of the capital-intensive nature of many manufacturing industries. In order to stimulate demand, money had to be made available for customers to make purchases. As the process became more ingrained, the finance companies became integral to the financial landscape. Without them, demand would plummet. Only when price became a matter of time payments did the actual costs of mergers and acquisitions become more prominent. If a deal contained too much water, consumers eventually would have to pay higher prices so that companies could recoup their investments.

While Henry Ford was producing cars in his customary range of colors—black only—Alfred Sloan began introducing concepts at

General Motors designed to ratchet prices higher. One concept providing some help on this score was product differentiation. Car models began to change every year to entice consumers to jettison old models for newer ones. The large manufacturers knew that such design changes were expensive and that only those companies with access to the capital markets would succeed.

Henry Ford came to the same conclusion. The public wanted something more than his simple black-only Model T. After producing over 10 million cars, he shut down his operations to gear up for the production of a new concept car. He introduced his new Model A in 1927, breaking the mold on his familiar color choice and adding new features as well. The timing was not good, however, since the market crash and the Depression would seriously curtail sales and the new model's potential popularity within a few years. The new marketing concept put GM in the top position in the industry because it had the best relationship with the major Wall Street investment banks and the most highly regarded management under Sloan. By the mid-1920s, Ford had slipped to the position of second-largest carmaker. General Motors was readmitted to the Dow Jones Industrial Average in 1925. It had previously been admitted after the first round of restructuring was complete in 1915 but kicked out a year later.

Why the money trust bankers were slow to recognize the automobile industry as the future engine of economic growth is not clear. Pierpont Morgan understood the navy buildup as a certain source of demand for steel products but did not see the same potential in autos. Perhaps there was an element of chauvinism involved. The motorcar was not an American invention: Models had been tested and used in Europe before the concept arrived in the United States. The American proponents of the auto were not inventors with established names but sales visionaries like Durant and Ford who could not lay claim to a tradition of their own.

What the money trust banks missed became another's fortune. The success of Clarence Dillon and the smaller bankers who participated in the M&A spree only added to the Wall Street bubble that was developing after 1926. Small investors and those unable to participate in big deals became susceptible to rumors of new deals and everyone began buying stocks, hoping to cash in on the bonanza. A bevy of popular books and movies appeared extolling the virtues and the lifestyles of Wall Street brokers, giving the impression that America was on the verge of a new era. Louis Brandeis, now sitting on the Supreme Court, recognized the trend because it was following the concept used in his book, entitled *Other People's Money*, published a decade before. But one other trend was emerging from the commotion caused by big deals. They became symptomatic of a market that was becoming top-heavy. Clarence Dillon and others realized it and became less active in the market as 1929 approached.

RETAILING REVOLUTION

Coinciding with the rise of the automobile was the rise of mass retailing in the United States. Henry Ford and his competitors discovered the virtues of the assembly line in producing quality products efficiently. The rise of chain store retailing was the equivalent in merchandising. Any store that could buy merchandise in large quantities could negotiate lower prices with producers and provide a service to both the public and the producers. The business may not have been as exciting as manufacturing consumer goods, but it was vital if big business were to find an outlet for many of its consumer durables and nondurables. By the time World War I began, mass retailing was on the rise and would become a hallmark of American business.

Retailers encountered two problems as they strove to extend their reach to a mass audience. The top bankers did not pay much attention to them because their businesses were somewhat commonplace despite the ingenuity some displayed in reaching their customers. Traditionally, their need for capital was short-term: they required cash to pay suppliers for goods until they could be sold. Capital for expansion was important but not crucial, as it was for heavy manufacturers or the telephone industry. Issuing securities was not vital for retailers as a result, and their businesses could be satisfied by smaller commercial banks willing to make working capital loans.

Social factors were equally important. Many of the retailers were Jewish and some top bankers did not want to deal with them directly because of this. Several Jewish banking houses sprang up in the nine-teenth and early twentieth centuries to deal with merchants and retailers and the two became intertwined as society and business grew larger over the years. Both Goldman Sachs and Salomon Brothers & Hutzler discovered that providing financing for mer-chants by buying their promissory notes at a discount and selling them to others was a crucial function. By providing cash to the mer-chants for their paper and then quickly selling it to banks and other financial institutions, they helped develop many small businesses in the period between the Civil War and World War I. Although not highly profitable, the function of discounting commercial paper (as the notes were called) allowed both firms to gain a foothold in the investment banking business. Once they were better established, they helped many of their small clients become larger.

These smaller businesses did not provide the sort of potential profits that Morgan and Dillon reaped from their M&A activities. In the first month of its operations, Salomon bought 41 loans totaling $7 million and earned commissions of $2,800 for reselling them. The profit margin on the turnover was a mere 0.04 of 1 percent. An investment banking fee on the same amount would have averaged between 4 and 5 percent, or $300,000, not including any stock for the underwriters. Money brokers operated for much smaller margins and were not dining at Wall Street's best restaurants as a result. Nor were they considered Wall Streeters in the strict sense of the word. They operated on the fringes, looking for the proverbial crumbs from the table. Even when Salomon invited Morton Hutzler to become a partner because he owned a stock exchange seat, his business was hardly glamorous. He operated as a two-dollar broker on the floor of the NYSE, executing trades for others for a flat fee. This was a far cry from the operations of James Keene, who conducted many of Mor-gan's floor operations. Hutzler would have had to execute 500,000 trades to match Keene's rate for the Big Steel deal alone.

Not all of the traditionally Jewish firms on Wall Street were small up-and-coming brokers looking for their first real break. J. & W. Selig-man and Kuhn Loeb & Co., headed by the already legendary Jacob Schiff, were top investment banks, and Kuhn Loeb was mentioned as one of the money trust banks by the Pujo committee when it wrote its final report in 1913. Small merchants were not likely to get much assistance from these firms any more than from Morgan, Kidder Peabody, or Lee Higginson. The top banks only worked for big fees and most operated with small staffs, meaning that many of their top executives (if not the partners) worked long hours, especially at Morgan. As a result, much of the retailing business was left to the smaller firms. Not all retailers or their bankers were Jewish, but many of them were, and they grew by using each other effectively.

The Jewish connection would also come under fire from the elements who saw conspiracy at every turn. Opposition to chain stores was also building in Germany and Italy, partially because of Jewish control of stores and strong nationalistic campaigns.[21] Congressman Louis McFadden of Pennsylvania suspected the Straus family, owners of Macy's department store, of being more than simple shopkeepers. And he considered Kuhn Loeb, the store's bankers, guilty of un-American activities. The Strauses were guilty by association since they dealt with the bankers and as "proprietors of R.H. Macy & Co. of New York, which is an outlet for foreign goods dumped upon this country at the expense of the United States Government, which is compelled to issue paper money on the said foreign goods of the Strauses."[22] In the emotionally charged days of the Depression, even such wild charges would be repeated by those looking for an answer to the country's economic problems.

Mass retailing was an expansion of the department store concept. A flagship store opened more versions of itself, expanding regionally and then sometimes nationally. Many department stores got their start before the Civil War but only began to get larger later in the nineteenth century. Others got their start in the mail order business. Aaron Montgomery Ward opened his mail order business in 1872 with $1,600 in capital, selling goods through his catalog. By purchasing direct from manufacturers, he eliminated the middleman and the expense of retailing. Ward's first venture began in Chicago with a one-page catalog. It quickly proved successful, in part because he instituted a liberal returns policy. The catalog expanded from year to year and by 1888 annual sales exceeded $1 million. Along with

Sears and Roebuck, Ward became one of the founders of mail order sales in the United States. The catalog became a staple in both rural and urban homes for years and epitomized the innovative nature of American retailing. In the early 1900s, over 3 million catalogs weighing approximately 4 pounds each were circulated annually. In 1926, Montgomery Ward began opening retail stores; by 1929 over 530 were operating.

Montgomery Ward's expansion was not unusual for the 1920s. Other stores began to expand nationally, including Sears and A&P. By the end of the decade, dozens of stores had national chains. The benefit to consumers was clear, but not everyone was enamored of the new style of shopping. Many critics saw it as a dilution of the American way and an invasion of Wall Street interests into the lives of ordinary people. In addition to stores, banks were also expanding their horizons. This process was also strongly opposed in some quarters. The reasons were obvious. The explosion in chain stores was changing the economics of selling and creating a new industry in the process. In 1920, there were 808 chain stores in the United States. By 1928, there were more than 1,700. At the time of the stock market crash, the retail industry employed over 5.7 million people and rang up sales totaling $48 million at a time when the average American salary was below $2,000 per year. The most popular type of chain store was the grocery store, but the most profitable were department stores, variety stores, and apparel stores.[23] With margins exceeding 30 percent, it was clear that the industry had appeal both to sellers and buyers.

Retailing also had a strong appeal for Charles Merrill, the founder of a brokerage house that eventually would become Merrill Lynch. He founded his brokerage at the beginning of the First World War and quickly used his customer base (mostly small investors) to underwrite several issues for retailers, including McCrory Stores, Kresge, and the Acme Tea Co. He and his partner, Edmund "Eddie" Lynch, both served in the military during the war and after being discharged took an equity stake in a French motion picture production company called Pathé Frères Cinema, one of the silent era's best known movie producers. Within several years, Merrill and Lynch controlled Pathé and had become movie tycoons.

The movie industry was rapidly changing in the 1920s as many production houses set up their own chain of cinema theaters in order to distribute their films. In 1927, *The Jazz Singer* was released starring Al Jolson. It was the first talkie. The public clamored for more movies with sound, and the industry had to adopt expensive technology to provide them. Merrill and Lynch recognized the trend and understood the increased costs they would face if they stayed in the business. The movie industry suddenly was becoming more capital intensive than before, and they decided to sell their interest in the company to a group headed by Joseph P. Kennedy and Cecil B. DeMille. The new owners used it to create RKO. Otto Kahn, senior partner at Kuhn Loeb, also was actively involved in the movie business and was known to enjoy the occasional foray into Hollywood. Merrill and Lynch's investment netted them several million dollars in profit and helped cement their fortunes.

Merrill and Lynch added more retailing clients during the 1920s, including Newberry, Walgreen Drugs, Western Auto, and Safeway Stores, all perfect examples of the retailing explosion. Merrill Lynch was on its way to becoming a solid second-tier Wall Street house. But Charles Merrill was becoming less enchanted with the rapidly expanding brokerage business and more enamored with general retailing, which would prove more stable in the years ahead. During his brokerage years, Merrill acquired an interest in Safeway Stores, which began an expansion into a nationwide chain. Merrill, slowly withdrawing from the brokerage and investment banking business to monitor his investments, retained a sizable interest in Safeway Stores, and by 1930 held a controlling interest. Over the course of the 1930s, he devoted his energies to expanding the chain through merger. Within several years, Safeway had become the third-largest supermarket chain and one of the most profitable. It was able to survive during the Depression by selling at low prices while generating high volume. Merrill would return to the brokerage business later, but the investment in Safeway became his prize possession during the

1930s. His other interests in retailers were also notable. He retained an interest in the department store chain S.S. Kresge as well as interests in Melville Shoe and First National, another grocery chain.

Lehman Brothers, one of Wall Street's notable Jewish investment houses, also loaned its name to the retailing trend, which paid off handsomely for the firm. Philip Lehman, senior partner and head of the firm, spotted many trends in American business in their early stages that other investment bankers failed or refused to recognize. The firm underwrote new issues for the Studebaker, F. W. Woolworth, and Underwood, the maker of typewriters. All were new companies in new industries and many traditional investment firms were reluctant to underwrite them. Lehman, which established itself as a commodities trading house on Wall Street after the Civil War, was a member of many of the important syndicates, which also included Kidder Peabody & Co., Clark Dodge, J.P. Morgan, Goldman Sachs, and Kuhn Loeb. The House of Lehman was able to achieve this lofty status rather quickly considering its history as a commodities trading house. Recognizing new industries and bringing these companies to market would help it crack into the ranks of investment banking.

Another Jewish investment bank joined Lehman in financing these new chain store expansions. Goldman Sachs entered into an agreement with Philip Lehman that allowed the two firms to share underwritings. As a result, their pooled efforts allowed many emerging companies to come to market. Founded by Marcus Goldman after the Civil War, the firm became the major underwriter and distributor of commercial paper on Wall Street but still had not entered the ranks of investment banking in a meaningful way. The new relationship would last 20 years. As a result of their combined effort, some companies that subsequently became household names came to market, among them Campbell Soup, May Department Stores, Endicott Johnson, Gimbel Brothers, and R.H. Macy & Co.

Goldman had already brought a new issue to market for United Cigar Co., and now Sears Roebuck was exploring additional financing. The presidents of both companies were personal friends of the Goldmans, and Goldman Sachs already had underwritten commercial paper for Sears. But the firm could not accomplish the deal without help and sought the aid of Lehman Brothers. Retailing became a specialty of Goldman Sachs as it did for Lehman Brothers. Family-run retailing stores, small and large, were expanding operations nationally and were constantly in need of money. Philip Lehman and Henry Goldman recognized the need as an opportunity to become full-fledged investment bankers and happily undertook the job of underwriting. The largest was Sears Roebuck & Co., founded by Richard Sears and Alvah Roebuck in 1886 as the R.W. Sears Watch Company. Selling goods purchased from a manufacturer directly to the public proved successful, and the name was changed to Sears Roebuck in 1893. The company added many household items and clothing sold by catalog, aiming at rural households located far from towns. But Sears was not the first mail order operation. That distinction was held by Montgomery Ward.

Sears sold literally everything including the kitchen sink through its catalogs. In 1898, its most popular item was an electric belt. When the device was strapped on, it was reputed to alleviate headaches, backaches, and other nervous disorders. By 1905, Sears reportedly sold over $1 million dollars worth of the belts. Roebuck declined an offer by Sears to take over the department that sold them because he did not have much faith in the product. "I tried one of the belts," he wrote, "and found that while it developed a strong current of electricity and produced a tingling sensation, it was so strong that if the battery cells became uncovered and touched the flesh it would burn and cauterize it."[24] Although Roebuck declined, Sears continued to sell the devices.

Although retailing deals were smaller, connections still proved important. Although Sears Roebuck continued to use his name, Alvah Roebuck left the company in the 1890s. Richard Sears took in Aaaron Nusbaum as a partner in 1894. Nusbaum's brother-in-law, Julius Rosenwald, also joined as a vice president. Both previously had been suppliers to Sears, Nusbaum of pneumatic tubes and Rosenwald of men's clothing. Nusbaum's share in the company was eventually bought out by Sears and Rosenwald. Substantial obstacles needed to be overcome, however.

Opposition was building to mail order houses in general, and many rural postmasters refused to accept merchandise from them. The mail order business traditionally had been rife with fraud, with all sorts of hucksters selling useless items cheaply to the unsuspecting. A favorite flim-flam was an ad that advertised a complete sewing machine for only $1.00. When the item arrived in the mail, the customer opened the package only to discover that a needle and thread had been sent, costing only a few pennies. In the South, a rumor spread quickly that Sears and Roebuck were in fact Negroes, in a vain attempt to kill their sales among the predominantly white farmers and landowners. As a result, the company embarked on a goodwill program, answering customers' complaints quickly and often helping them out of personal difficulties, especially if they complained about the quality or safety of a Sears product. After learning of the local postmasters' wrath, many merchants began sending catalogs in plain brown wrappers so that the curious could not see what was inside.[25]

Montgomery Ward attacked the problem differently, appealing to customers' political sensitivities. One of the company's catalogs stated: "Trusts. Every day in country towns little trusts are formed by the merchants who stand by each other and dictate to you what you should pay for sugar, coffee, groceries, etc. and when you come to sell, you will almost always find they all pay the same price for your butter, your eggs, your produce and your stock . . . We belong to no trust."[26] The company turned the provincials' argument on its head, evoking the major trusts of the day that frequently found their way into the newspapers.

Sears and Nusbaum succeeded in their campaign but needed capital for further expansion. Fortunately, one of Rosenwald's childhood friends was Henry Goldman of Goldman Sachs, son of the firm's founder. Goldman and his friend Phillip Lehman asked Rosenwald to take Sears public. The bankers initiated the deal but did not significantly cut themselves in for control of the company. The deal would be the first public offering for a mail order house. Rosenwald readily agreed.

The greatest retailing coup of the twentieth century to that time occurred when Lehman and Goldman Sachs brought the Sears offering to market. The deal was large for a retailer, even one of Sears' reputation. The company sold $10 million of 7 percent preferred stock and $30 million of common stock. The underwriting fee was $500,000 in cash and $5 million worth of common stock for the two underwriters. The offering prices were hefty in dollar terms: The common stock was sold at $50 per share and the preferred stock at $97.50. Sears and Rosenwald made $4.5 million each in the deal.

Goldman Sachs sold much of its allocation in the deal in Europe. Since the end of the nineteenth century, the firm had had an established connection with Kleinwort Benson, the English merchant bank and affiliate of J.P. Morgan & Co. As a result, Henry Goldman was able to place a large portion of his underwriting in the hands of British investors. Until the outbreak of World War I, the British were still avid investors in American stocks, and the connection between the two investment banks became stronger. Other notable underwritings followed on the heels of the Sears success, including Woolworth, and many were placed in Britain. Between them, they brought over 100 issues to market in their 20-year collaboration.

The Woolworth deal followed the success of Sears. The variety store chain was founded by Frank W. Woolworth in 1880. Previous stores opened by the 28-year old had met with mixed success, but a store opened in Lancaster, Pennsylvania in 1879 proved to be highly successful. Woolworth's business model was simple. His store, which measured only 14 by 35 feet, offered merchandise stacked on tables at either 5 cents or 10 cents, leading to the nickname "five and dime stores." Within 15 years, Woolworth's empire extended to 28 stores with combined sales of over $5 million. Stores were opened in Britain as well, and the name *Woolie's* became accepted in British shopping. Many Britons thought the company was local. Woolworth incorporated in 1905, and a limited number of shares were held by management and employees. A $65 million consolidation in 1912 with S.H. Knox & Co. and several smaller stores expanded the chain. The public offering through Goldman Sachs and Lehman raised

$6 million of preferred stock and $7 million of common stock. Another $9 million of preferred stock and $43 million of common stock were kept by Woolworth and his close colleagues. The company's performance continued to please investors. The year after the offering it reported profits of $5.4 million on sales of $60.5 million.[27]

Woolworth was flush with cash, and in 1913 he opened the Woolworth Building, a skyscraper in lower Manhattan that was the distinguishing building on the skyline at the time. The opening marked a long journey for a retailer who once referred to himself as a "boob from the country." Woolworth died in 1919, leaving an estate worth approximately $65 million. In 1924, the company was added to the Dow Jones Industrial Average, where it remained until 1997.

The chain stores also suffered from adverse public opinion. But this time the opposition was much better organized than those who originally opposed the mail order houses. By the end of the 1920s, over 260 local and national organizations claiming over 8 million members existed opposing the chains.[28] The arguments they employed were becoming familiar but were emotional nevertheless: The stores were siphoning money from the local communities, avoiding taxes, and using big-city banks and Wall Street for their financing. The latter point was at the heart of the matter. Banks were expanding at the same time and the combination of the stores and their bankers invading small-town America made local businessmen very nervous. It would only be a matter of time before opposition to bank expansion occurred as well.

HINDERING EXPANSION

Despite the retailing explosion in the 1920s, not all industries expanded as freely as they wished. Bankers wanted to participate in the move toward nationwide branching but had more regulations to contend with than the average seller of groceries or dry goods. The banks desperately seeking to expand were the rapidly growing retail-oriented commercial banks. Realizing that installment credit companies were reaping large rewards by offering time payments to customers, some of the banks decided to cash in on the trend.

The most aggressive retail bank in the country at the time was A.P. Giannini's Bank of America, based in San Francisco. A smaller institution of the same name had existed in New York since the early nineteenth century. The son of Italian immigrants, Giannini transformed the Bank of Italy, a California bank operating in Italian-American neighborhoods, into the Bank of America. Aggressively expanding during the 1920s, Giannini had already bought a Wall Street brokerage and was moving into consumer financing in the late 1920s. His attitude was definitely a harbinger of the future in American consumer financing. "It does not take much of a credit man to say 'No' to a borrower," he was fond of saying, "but it does take time, labor and understanding to find a basis on which a loan can be made."[29]

While nationally chartered banks were among the largest, they were vastly outnumbered by the smaller, state-chartered banks.[30] The power of the money trust alarmed many of the smaller banks, and their legislators were opposed to the expansion trend, which would have allowed the larger banks to cross state lines seeking business. Banking was primarily a local business in the postwar years, and many small bankers lobbied their local politicians to stop the expansion trend. The fear was misplaced because the money trust had passed the peak of its power. However, it still had a formidable reputation among small-town and rural bankers around the country.

The 1920s were also the decade of bank failures. About 8,000 banks with national charters existed in 1920, compared with almost 23,000 state and local banks. Over the course of the decade, over 4,000 state-chartered banks failed, representing about 20 percent of the total. About 500 national banks failed during the same period.[31] Many fell under the weight of failed commercial loans and unwise real estate lending. A movement quickly developed to halt the spread of the national banks in order to preserve the integrity of the smaller institutions. The logic appeared faulty, however, in that many areas of the country could have benefited from the presence of larger banks and the banks could have benefited from the diversity.

A bill appeared in Congress in the mid-1920s designed to make the Federal Reserve a permanent institution not requiring a renewal every 20 years as its nineteenth-century predecessor—the Bank of the United States—originally had. The bill also contained many provisions for redefining national banks, clearly specifying their ability to branch and engage in new sorts of lending activities. The original bill was introduced by Representative Louis T. McFadden, a Republican from Pennsylvania, later to become one of Congress's most avid opponents of the Federal Reserve.

McFadden was born in Pennsylvania in 1876. He graduated from a business college and as a young man worked in the National Bank of Canton, Pennsylvania. After several promotions, he became president in 1915 and held the job until 1925. In 1915, while serving as the president of the Pennsylvania Bankers' Association, he was elected to Congress, where he served for the next 20 years. While in the House, he served as chairman of the banking and currency committee. Being one of the few congressmen with actual finance experience, he was in a unique position to influence the course of public policy. On the surface, his bill was a reform bill, dedicated to preserving the Fed and outlining the power of national banks. It was clearly on the side of national banks, extending their powers and putting them on a level playing field with the state banks in expansion and lending. But the bill was remembered for something quite different. The McFadden Act prevented national banks from opening new branches across state lines. From the date it was passed, the national banks were effectively confined to their home states, just as the state banks were since the new legislation did not affect them. The bill had the full support of the Treasury and the American Bankers' Association.

In order to get passed, the original McFadden bill had an amendment tacked on called the Hull amendment, named after Republican Representative Morton Hull of Illinois. The amendment prevented the national banks from branching across state lines. The debate on that point was bitter and held up passage of the bill for several years. The *New York Times* reported that several congressmen called that portion of the bill un-American and the product of selfish interests designed to curtail the growth of the nationally chartered banks.[32] In order to pass, the bill needed to appease those who were fearful of the money trust. While small banks like McFadden's were nationally chartered, so too were larger ones in New York.

McFadden's career became even more quirky after the bill that bore his name was passed. He was always a firm believer in the powers of the money trust. As a small-town banker, he, like thousands of others, was concerned about the powers of the big-city banks, even after the Federal Reserve was created. After World War I, McFadden vainly tried to unseat Comptroller of the Currency John Skelton Williams. The *New York Times* went so far as to suggest that McFadden pursued Williams simply because "some of Mr. Williams' examiners had investigated the McFadden bank and made certain criticisms of it. The headlines were black about the matter at the time."[33] As time passed in the 1920s, it was becoming obvious that branching and chain stores were bringing out the best and the worst in many in Congress. McFadden supplied many more conspiracy theories and distrust of international bankers in the early 1930s after the Crash.

Supplying credit to small banks was a power traditionally vested in the money center banks in New York prior to 1913, and many state bankers still suffered from the memory of New York and Chicago banks controlling the amount of funds smaller banks could access, especially when credit was generally tight. Despite having been the president of a small, but nevertheless national, bank, McFadden also had other complaints about the national finance system as it existed before the 1929 Crash. In the early 1920s, he also denounced municipal bonds, which were currently undergoing substantial debate concerning their income tax status, as a "growing evil." But many of these comments paled in comparison to those he made after the Crash.

An irascible personality aligned McFadden with the neo-Progressives in Congress who distanced themselves from the mainstream Republicans, especially after Herbert Hoover was elected. The McFadden bill, sponsored in the Senate by Republican Senator George W. Pepper, also of Pennsylvania, was seen by many as a sensible amendment designed to extend the power of national banks in select areas, such as real estate lending. A leading investment periodical, *U.S. Investor,* supported it, saying that the bill "would help to keep the national bank system alive by giving national banks the right to compete with state banks and trust companies on equal terms." But for each forward step the bill gave the national banks, it took two steps backward by limiting their right to branch across state lines. That provision proved to be its Achilles' heel and its legacy.

The McFadden Act allowed national banks to branch within states but made crossing state lines difficult if not impossible. As a result, the United States never developed a national banking system of commercial banks that were allowed to open branches across the country. When the full implications of the law became widely understood, it became clear that department store chains, gas stations, and grocery stores could open branches wherever they pleased but banks were restricted. Arguably the most important chain expansion of all was hamstrung in a clear attempt to turn back the tide of branching. Even higher education got into the act when New York University opened seven overseas summer schools at European universities. The great irony was that American banks were allowed to branch overseas with the permission of the Fed; they just could not do so domestically. McFadden proved to be a thorn in the side of international banking as well.

The ban on interstate banking would take 67 years to repeal. The American banking system became highly fractured as a result and was dominated by small banks that primarily served their local communities. In 1927, the new law was more protective than anything else. The massive bank failures of the 1920s, when about two banks were failing daily, were concentrated in small banks with capital of under $50,000. With so many banks failing, a consolidation movement was bound to occur in which larger out-of-state banks could move in on the smaller institutions.

Another major concern was that national banks were beginning to acquire brokerage subsidiaries, bringing Wall Street closer to the commercial banks than at any time since the Civil War. National City Bank acquired Halsey & Co., a New York securities dealer, and the Bank of America acquired William Blair & Co., a medium-size

New York securities dealer. Almost all of the securities traded were bonds, but the McFadden Act also allowed the comptroller of the currency to decide whether the banks could begin dealing in common stocks as well. This was a clear backdoor attempt to allow national banks to become involved in the stock market. As the details of the act began to emerge, it appeared that it was loaded with implications for the banking system, buried under a mass of legalese and technical language.

Provincial bankers saw the expansion trend of the 1920s as a threat to their businesses and way of life. World War I was crucial to understanding the nature of the perceived threat that reverberated throughout the heartland of America. The money trust bankers were already well known in the press since congressman Charles Lindbergh Sr. of Minnesota had dubbed them with the name in 1913. The trust as such was the cornerstone of a larger conspiracy theory that traced its immediate origins to the war. In 1916, Woodrow Wilson offered to broker peace talks between the European Allies and the Central Powers. The Americans had been doing very well by the war because exports of manufactures and agricultural products were very strong. When word of the peace talks circulated, the markets did not take it well and fell heavily. Wilson made a public announcement of his intentions on December 20, 1916 at 8:00 P.M. in Washington. The stock and commodities markets dropped precipitously as a result of what became known as the "peace scare." Anti–Wall Street politicians were annoyed because news of the offer appeared on the news wires several hours earlier, allowing short sellers to begin dumping shares in many war-related industries. The shares of International Mercantile Marine were especially hard hit after the British government announced that it was thinking of putting all British shipping under government supervision.

Matters were complicated by the fact that the announcement had been released to some wire agencies four hours earlier, at 1:00 P.M. Some in Congress feared that financiers had advance information of the announcement and began short selling stocks to take advantage of what were sure to be falling markets. For years short selling had been the bête noire of the agrarians, who forcefully and unsuccessfully argued against its use in the futures markets in Chicago and New York. Suspicions immediately arose that bankers were using the war to make inordinate gains by supplying war materiel to the Allies and then by short selling when the prospect of peace was being raised. The prospect became unbearable for many of them and a congressional investigation was called. When its results were finally published, government officials were absolved of any blame, although it was acknowledged that a leak did occur through the press wires. While the official inquiry ended tamely, the basis for a long-standing conspiracy theory was born.

Wall Street's popularity was falling rapidly even before the war was over. The Washington correspondent for the *Times* of London described the House of Morgan as "the most unpopular house in the country, the personification for the radical West of the malign money power of Wall Street, it has done nothing to propitiate either the people or the politicians."[34] Those who believed that the world war was orchestrated by bankers vastly overstated their case, although there clearly was some evidence that Wall Street had a vested interest in war efforts, as events certainly proved.

From the beginning of the "conspiracy," several congressmen and senators were convinced that Wall Street and Washington had acted in concert to make illicit gains at the expense of everyday citizens. Among them were McFadden and the group in the Senate known collectively as the "Sons of the Wild Jackass." They would be joined by Representative Wright Patman of Texas in the 1930s. Clearly, they represented a loosely organized fringe group in Congress, but their influence was much greater than anyone would have expected in the 1920s. They played prominent roles in all major congressional investigations and legislation passed until the New Deal assumed the reform mantle in 1933.

The disabling part of the McFadden Act was the only success the antiexpansion forces had in the 1920s. In order to stem expansion of commercial enterprises nationally, a prior set of rule and regulations was needed so that they could be amended, as was the case with the McFadden Act. Trying to write new antiexpansionist laws against unregulated industries like chain stores was not feasible because the economy was booming. Attempts would be made in the 1930s, however. In a speech delivered over WJSV radio in Washington, D.C., McFadden went on record against the expansion of chain stores in general. "We are indeed today involved in an economic battle between the chain store and independent merchandising," he declared. "In my judgment, it is high time that Congress, as well as the people of the United States, should give serious attention to what is unquestionably a vital factor in the living costs of not only the present day but of the immediate future."[35] He suspected that the presence of chains would raise rather than lower the cost of consumer goods.

Of all the businesses attempting to expand, banking was the one suffering economically and became an easy target for the antichain group desperately trying to preserve what it understood as the American way of life. The postmasters refusing to deliver catalogs of the mail order merchants and the small shop owners protesting the expansion of Montgomery Ward and Sears stores experienced little joy as the stores expanded into their towns and counties. But banking was another matter. Existing banking laws bore the seeds of hope if they were amended properly. The McFadden Act was the first opportunity in the 1920s to stem the tide. But it would pale in comparison to some charges that McFadden began to make after the market crash in 1929.

The idea of branch banking across state lines was not dead, however. Senator Carter Glass of Virginia tried to have it included in legislation introduced in the early 1930s, but the idea never gained any additional support in Congress. In fact, Glass went as far as to say that state banking interests had paid off some congressmen to oppose full branching in 1927 when the McFadden Act was finally passed. "They hired a professional lobbyist and paid him a large salary," Glass declared in 1932. "More than that, they hired some congressmen, to my certain documentary knowledge," he added, holding up a wad of more than 2,000 telegrams sent to him opposing branch banking nationwide. Acknowledging the bulk of the telegrams as "pure propaganda," Glass added that "there will be bank failures" if the branch banking bill did not pass Congress the second time.[36] It did not pass, and many failures did follow during the Depression.

Wall Street profited by the expansion of the stores in the 1920s as it had by the consolidation of the auto industry. A by-product of the success was an almost rabid dislike of merger bankers that was developing across the country. While the reaction was natural, it would become more odious for Wall Street in the 1930s as the economy faltered badly. Class warfare was simmering in the United States in the early 1930s and those at the lower end of the socioeconomic scale did not want to be reminded that the old car in the garage and the store in which they shopped had made a Wall Street investment banker rich. Reaction came from unanticipated places.

NOTES

1. Neill Baldwin, *Henry Ford & the Jews: The Mass Production of Hate* (New York: Public Affairs, 2001), p. 106.
2. Bernard A. Weisberger, *The Dream Maker: William C. Durant, Founder of General Motors* (Boston: Little, Brown, 1979), pp. 129–130.
3. Axel Madsen, *The Deal Maker: How William C. Durant Made General Motors* (New York: John Wiley & Sons, 1999), p. 133.
4. Ibid., p. 137.
5. Weisberger, p. 152.
6. Lawrence H. Seltzer, *A Financial History of the American Automobile Industry* (Boston: Houghton Mifflin, 1928), p. 171.
7. *San Francisco Examiner,* October 31, 1913.
8. Ron Chernow, *The House of Morgan: An American Banking Dynasty & the Rise of Modern Finance* (New York: Simon & Schuster, 1990), p. 222.
9. *New York Times Magazine,* January 11, 1914.
10. *New York Times,* January 7, 1914.
11. Seltzer, p. 132.
12. Weisberger, p. 258.
13. Earl Sparling, *Mystery Men of Wall Street: The Powers Behind the Market* (New York: Blue Ribbon Books, 1930), p. 39.
14. Chernow, p. 224.
15. Seltzer, p. 65.
16. United States Department of Commerce, *Historical Statistics of the United*

States: Colonial Times to 1957 (Washington: U.S. Government Printing Office, 1957), p. 462.

17. *New York Times,* November 15, 1925.
18. Seltzer, p. 57.
19. Vincent Curcio, *Chrysler: The Life and Times of an Automotive Genius* (New York: Oxford University Press, 2000), p. 378.
20. Seltzer, p. 5.
21. Robert Hendrickson, *The Grand Emporiums: An Illustrated History of America's Great Department Stores* (New York: Stein & Day, 1979), p. 261.
22. Speech made by McFadden in the House of Representatives, January 24, 1934.
23. *Historical Statistics,* pp. 520–521.
24. Hendrickson, p. 218.
25. Tom Mahoney and Leonard Sloane, *The Great Merchants* (New York: Harper & Row, 1966), p. 228.
26. Hendrickson, p. 215.
27. Mahoney, p. 202.
28. Hendrickson, p. 262.
29. Marquis James and Bessie Rowland James, *Biography of a Bank: The Story of the Bank of America* (New York: Harper & Row, 1954), p. 416.
30. A nationally chartered bank fell under the National Bank Act of 1864 and reported to the comptroller of the currency. A state-chartered bank was chartered by the state in which it legally resided.
31. *Historical Statistics,* pp. 628–630.
32. *New York Times,* January 25, 1927.
33. Ibid., December 20, 1931.
34. Chernow, p. 201.
35. *New York Times,* March 27, 1930.
36. Ibid., May 11, 1932.

CHAPTER 3

POWER PLAYS AND CONSPIRACY THEORIES

The following is [among] my own glossary of Wall Street phrases:
Merger—a shotgun wedding.

Eddie Cantor, 1929

T he 1930s proved to be a watershed for Wall Street in more than one respect. Finance capitalism came to the foreground more than at any other time since the early days of the century. The empires of J.P. Morgan & Co., and to a lesser extent Kuhn Loeb, Dillon Read, and Lehman Brothers, elicited criticism from many quarters. Populist agrarians thought these firms to be part of an international banking conspiracy destined to enslave the farmer and average citizen. Others saw them as a genuine threat to American democracy, agents of the corporate state that was growing in Europe. Their detractors feared that their influence was the back-door to fascism without the accompanying European ideology.

Since the late nineteenth century, Progressives and Democrats had been criticizing large corporations for their negative effects on American life. Dozens of books and studies appeared indicating that American corporate wealth was more concentrated and inequitable than appeared on the surface. There obviously was a difference between a company's public relations and its true nature. Consolidated industries were destroying competition and the American sense of fair play by swallowing smaller competitors. Wall Street

92

bankers grew rich off the trend, helping create large companies simply to reap fat underwriting fees while disregarding the implications for society at large. The lament was as old as the merger trend itself, but in the 1920s it began to assume a greater degree of credibility than ever before.

The irony was that while the merger trend began to snowball in the 1920s, critics fell silent in the general euphoria surrounding the consumer boom and the stock market rise. While some well-known market operators began preaching caution in 1929, the early years of the boom elicited few complaints. When times were good, criticizing the boom was not considered in the best of taste. More people appeared to be progressing economically and capitalism was extending its reach to the newly discovered American consumer, whose spending would soon account for two-thirds of the gross national product. What could possibly be wrong with the trend?

The prosperity did not extend to all quarters of American society, however. The decade was also known for a farm depression followed by years of flat agricultural prices that forced many farmers off their land. Neo-Progressives, mostly from the agrarian states, joined to keep pressure on Congress, bankers, and the markets. Members of this group, mostly sitting in the Senate, were labeled "Sons of the Wild Jackass" by one of their colleagues, George Moses from New Hampshire. Viewed as a fringe element by most of the public and its colleagues, this mostly Republican, neo-Progressive group wielded influence out of all proportion to its numbers. Its constant references to conspiracies among Wall Street bankers combined all the ingredients of agrarian populism with distrust of the federal government and the occasional twinge of nativism and anti-Semitism. In the late 1920s, these attacks began to take on more credibility as the stock market bubble became more inflated while agricultural prices remained moribund.

The merger trend continued in industries other than retailing and manufacturing. The greatest concentration of the decade occurred in the utilities industry, where several large utilities holding companies controlled almost 50 percent of national electric power production. This particular twist in the merger movement began to evoke serious concern among those who believed that the concentration of political and electric power was increasingly held in too few hands. The future of democracy could not rest solely in the hands of the House of Morgan or an expatriate Briton who had formerly worked for Thomas Edison. To extreme critics the problem was clear: Bankers were literally stealing power and money from the public in the boldest grab for wealth and fame seen since the days of the robber barons 50 years before. The claim would become all the more dramatic when one of the critics died under what his supporters claimed were suspicious circumstances in 1936.

After the Crash, the mergers and acquisitions business on Wall Street dried up. By early 1929, it was clear that issuing new securities for a merger depended upon values in the stock market. High equity prices were needed to entice investors to lay down the cash necessary to pay for a deal. One statistic lost in the maze of discussions about 1929 was particularly important: That year witnessed the largest number of mergers since 1899—1,245, exceeding the 1,208 consummated in 1899.[1] Without the strong stock market, the old principle of other people's money could not operate. The mergers and acquisitions business was about to slip into its dark ages, from which it would not emerge until the 1950s. But investment bankers proved to be an indomitable group. When traditional methods of fashioning mergers could not succeed, they resorted to an old, time-proven method that needed to be disguised well. Although the days of the robber barons had long since passed, the occasional bear raid could force a company into the arms of potential buyers through the backdoor by pushing down stock prices to a point where they became easily affordable for potential raiders. The problem was that the two securities acts, passed in 1933 and 1934, put a quick end to the hangover of nineteenth-century piracy. The one area they did not affect finally would be regulated by a 1935 law limiting ownership of public utilities.

Even after the Crash, some on Wall Street maintained that money could still be made through shrewd investing. In January 1931, *The Magazine of Wall Street* named its 10 outstanding investments for the year. The group included the best-known names on Wall Street, with several Morgan companies and utilities among them. They were United States Steel, United Corporation, Electric Bond and Share Co., Standard Oil of New Jersey, Union Carbide, Liggett & Myers, National Dairy Products, American Can Co., Chesapeake & Ohio, and Sears Roebuck. The magazine's comments on United Corp. were particularly revealing since it assumed that "over a reasonable period [it will] show record substantial gains in price." Only 15 months after the Crash, the prospects for the market and the economy were not as bleak as they would be a year later. It would be another year and a half before the Depression became recognized as an event much more serious than the previous recession in 1920 to 1921.

EMERGING TRENDS

Although the auto industry was booming during the 1920s, it was sharing the limelight with the utilities. It did not take Wall Street long to spy opportunity. During the 1920s, many utilities companies doubled in size and their electric output quadrupled. Electricity was the new infrastructure play of the decade because it provided all of the necessary ingredients for mergers and consolidation. The industry required massive doses of capital to provide power-generating facilities to satisfy demand throughout the country. Not since the growth of the railroads and the creation of U.S. Steel had such an infrastructure opportunity arisen. The rise in utilities would be as rancorous as the debate over the railroads 40 years before. The utilities also inspired the most strenuous legislation restricting their activities in the mid-1930s; legislation on par with the two securities acts passed several years before.

What became known as the "utilities wars" of the 1920s and 1930s was the last great hurrah for the merger specialists until the 1950s. In the 1920s, big business was considered very healthy and its leaders were among the best-known personalities in the country. After the Crash, the picture changed substantially. Revelations about executives avoiding income tax and living richly while the average worker suffered touched a radical nerve in many Americans who saw their wide panoply of consumer products and installment credit collapsing. When it became clear that the electricity powering their homes was also under the influence of Wall Street, the response became even more shrill. Louis T. McFadden made inflammatory remarks on the floor of the House attributing the problem to Jews on Wall Street that would have been more appropriate for Henry Ford's *Dearborn Independent* 10 years before. As unemployment grew and the economy slid deeper into depression, this view began to take on some credence for those who would have dismissed it only several years before. The early 1930s were quickly becoming the years of the demagogue, and Wall Street was the favorite bête noire.

The state of the utilities industry at the beginning of the 1920s was similar to that of steel at the turn of the century. Many small operating companies existed and were begging to be consolidated into larger, more efficient systems. The utilities industry was poised for consolidation after World War I and there was no shortage of volunteers to help. There was a rapid growth in the number of electric generating plants from 1900 to 1920, with numbers increasing by about 80 percent. Then, in the 1920s, growth slowed. Between 1921 and 1930, only 300 new plants were added nationwide. In the earlier period, almost 1,800 were brought online to serve increased demand. The number of residences having electricity doubled in the 1920s, so that by 1930, 85 percent of urban residences had service. The number of farms having electricity was another matter entirely. In 1920, only $1\frac{1}{2}$ percent of farms had service and by 1930 the number had only risen to 10 percent.[2] Vast discrepancies like these gave further indication of the farm sector's general discontent with Wall Street and the East in general. Electricity was a luxury on the farm until the 1950s when the percentages began to catch up with urban and suburban homes.

Investment bankers and consolidators saw the number of power-generating plants and the small companies that operated many of them as candidates for consolidation. Linking the power generators together into large systems was the last opportunity bankers would have to generate large fees before the Depression struck. The Republican administrations of the 1920s provided halcyon days compared to the turbulent 1930s, when the New Deal began to actively intervene in the economy in an attempt to stimulate demand and prices. The fact that many Wall Street merger bankers were Republicans would not help their prospects as the 1930s wore on.

The 1920s also became the decade of incorporation. Thousands of companies incorporated in order to cash in on the economic boom and limit their own liabilities at the same time. Many of the incorporations took place in states of convenience. New Jersey and Delaware were the two favorites, both having relatively lax registration procedures. The numbers were truly astounding. In 1920, the entire United Kingdom had around 79,000 registered corporations while Delaware alone had 70,000. In 1925, New York registered almost 25,000 companies and Delaware added 5,000.[3] New Jersey also continued to be a leader. The state was the home of the original holding company, registering the first one—the Standard Oil Company—in 1889. On a clear day, many company headquarters could be seen across New York Harbor from Wall Street.

The strident debate over the control of utilities and the influence of bankers fell under the scepter of the two bugaboos of the period, xenophobia and anti-Semitism. The Progressive Republicans appealed to fears in their speeches and campaigns, assuring at least some of their constituents that a Jewish plot existed to destroy American institutions and undermine the culture. When a case could be made for including foreigners in the mix, the argument became even more volatile. The attacks could then include anyone suspected of thinking differently from the agrarians. Mergers and acquisitions bankers naturally came under suspicion because they were often allied with foreign bankers whose loyalty was constantly brought into question. As Frederick Lewis Allen succinctly wrote, "Prejudice became as pervasive as air. Landlords grew less disposed to rent to Jewish tenants, and schools to admit Jewish boys and girls . . . Harvard College seriously debated limiting the number of Jewish students; and all over the country Jews felt that a barrier had fallen between them and the Gentiles."[4]

Barriers certainly appeared, and no one suffered worse than Wall Street investment bankers and brokers. Anyone who was in any way affiliated with Jews or with international bankers was tainted by the xenophobic distrust imbued by a long line of prejudice and invective like Henry Ford's "The International Jew," which appeared in his *Dearborn Independent* in 1920. On Wall Street that meant almost everyone of any consequence because foreign investors traditionally had been crucial to its success in selling securities. Although overseas investors were less important to Wall Street's growth after the world war, the long tradition of foreign influence in American investing was seized by critics who maintained that an international conspiracy was afoot to destroy the wealth of the United States. While ideas like that were taken lightly during the 1920s, during the Depression they gained additional credence and had unexpected results.

WHEELER-DEALERS

The bull market in the 1920s provided the ideal atmosphere for deal makers, who set the tone for the market run-up lasting until October 1929. Some were well-publicized bankers who often appeared on the society pages of the newspapers, while others preferred the anonymity of working behind their desks. Regardless of their profile, they all capitalized on rising stock values to entice small investors into the market to provide the basis for stock values. As they discovered, high profiles did not provide much comfort after 1933, when their antics were revealed publicly by a Senate investigation.

One firm that maintained a very low profile on Wall Street was Brown Brothers, the private bank founded by Alexander Brown before the War of 1812. The family-run institution was involved in many of the major merger deals and investment banking transactions on Wall Street during the nineteenth century. In 1930, the bank decided to merge with Harriman banking interests in a clear attempt to maintain its business and add to its partners' capital. The announcement of the merger came on the same day that the Bank of United States, located in New York City, failed, becoming the largest bank failure in the United States. The *New York Times* ran the two news stories in adjacent columns. One headline read, "Bank of U.S. Closes Doors; State Takes Over Affairs; Aid Offered to Depositors." The other announced, "Big Banking Houses Decide on Merger." The contrast could not have been more stark. International investment banks were consolidating while a retail bank was shuttered. The institutional side of Wall Street seemed to be prospering while banks catering to small depositors were in trouble. Although the story was considerably more complicated, the image conveyed in the press was that small savers suffered while the big institutional banks enjoyed the luxury of merging.

The 1920s also illustrated that many large merger deals could be consummated far from the corner of Broad and Wall Streets. Many significant deals were fashioned in Cleveland, not the likeliest of locations for big deals but certainly the traditional home of men of large ambition. The city's most prominent citizen was John D. Rockefeller, one of whose protégés became the investment banking king of the Midwest, structuring deals through a local securities firm that made Wall Street green with envy. His experiences were far from the norm, however, because Wall Street's reach was considerable.

Cyrus Eaton was born in Pugwash, Nova Scotia in 1883. The son of a merchant, he was the fifth of nine children. After graduating from McMaster University in 1905, he moved to Cleveland to work for John D. Rockefeller at the East Ohio Gas Company, a company in which the oil magnate had a substantial interest. Eaton had been introduced to Rockefeller by his uncle Charles Aubrey Eaton, a Baptist minister who was the pastor of Rockefeller's parish church. Rockefeller gave the young man a summer job as a personal assistant and golf caddy before he graduated from college. As Rockefeller was duly impressed with the young man's work ethic, the offer was extended to full-time and Cyrus went to work for him after graduation.

Pastor Eaton was destined for greater things as well. He transferred to the Madison Avenue Baptist Church in New York in 1909 and soon after became a magazine editor, a member of the War Shipping Board during World War I, and director of industrial relations at General Electric. In 1924 he was elected to the House of Representatives from a New Jersey district and served 28 years before retiring. Rockefeller may well have influenced his career as he did that of Cyrus, 15 years his uncle's junior. Within two years of joining the gas company, Cyrus made his first deal. He acquired and sold a number of small utility franchises in Canada and used the profits to buy other franchises in the Midwest. By 1912, he organized the Continental Gas and Electric Co. Four years later he became a partner in the Cleveland securities firm of Otis & Co. Within 11 years of graduating from college, the boy from the small rural town in Nova Scotia had become a millionaire several times over.

Eaton's early career began without any New York or Wall Street influence and the trend would continue for his entire career. His interest in patching together utilities companies continued, and by the time he was 40, he had put together about $1 billion in utilities mergers, mostly in the Midwest.[5] By the mid-1920s, he was developing other interests as well, including steel companies. But it was in utilities that he would leave his mark, both by the utilities empire he created as well as the effect he had on the even larger empire of his major rival Samuel Insull.

Eaton's interest in steel arose because of the fragmentation of the industry in the Midwest and the declining interest in steel by New York investment bankers. At the time, U.S. Steel was still the country's largest company, followed by Bethlehem Steel. Eaton spied an opportunity when a local Ohio company, the Trumbull Steel Co., fell upon hard times. Eaton bailed it out with an infusion of $18 million. Then he and his partners at Otis went about buying other smaller companies and also began acquiring stock in Republic Steel, a much larger manufacturer. In order to do this, Eaton created an investment trust called Continental Shares. The trust was a popular financing shell of the 1920s, used purely to invest in other companies. Selling shares in Continental, Eaton was able to finance these acquisitions and others. By 1929, he had created the new Republic Steel Corporation, the third-largest producer in the country behind Big Steel and Bessie. Among his other interests was a majority share in the Goodyear Tire & Rubber Co., which had almost gone bankrupt less than a decade earlier before being rescued by Clarence Dillon. Eaton was clearly playing the mergers and acquisitions game in traditional

New York style from his Cleveland base. His activities were watched with considerable interest by larger Wall Street investment banks jealous of their traditional preserve.

Eaton put the anti–Wall Street sentiment of the decade to good use. He later stated that finance needed to be separated from Wall Street: "How are we going to have leadership in this vast country if everything must be directed from Wall Street? It would make clerks of us all here in the Middle West." On another occasion, he evoked the chain store argument in the same vein. "With the coming of the chain store, [the local town merchant's] place is taken by a well-trained clerk whose policies are directed from a far off place and by persons whom he knows not. I have no opposition to business on a great scale, but I maintain that control of great industries should remain in the communities that created them and not follow a great banking power to some distant point."[6] His remarks added a new dimension to traditional investment banking—local control. It was not clear whether he was serious or just using the tenor of the times to his own advantage. Wall Street had already reached its own conclusion about him, however.

Eaton certainly practiced what he preached. After a failed bid to acquire the Detroit Edison Company in 1926, he persisted in pressuring the company until it allowed him to participate in syndicates underwriting its bond issues. The company had one of the healthier utilities balance sheets in the mid-1920s. Traditionally, Detroit Edison bonds were handled by Morgan and his affiliated banks in New York, so eyebrows were raised when Eaton muscled his way in. Even before beginning his incursions into Insull territory, he had already acquired a reputation as an interloper on traditional Wall Street turf.

By 1930, the Eaton empire was extensive. In addition to Republic Steel, his interests also included substantial holdings in utilities companies in the Midwest. The utilities acquisitions also were financed through Continental Shares. Investors eagerly bought the shares based upon Eaton's growing reputation as a financier in the same league with Morgan and Dillon. Midwesterners especially were attracted to the company because Eaton was one of their own. At the time of the Crash, he was worth a reputed $100 million and served as the chairman of Inland Steel, United Light & Power Company, Continental Shares, the Sherwin-Williams Paint Company, and the usual array of philanthropic and cultural organizations in Cleveland. But the Crash and the battle with the Insull utilities empire would prove damaging to his fortune and reputation in the early 1930s when public attitudes toward finance and financiers took a distinct turn for the worse.

THE INSULL EMPIRE

The second-largest utilities empire in the country in the 1920s was a conglomeration of operating companies run by Samuel Insull of Chicago. Unlike many of the other barons of industry, Insull was a true utilities man, not a banker sniffing for an opportunity. He was a legend in his own time in Chicago, where he displayed an enormous amount of civic pride, helping the city financially on more than one occasion. He had also experienced the Morgan influence once earlier in his career and learned to be wary of Wall Street.

Insull was born in Britain in 1859 and attended private school before moving to London with his parents. He began work at age 14 as an office boy in order to help his family pay the bills. He also worked part-time for the editor of *Vanity Fair* magazine as a stenographer, learning something of politics and current affairs in the process. His second job brought him into contact with the London representatives of Thomas Edison, who happened to be the young Insull's idol. After a brief period, Insull was invited to the United States to become Edison's private secretary. He emigrated in 1881, arriving in New York to begin a long business career that would take him to the pinnacle of his adopted profession.

Working as Edison's secretary in New York introduced Insull to the world of finance. Edison's first customer in the city was Pierpont Morgan, who purchased electricity provided by a power-generating substation operated by Edison on Pearl Street. As a result of the relationship, power generation was one of the few areas in which Morgan had an inside track, and he exploited it fully in the years ahead, much to Insull's chagrin. In an era when professional allegiances were heavily based on personal loyalties, Insull's job with Edison was secure only as long as the inventor remained at the helm of his electric company. Morgan eventually took over Edison Electric and created General Electric after the merger with the Thompson-Houston Electric Company that forced out Henry Villard. Insull also eventually found himself out of a job as a result and had to seek greener pastures elsewhere. He gravitated to Chicago, where the utilities industry was less concentrated than in New York. In 1892, he became president of the Chicago Edison Company.

Leaving his position as a vice president of Edison Electric convinced Insull that Wall Street bankers and New York in general were anathema. As a result, he never again used a New York investment bank for raising funds but insisted on using Chicago banks at every opportunity. At first, many of the established banks would not deal with him, so he turned instead to a smaller securities dealer that was eager for the business. His main investment banker became Halsey Stuart & Co. of Chicago. The firm's principal, Harold Stuart, shared a common philosophy with Insull that dictated that Midwestern utilities should be run and financed by Midwesterners. The New York syndicates, dominated by Morgan and Kuhn Loeb before World War I, did not bother with small and medium-size utilities in the Midwest, and Stuart actively sold and promoted utilities bonds to the investing public. Disavowing the New York moneyed elite was a local source of pride and profit.

The empire was assembled mainly through two holding companies, the reorganized Commonwealth Edison Company, founded in 1907, and Middle West Utilities Co., the main Insull operating company, founded in 1912. Like many of his counterparts in the steel and automobile industries, Insull was a firm believer that monopoly concentration was necessary to eliminate ruinous competition. He considered the utilities a "natural monopoly," a business that needed to be concentrated in only a few hands in order to provide efficient service. He was fond of saying, "All the electrical energy for a given area must be produced by one concern," and he certainly practiced what he preached in Chicago and the Midwest. Insull became the main power supplier for a vast stretch of the central United States, extending into Mexico as well, and patched together his companies in traditional prewar fashion, using the holding company to acquire operating companies. He casually remarked to a Harvard professor that he was "personally responsible for one thousand million dollars [$1 billion] of other people's money." The formula worked famously well, and Chicago became his own personal fiefdom. Chicago had inherited New York's earlier reputation as a wide-open city of opportunity, dominated by its commodity futures markets.

While Eaton was certainly a power in utilities in his own right, Insull ran the nation's second-largest utilities combination from his Chicago base. Even before World War I, the city was referred to as "Insullopolis." Despite his many contributions to the city, Insull was still considered something of an outsider because of his nationality. After years of investments from Britain and many complaints from Midwestern farmers and manufacturers about absentee British landlords, the United States was dragged into World War I to save the British and the French from Germany. The affair did not sit well with many detractors who criticized the U.K.'s privileged status in the U.S. Insull personally led Britain's propaganda efforts in the United States during World War I and later took some criticism for it, especially since he was otherwise the head of a large American corporation. During the mid-1920s, the utilities were being widely criticized for influence peddling, dictating their wishes to politicians through campaign contributions and even influencing the writing of American history schoolbooks so that they would appear as magnanimous benefactors to the country as a whole. Insull's role as both corporate chieftain and foreigner at the same time made him especially vulnerable despite his good works in Chicago.

After having a tight grip on the city for over 20 years, Insull was not accustomed to competition. Suddenly Eaton began acquiring shares in Insull interests using his Continental Shares Corp. as the investing vehicle. His main targets were Commonwealth Edison, Public Service of Northern Illinois, Peoples' Gas, and Middle West Utilities. From the outset, it was clear that outright control of the companies was out of the question, but Eaton devoted considerable resources to the acquisitions. He accumulated a substantial amount of stock. What made Insull extremely suspicious was the manner by which he accumulated it.

Insull and Cyrus Eaton crossed paths in the 1920s on more than one occasion. By coincidence, they both shared an Atlantic crossing in 1928 and socialized on the trip. The Chicago tycoon was already aware that Eaton was buying his stocks, but apparently Eaton did not know that Insull knew. Eaton never divulged the fact while otherwise sharing cordial relations with his older counterpart during the voyage. Upon their return, Insull reacted as expected and began buying shares of the companies himself to fend off Eaton.[7] After spending some of his personal fortune in the battle, he raised extra capital by forming two investment trusts—Insull Utility Investment Inc. (IUI) and the Corporation Securities Company. Both borrowed heavily to fund the purchase. Eaton responded by raising additional funds through Continental and the battle was joined. Insull raised an additional $300 million and the stocks of his companies soared to unheard-of prices. The buying spree continued into 1930. Then Eaton visited Insull personally and offered to withdraw from the battle for a price. He demanded $400 per share for his holdings, a premium on the current market price. Insull responded by offering $350. Finally in June 1930 they reached an agreement by which Eaton was paid $350 per share for the 160,000 shares he held in the Insull companies. The amount was $6 million above the market price prevailing at the time. The deal smelled bad and prompted an investigation by the Federal Trade Commission several months after it was completed. The inquiry proved of no consequence, however. After the smoke cleared, the Eaton investment trust made a $19 million profit through its Insull investments, a tidy sum considering that the country was plunging into Depression.[8]

Eaton certainly needed the money, for the price of Continental Shares plunged after the stock market debacle. Insull was momentarily safe but his real problems were only beginning. The pyramid he had created had become unsustainable and began to wobble badly under the weight of too much borrowed money. In 1930 and

1931, the utilities magnate helped Chicago out of financial difficulties by providing financing from his own resources so that the city would not have to declare bankruptcy. He was also embarking on several other capital projects after the Crash, which were not immediately relevant to his operating companies; risky ventures given the declining state of the economy. After the market crash, equity financing was not possible so he turned to debt financing to raise the necessary money instead. Each of his operating companies increased its debts by about 10 percent for a total of slightly less than $200 million in 1930 alone.[9] Then the two Insull trusts borrowed the necessary money to fend off Eaton. When local Chicago banks failed to provide the necessary loans, Insull had to raise about 40 percent of the money from New York banks. The collateral supporting the loans was stock in his major operating companies.

The debt securities were sold by Halsey Stuart and earned the investment bank between $10 and $20 million in underwriting fees. The amount raised eyebrows in New York because substantial fees were becoming less common during the Depression as capital spending declined. Insull then added insult to injury by delivering a salvo against New York bankers at a speech at the Chicago Stock Exchange in May 1930 in which he blasted the power of New York and called for "a war of financial liberation against Wall Street."[10] His tone was becoming more strident as it became clear that his empire was being squeezed. In the Senate investigation begun by Herbert Hoover in 1932, Insull's son Samuel Jr. was questioned about the nature of the IUI and the Corporation Securities Co. He freely admitted that the purpose of the two investment trusts was to maintain control of the utilities empire. Under questioning from Ferdinand Pecora, the committee counsel, he also added, "If the public generally were sympathetic with the operating management there should be, in these investment companies, a large enough block of stock, together with the general public, to offset any other interests that might want to come in and get control."[11] Clearly, the two investment trusts were viewed as shark repellents.

After borrowing to support the Eaton purchase, Insull also had to borrow personally to keep his empire afloat. He was so hard-pressed for money that he borrowed several million from the National City Bank of New York and from the General Electric Co. National City was run at the time by the decade's greatest stock promoter, Charles Mitchell, a known ally of Jack Morgan. General Electric was founded by Pierpont Morgan and was run by Owen Young. Young remarked to the Pecora committee, "I should like to say here that I believe Mr. Samuel Insull was very largely the victim of [a] complicated structure which got even beyond his power, competent as he was, to understand it."[12] The theme was repeated time and again in an attempt to show that the empire was too big for even its founder to understand. Insull supporters would counter that it was just a story concocted by Morgan interests to show that he was not competent to run it properly.

Unlike many investment bankers and securities dealers, Insull adopted the investment trust as a defense against an unwanted takeover, not merely as a vehicle to pyramid and run up stock prices. Unfortunately, the result was the same for all of the investment trusts created in the 1920s: their prices plummeted, leaving investors with millions in losses. For his part in the debacle, Eaton assumed a reputation for being what decades later would be called a greenmailer. He accumulated enough stock in the companies to become annoying but never a serious threat to the Insull empire. However, if he decided to sell his holdings precipitously without a deal from Insull, then the stock prices would have fallen quickly, something that the Chicago utilities king certainly did not want to occur. Eaton became the first major greenmailer of the twentieth century and the reputation followed him for the rest of his career.

BEAR RAIDING

The downfall of the Insull empire was the major news story of the early 1930s. It dwarfed even the Pecora hearings in the shenanigans of Wall Street before and after the Crash. The vast empire that had taken Insull decades to assemble came crashing down under a heavy load of leverage and pyramiding. The expatriate Briton was accused of skullduggery and violating the public trust, not to mention a more specific host of felonies filed in Chicago courts. How his empire came to crumble became less important at the time than the fact that it did crumble. The unraveling of Middle West Utilities caused serious concern in Chicago. While Insull's empire was enormous, it was already stretched thin when Eaton began making overtures.

The financing that Insull used to fend off the intruder was the straw that broke the proverbial camel's back. The New York investment bankers took stock worth about half the value of the loans made to Insull as collateral. That alone would not have threatened his empire unless the value of the collateral declined sharply and they asked for more stock as a result. Declining stock prices would mean relinquishing more and more of his certificates to creditors. If someone were able to "bear" his stock effectively on the stock exchange, then control of the company could slip from his hands. In order for that to happen, a bear raid would have to be mounted in which the stock of his major companies was sold short in significant amounts.

After the Crash, business on the stock exchanges began to slow considerably. The amount that Insull paid Eaton for the shares—$56 million—attracted considerable attention on Wall Street because it included all of the investment banking fees attached to the borrowing. At the time, the Depression was still in its early stages and most businessmen and commentators believed that it was nothing more than another cyclical slowdown. As stock prices declined in the aftermath of the Crash, many bear raids were mounted on the floor of the NYSE and the regional exchanges as traders attempted to cash in on declining prices. But forcing a company to the brink of insolvency was a tactic that was not that common. The mergers and acquisitions business was on the verge of taking a new tack. Instead of using inflated stock prices to purchase other companies, investment bankers now were shorting the stock of a target company. When its price dropped so low that liquidation appeared on the horizon, they could then dictate their own terms to the management they sought to displace.

The key to seizing a company down on its luck was short selling. Prior to 1934, there were no prohibitions against the practice as long as there was enough existing stock to borrow so that any short sales could be delivered to the stock exchange. A concerted selling effort could easily plunge a stock to historic lows. Short sales did not have to be interrupted by upticks as they did after the Securities Exchange Act was passed in 1934.[13] Although the practice was clearly an insiders' technique that had been decried by stock exchange critics since the early nineteenth century, it had been used widely in takeover battles and stock manipulations ever since. Usually it was associated with Wall Street culture of the previous century, although some short sellers were operating in the market in the 1920s, notably Jesse Livermore, the king of the bears. He was joined by other market manipulators such as Michael Meehan, "Sell 'Em" Ben Smith, and Arthur Cutten, to name but a few. Making many Midwestern industrialists apprehensive was the fact that some of the short sellers, including Livermore, had bought seats on the Chicago Board of Trade, a futures exchange, where they could also trade Chicago Stock Exchange (CSE) stocks. Insull's IUI and Corporation Securities were both traded on the CSE, so Samuel Sr. had reason to worry about the value of his holdings as the great bears migrated west.

Many pools operated on the floors of the stock exchanges in the 1920s and 1930s. The best known were those that took investors' money and ran up the price of a stock, usually behind the specialist on the stock exchange who was assigned to trading it. Others were bear pools dedicated to selling stocks short. Either type could have a serious impact on prices. They came to light during the Pecora hearings in 1933 when the details of several of them were divulged. Specialists and floor traders were often in the employ of companies or their bankers and were given instructions to move the price up or down, depending upon the wishes of the bankers or investors' pool. It came as no surprise when Insull's companies were beared. George Whitney, a Morgan partner, divulged to the Pecora committee that Morgan had 32 securities dealers acting as allies on the floor of the NYSE, one of which was the firm of his brother Richard Whitney, president of the NYSE. The others were not named.

Bear raiding was normally associated with floor traders who took positions opposite the bulls but was not normally linked with takeovers. After the SEC was installed, the process was curtailed because of the uptick rule that required a stock to have been purchased on the transaction preceding any short sale. The rule went into effect in 1938 and was the subject of much discussion on Wall Street. One commentator remarked, "The new rule will prevent powerful raiding in this country," but went on to say that it "leaves the question of selling abroad unsettled."[14] While traders were restricted on the domestic markets, those with influence and considerable international reach could still sell short through a foreign exchange such as London or Toronto, accomplishing a raid despite the SEC rule.

The Pecora hearings, later summarized as the Fletcher report after Senator Duncan Fletcher, a Florida Democrat, also revealed that the activities of floor traders in the late 1920s and early 1930s were highly concentrated. Almost 27 percent of total volume generated on the NYSE as well as the 27 regional exchanges and the New York Curb Market were attributed to professionals trading for and among themselves. The clear implication was that the public was at the mercy of the insiders. So too were Insull's companies that the bankers happened to hold as collateral. In April 1932, Insull finally threw in the towel and declared bankruptcy. His companies were no longer able to operate without assistance. He did not file for personal bankruptcy but did turn over to his creditors most of his personal assets not directly involved in his companies. Two months later, he sailed to Europe to get away from it all. After the smoke cleared from the ruins of Insull's empire, Morgan interests, including Bonbright & Co., held substantial holdings in his companies. Unfortunately, Insull had learned vaudeville comedian Eddie Cantor's definition of collateral after the Crash—"A form of security, viz: your right eye."

ENTER MORGAN

Insull was not alone in forging a vast utilities empire. J.P. Morgan & Co. under Jack Morgan entered the field in January 1929 when it formed the United Corporation, a holding company that would rival those of the Chicago utilities baron in size and ambition. Coming in the middle of Insull's war with Cyrus Eaton, the competition seemed to be increasing, putting additional pressure on Insull to ward off unwanted suitors. It was also particularly odious to him coming from the House of Morgan, which had displaced Edison years before.

Morgan formed the corporation along with two other investment houses, Bonbright & Co. and Drexel & Co., both close allies. The operating companies it acquired became known as the Morgan group. The group included Mohawk-Hudson Power, United Gas Improvement, and Public Service of New Jersey, and subsequently grew to include Consolidated Edison of New York City and the Commonwealth & Southern Corporation. Technically, the holding company bought controlling interest in the utilities from their major shareholders, all of whom were Morgan cronies. But the method of offering new stock in United differed somewhat from other public offerings made by Insull and Eaton.

The stock of United Corporation was distributed to its shareholders via a private offering. The list of investors to whom the stock was offered became known as a *preferred list*. In order to be included, one had to have some business relationship with Morgan. Generally, the offer was a package of one common and one preferred share at an offering price of $75 each. Subscribers did very well after they made their purchases: By the end of January 1929, the units were offered at around $99 on the stock exchange. Naturally, Morgan took warrants on the deal, which were considered separately and not reported. The warrants became the best part of the deal by far. Morgan received 1,514,200 option warrants on United stock, paying $1 each. Two months later, the warrants soared to over $40 each, presenting the firm with a profit of $68 million. The amount of money involved prompted Duncan Fletcher to remark, "It is beyond belief that any form of service an investment banker can render, entitles him to so stupendous a profit."[15] The amount was for the sale of options only. Other fees were not included.

The preferred list for United contained a veritable *Who's Who*. Included were John Raskob, Albert Wiggin, Charles Mitchell, Richard Mellon, and the heads of General Motors, Standard Oil, U.S. Steel, and Alcoa. Also included was George W. Pepper, the Senate coauthor of the McFadden Act. In many cases, these people were not in Wall Street positions that Morgan needed to cultivate, so the assumption was that they were merely included to pay off past favors. Other investment bankers who maintained such lists also spread the wealth around among colleagues and cronies.

Further offerings done on a similar basis followed during 1929, including some for the common stock of the operating companies themselves. In August 1929, a deal was done for Niagara-Hudson. Clearly, the offering prices were too low when compared with the prices subsequently fetched in the marketplace. The preferred lists became a hot topic during the Pecora hearings in 1933, when senators on the committee began to openly wonder why Morgan would have offered the stock to so many influential people so cheaply, except to curry favor with them. George Whitney, a Morgan partner, denied that there was any other motive to the offer than good business practices. His remarks prompted Senator James Couzens, a Republican from Michigan, to respond, "I have never heard of anybody quite so altruistic in my life before." Whitney responded by stating, "It is not a question of altruism; it is a question of doing a legitimate, straightforward security and banking business."[16] Given the state of the economy, he made few converts among his inquisitors. Couzens, one of the Sons of the Wild Jackass and described as a man "who prefers a fight to friendship," clearly was not impressed.

Preferred lists were also extended by other notable investment bankers, including Kuhn Loeb & Co. No banker admitted that the lists were anything more than a legitimate form of distributing securities. Clearly, the United offering and similar deals were designed to cash in on the surging stock market and the reputation of the promoters themselves. Morgan and his allies had achieved a double victory by pleasing friends and colleagues while using the market to provide most of the excess compensation. But once the offerings were complete, Morgan claimed that the newly traded public companies were free of his influence. The private offerings were now public companies owned by a wide array of shareholders.

The argument was similar to the one made after 1934, when the House of Morgan claimed that the newly created Morgan Stanley &

Co., headed by Jack Morgan's son Henry S. Morgan, was independent of J.P. Morgan & Co. The Glass-Steagall Act of 1933 mandated that commercial and investment banking be permanently separated, and Morgan Stanley was created to comply with the law although its preferred shareholders were Morgan partners and its offices were adjacent to J.P. Morgan & Co. at 23 Wall Street. United Corporation shared a similar link. Jack Morgan testified at the Pecora hearings that three of his partners were directors of United. George Howard, the president of the company, further testified that United's offices were shared with those of Niagara-Hudson and adjoined the offices of the bank at 23 Wall Street. There was even an interior passageway between their offices.[17]

Even by contemporary standards, the United empire was extensive. The company had a market capitalization of $5 billion by the early 1930s and controlled slightly less than 25 percent of the country's electric generation. When combined with Insull's companies and the Electric Bond and Share Co., the other major utilities system, the group controlled almost half of American power production. The prospect of a combined system, with Insull effectively out of the picture, certainly was inviting. Eaton was not able to achieve his goal but certainly set the ball in motion, and the House of Morgan seized the opportunity after 1931 to ensure that the Insull companies came into the Morgan fold.

Despite the pyramiding and concentration of power at the top of the holding companies, many of the operating companies did increase their common shareholders in the 1920s and early 1930s. Generating electric power was a growth industry in the 1930s, and some estimates projected that the amount of kilowatt-hours generated would increase threefold over the decade. *The Magazine of Wall Street* proclaimed that over one-third of the utilities were customer (small shareholder)–owned in the early 1930s. While the numbers were accurate, they overlooked the actual control of the operating companies, residing in the holding companies, which were not widely held. Nevertheless, the utilities were an investment favorite of depository institutions and insurance companies where small investors kept their money. Calvin Coolidge noted the importance of the funds and the institutions in developing the American infrastructure and of keeping government hands off the institutions: "If these great accumulations are to be conserved for the benefit of their scores of millions of owners," he remarked, "they must have the constantly sympathetic consideration of the government. Public officials can confer no greater benefit on the people than by protecting the property of these institutions."[18] Unfortunately, the institutions needed protection not from the heavy hand of government but from the owner-operators of the utilities themselves.

The Pecora hearings revealed the scope and extent of the Morgan empire. Despite the Clayton Act passed almost 20 years before, the reach of the Morgan bank was considerable. The final report of the committee stated that the ownership situation among utilities and other companies dominated by investment trusts "has resulted in the domination of corporations by small groups of individuals controlling a comparatively insignificant part of the voting stock. These groups dictate the selection of directors and consequently the management and control of these corporate institutions." The numbers provided about J.P. Morgan & Co. were impressive. "The partners of J.P. Morgan & Co. and Drexel & Co. held 126 directorships and trusteeships in 89 companies . . . with $19,929,396,475.39 total resources for 75 of these companies . . . including 20 directorships on 15 banks and trust companies . . . 9 directorships on 5 utility holding companies, 10 diectorships on 8 utility operating companies." The total tallied by the committee staff was staggering. In addition to Morgan and his partners, Morgan personnel who were not partners—an additional 537 executives—held directorships in 2,715 companies with assets of around $101 billion.[19]

The total was impressive. In addition to the moribund stock market, the numbers showed that, despite the best intentions of Congress in the Clayton Act, corporate America was solidly controlled by the Morgan empire with some assistance from other investment bankers, notably Kuhn Loeb and Dillon Read. The mergers business lay at the heart of the vast empire and it was clear to Congress that it would have to be dismembered. But the problem of corporate control through mergers and acquisitions activity was not one that could be effectively combated with the antitrust laws; it would have to be dealt with on a case-by-case basis. Strong banking laws would be needed to keep the foxes out of the henhouse. The laws would also need to be strong enough to ensure that the foxes did not actually build the henhouses either.

The formation of the United Corporation was the greatest coup for Morgan since the U.S. Steel deal almost 30 years before. Unlike Big Steel, United was much less visible to the public eye. The tenor of the times had changed substantially since the beginning of the century. While there had always been critics of big business combinations, many of those in the 1930s were especially shrill and their arguments began to reverberate against the background of the swiftly declining economy. Discretion became the byword for bankers in the early 1930s. Big deals could still be done but bankers had to be seen at arm's length from the megadeals. The reason was simple. The $68 million value of Morgan's warrants in United represented one month's wages for almost 1.5 million farm workers. Numbers like those would prove explosive fodder for Wall Street critics in the years ahead.

TENTACLES

Samuel Insull planned a European trip as a vacation from the distressing business of filing for bankruptcy, but the sojourn proved to be even more distressing and short. While Insull was out of the country, pressure began to build to charge him with fraud and deception over the unraveling of his empire. Accordingly, in September 1932 the United States Attorney in Chicago began an investigation into the Insull companies and several weeks later in October a Cook County grand jury returned indictments against Insull and his brother Martin, who was also active in the companies' affairs. The federal indictments followed in February 1933, charging Insull and 16 other defendants with mail fraud. Included were his son Samuel Jr. and Harold Stuart. Further charges followed charging father and son as well as Stuart with illegally transferring property to avoid having it included in bankruptcy hearings. Insull was living with his wife in Paris at the time.

Fearing extradition when he learned of the indictments, Insull left France for Greece and then departed again, sailing around the Mediterranean to avoid being extradited. He was finally apprehended and sent home in April 1934. Upon returning to Chicago, he told reporters, "I have erred but my greatest error was in underestimating the effects of the financial panic on American securities and particularly on the companies I was trying to build." The first trial began in October 1934 and included extensive testimony from Insull himself, who maintained his innocence in the face of dubious business practices and a hostile public. The federal case collapsed when the jury returned a not guilty verdict after only two hours of deliberation. Other trials followed on state charges and Insull was found not guilty in all of them.

Reflecting on his career and the trials, Insull stated, "What I did, when I did it, was honest; now through changed conditions what I did may or may not be called honest. Politics demand, therefore, that I be brought to trial; but what is really being brought to trial is the system I represented." The juries obviously agreed. The *Chicago Times* summarized the affair in much the same way: "Insull and his fellow defendants—not guilty; the old order—guilty. That was the Insull defense and the jury agreed with it."[20] But exoneration was small comfort for a man who was once the toast of Chicago. He voluntarily exiled himself again after the affair and died of a heart attack in the Paris subway in 1938. When his body was discovered, he had only eight francs in his pocket.

Insull's problems and the lingering Morgan presence finally forced Congress into action. In the early 1930s, the utilities companies were something of a sacred cow on Wall Street. Their consolidations had reaped large fees and their stocks stood up better after the Crash than those of many industrial companies. Having radical agrarian Progressives as their enemies also incensed many conservative elements on the Street who feared that the companies would become the targets of federal meddling. One investment magazine wrote, "the utilities corporations are public servants and they have served the public well. Their record constitutes, in fact, an impregnable argument from experience for the entrustment of public services to private management instead of bureaus and bureaucrats."[21] Within several years, the attitude in Congress would not countenance such a friendly view. Using the two securities acts passed in 1933 and 1934 as a template, Congress passed the Public Utility Holding Company Act (PUHCA) in 1935. In many respects, the Holding Company Act was far tougher than the securities and banking laws passed earlier. It provided the final blow to the Morgan empire that the banking laws could not fully achieve. Although J.P. Morgan & Co. had earlier divested itself of investment banking by forming Morgan Stanley & Co., the utilities companies had remained under the bank's effective control. Now under the new law, utilities were effectively under the aegis of the Securities and Exchange Commission (SEC), itself created a year earlier by the Securities Exchange Act.

The PUHCA required utilities engaging in interstate commerce to register with the SEC. The SEC would review its organizational structure as well as all requests to issue new securities on behalf of the holding company. The PUHCA also contained the famous "death sentence" provision that effectively limited all holding companies to a single integrated system. This limited the scope of their empires, reducing them to more manageable size. Although the utilities raged over the provisions of the act and sued to have it overturned, they were unsuccessful. A Baltimore dentist, Dr. Ferd Lautenbach, who held $2,500 in bonds of a small utility company, sued to have the law declared unconstitutional. He was represented by John W. Davis, the Democratic presidential nominee in 1924, representing the utilities industry. Davis also was a close associate of Jack Morgan and critics of the industry naturally suspected that the dentist was supported by "higher forces." Davis admitted that he had never met his client before entering court on the day the lawsuit began. The *New York Times* reported tongue-in-cheek, "Mr. Davis admitted that he had never seen Dr. Lautenbach and later the court room witnessed the unusual incident of a lawyer being introduced to his client during trial of a case."[22]

Despite the suits and heavy lobbying, the PUHCA became the harshest law ever enacted against a single industry. It superseded the laws passed regulating railroads, banks, and (most lately) the securities industry. Like its banking and securities predecessors, it did more to aid the antitrust movement than either of the two antitrust laws on the books. The utilities industry inadvertently had returned to the local control that Insull and Eaton pined for in the 1920s despite the fact that they were empire building at the same time.

After the PUHCA was passed, the utilities wars between the Roosevelt administration and the power industry came to an end. The utilities' influence on American life had been throttled. Large-scale contributions to political parties and money spent to influence American life were scaled back severely since the companies now had the SEC as their watchdog. George Norris later summed up the first Roosevelt administration succinctly when he stated, "Among the reforms in the first years of Mr. Roosevelt's administration that I think represent a great improvement in American life were the act providing for the regulation of the New York Stock Exchange; the act establishing a securities commission; and finally, the utility holding company death sentence act."[23] The ironic part of the remark was that it turned 50 years of Wall Street consolidations on their head. In the dark days of the 1930s, no one was giving merger bankers much credit for the changes they brought to American industry and economic life. In the 1930s, the proverbial glass was half empty.

The Depression brought a wave of severe criticism of American culture and institutions. The criticism was particularly acute when Wall Street and the House of Morgan were mentioned. It came from two directions—from the right through the neo-Progressives in Congress and from the left through Socialists and muckrakers. The combination was powerful since both groups had a common enemy in their sights. Whether the critic was Leninist or an agrarian radical, the common enemy was "finance capitalism." In the 1930s that was shorthand for mergers and acquisitions.

While the agrarians and neo-Progressives were busy criticizing Wall Street and the House of Morgan for the country's problems, the socialists and muckrakers mounted a more systematic campaign that was focused on the amount of money the top financiers had accumulated through their ventures in finance capitalism. In 1937, Ferdinand Lundberg, a reporter for the *New York Herald Tribune*, published his first book exposing the super rich, listing America's 60 richest, most powerful families. Topping the list were the Rockefellers, followed by the Morgan group of partners and associates, and the Fords. Rockefeller's gross fortune was estimated at somewhere between $1 billion and $2.5 billion, Ford's between $660 million and $1 billion. The Morgan group was more difficult because of its extended size, but an estimate was made of around $780 million.[24]

Other investment bankers and their families included in the group were the Bakers of First National Bank of New York ($350 million), the Lehmans of Lehman Brothers ($130 million), the Stillmans of National City Bank ($100 million), the Warburgs of Kuhn Loeb ($97 million), the Kahns of Kuhn Loeb ($86 million), the Drexels of Drexel & Co. ($21 million), the Schiffs of Kuhn Loeb ($66 million), George Blumenthal of Lazard Freres ($54 million), James Storrow of Lee Higginson ($34 million), and several stock market operators including Thomas Fortune Ryan ($108 million), Charles Hayden ($60 million), and Bernard Baruch ($37 million). Being drawn from tax figures released in the mid-1920s, the list did not include Clarence Dillon or Cyrus Eaton, the bulk of whose fortunes were yet to be made. But clearly 20 percent of America's richest families and individuals attributed their fortunes to the investment banking business or the stock market. In the 1930s, simply listing the numbers was enough to set off a wave of criticism based upon the theory that where there was that much smoke there certainly was a concentration of political and financial fire.

Coming in the wake of Huey Long's "share the wealth" campaign, the Lundberg book's thesis was taken up by presidential advisor Harold Ickes. Speaking in a radio address in 1937, Ickes attributed the economic problems of the 1930s to a constant struggle between democracy and plutocracy. "It must be fought to a finish," he railed, "until plutocracy or democracy—until America's 60 families or America's 120 million people—win."[25] The speech became very controversial since it echoed the sentiments of other muckrakers on the left, including Gustavus Myers and Matthew Josephson. Ickes admitted that his use of the list was dictated by politics at the time since he needed a controversial topic to rally a languishing campaign and the publicity helped support Lundberg's thesis. Myers later expanded on the theme in a similar book in 1939. Most important, a congressional committee reopened the issue one last time before World War II.

The most compelling description of that oligarchical power came from a Socialist, using Lenin's analytical style and categories of the historical development of capitalism. When Pierpont Morgan died in 1913, he left a personal estate of around $68 million, an amount that prompted Andrew Carnegie to remark that the legendary banker was not very rich. World War I presented the bank and many Morgan-related companies with a plethora of profit so that 11 years later Lundberg could arrive at his much higher aggregate figure. In 1936, Socialist writer Anna Rochester described Morgan's power in broader terms in another book examining the power and financial structure of the United States. "The Morgan power represents the most advanced stage of capitalist development and concentration," she wrote. "It is largely separated from stock ownership. Industrial companies drawn in originally through Morgan investment banking are held in line through Morgan dominance in the banking world, but at the same time the Morgan banking power is now supported by the great Morgan industrial companies."[26] Anyone who heard Jack Morgan's testimony before the Pecora committee in 1933 or could remember his father's testimony 20 years earlier before the Pujo committee could easily understand how the House of Morgan could disavow any charge of controlling companies by simply stating that it held no serious vested interests. But the structure of power was very different from simply examining the stockholder lists to see who owned companies. Even though the Clayton Act of 1914 outlawed interlocking directorships in a clear attempt to curb the power of the money trust, the influence exerted by investment bankers was as strong as ever.

NYE-SAYERS

The old argument about banker influence and World War I refused to die in the 1930s. Aside from the socialists and muckrakers, other

American writers were beginning to question the past, focusing on Wall Street and the events it had wrought on American society. Many believed that Woodrow Wilson had been seriously misled by bankers and their lobbyists concerning German intentions that led to American intervention in the war in Europe.

Economic conditions and public opinion sided with the new revisionist interpretations. A few Sons of the Wild Jackass remained in the Senate and books appeared providing fodder for their salvos. War clouds in Europe suggested that another potential conflict was looming and the few Progressive Republicans still sitting in Congress used the opportunity to revisit the past. One contemporary account called them "the strongest and weakest element in American national affairs. Individually they are the strongest. Collectively they are the weakest."[27] The assessment was on the mark because their individual efforts on behalf of farmers and the downtrodden came in the early 1930s. By the mid-1930s, their principles had become enshrined in some notable legislation that many would not have thought possible. After the two securities acts, two banking acts, and the Public Utility Holding Company Act had been passed, their prominence grew to the point where calling a Senate investigation into alleged abuses of power 20 years before was not considered extraordinary.

The Senate hearings into war dealings by bankers were significant because the future of the mergers and acquisitions industry hinged on its deliberations and results. Public opinion had turned against Wall Street after the Crash and financiers had not regained any lost ground in the eyes of the average citizen. The extent of Morgan's power in particular was better understood than at any time in the past even though it had been severely curtailed by the legislation passed between 1932 and 1935. But at the heart of the matter was another conflagration. The United States was in an isolationist mood and did not want to experience another European war. *Time* magazine put it succinctly, stating that "the Senate Committee on Investigation of the Munitions industry set out last week [mid-January 1936] to prove, if possible, that the U.S. had gone to war in 1917 because Wall Street's international bankers needed U.S. troops in the field to secure repayment of their Allied loans."[28] The idea was resurrected because of a book published in 1935 by Walter Millis, a reporter for the *New York Herald Tribune,* entitled *Road to War.*

The Nye Committee, as the investigation was called, drew Jack Morgan and his partners to Washington for only the second time in their careers. The bankers decamped to the Shoreham Hotel, where they occupied an entire wing of the eighth floor, surrounded by armed bodyguards. One news account described the group by saying, "If the presence of the House of Morgan in Washington was like that of an expeditionary force, the witnesses before the Senate Committee looked more like the survivors of the Grand Army of the Republic." Clearly, the surviving partners were aging and their memories of events 20 years before were not particularly vivid. But the committee members realized that they were up against perhaps the most formidable group of senior bankers ever assembled. Included in the party were Jack Morgan and his partners Thomas Lamont, George Whitney, and Russell Leffingwell as well as Frank Vanderlip, formerly of National City Bank. Two of the key members of the House of Morgan during the war—Edward Stettinius and Henry Davison—had since died.

Millis wrote an account of World War I financing that accused bankers of growing rich off the conflict. He was not complaining as much about finance capitalism as the money made by Morgan and others, especially when acting as the British agent in the United States for war materials. Unlike the direct approach used by Lundberg and Rochester, Millis' account was more subdued. He painstakingly laid out his narrative, citing the inextricable relationship between business and politics that slowly led to the war loans and eventual American involvement. Certainly not everyone was convinced by the argument, but it proved a valuable polemic for war critics and vaulted Millis into prominence. It provided more tangible substance for those seeking to discredit Wall Street and, if not totally convincing, provided an excuse for congressional inquiry. But after all the testimony had been heard, the hearings ended tamely and most observers realized that the main contention had not been proved in the slightest. It was one of the few times that the thesis of a popular book got such an acid test in order to see whether it would stand the light of day.

The Millis account nevertheless touched a sensitive nerve in Congress, where some of the Sons of the Wild Jackass had been complaining about the bankers' activities. During the war, Senator George Norris of Nebraska, a Progressive, had been complaining about the role of financiers in determining U.S. economic policy but had received little attention at the time. In 1917, he made a speech in the Senate that was highly reminiscent of William Jennings Bryan's "cross of gold" speech during the presidential campaign of 1896 against William McKinley. Norris warned, "You shall not coin into gold the lifeblood of my brethren. . . . I feel that we are about to put the dollar sign upon the American flag." This played well along with the suspicions that Wall Street was profiting on advance news reports concerning the war. The theme was picked up in Henry Ford's series of anti-Semitic articles printed in the *Dearborn Independent* and was later continued by Louis McFadden in a series of bombasts against international bankers and the Federal Reserve in the early 1930s.

Although the Nye committee was not able to prove any of the allegations made in the Millis book or to prove that any conspiracy existed among Morgan partners to profit unduly by the war effort, over a decade of charges came to the surface and were finally laid to rest. As the Depression lingered, charges were being made that American capitalism bore the seeds of its own destruction and that financiers were leading the charge. Needless to say, the mergers business was moribund for most of the 1930s, especially after the bear raids of 1931 and 1932. Mergers led the stock market to a bubble, but they no longer had the necessary impetus or the means to continue functioning in a deflated economy. But that did not mean that money should not be invested in mergers during the Depression. *The Magazine of Wall Street* suggested that its readers invest in "Depression mergers." It advised that "There is little to be lost and much to be gained" by investing in mergers arranged during Depressions, but failed to mention any possibilities in the current climate. The only precedent it could find was the depression of 1920 to 1921, which, while severe, was only a recession when compared to the 1930s experience.

McFadden's diatribes against bankers became increasingly heated after the Crash. He had become increasingly unpopular in the Republican Party for introducing impeachment proceedings against Herbert Hoover in 1932. Interpreting Hoover's moratorium on Allied war debts from World War I as a capitulation to foreigners, he charged the president with high crimes and misdemeanors on December 13, 1932, after Hoover had already lost the presidential campaign to Franklin D. Roosevelt. The charge was never acted upon, with only eight congressmen voting in favor. The Republicans did not embrace McFadden after that, although he did win reelection from his district for another term.

Six months later, McFadden introduced a resolution into the House to impeach every member of the Federal Reserve Board. His problem with the Fed went back to the 1920s, when he vigorously opposed the nomination of Eugene Meyer to be Fed chairman. He described Meyer as "a Wall Street man." That was putting it mildly. McFadden and Smith Brookhart in the Senate led the charge against Meyer, a Yale graduate and former stock market operator. The affair did not exactly cast either man in a tolerant light since Meyer was a Jew who had studied finance in Germany as a postgraduate. Journalist Clinton Gilbert summed up the affair by writing, "In the Senate the noble Brookhart led the sortie . . . he is a perfect example of the type of biped who travels from the cradle to the grave without having been aroused from a state of invincible ignorance." Concerning McFadden, Gilbert was somewhat kinder: "Those who have made a study of Tiny's various mental attacks during the last few years, those who knew him as a plump, pleasant nonentity during his earlier terms in the House, trace his gall-tinctured idiosyncrasies to his experience in a primary campaign . . . his opponent was Mrs. Gifford Pinchot. Although renominated by a small majority, he, like some others who have come in contact with the flaming haired, effervescing mate of the Governor of Pennsylvania, has never quite recovered his equilibrium."[29]

After Meyer's confirmation, McFadden continued to berate the Fed for acting in unison with international bankers whom he accused of profiting at the expense of the American people by granting unnecessary export credits to foreign governments. In his opinion, the Fed also was too lax in its credit policies to banks in the 1920s and the policy led to the market crash. He was not the only legislator to criticize the Fed for fueling the bubble, but as chairman of the House Committee on Banking and Currency he was the most prominent. Writing in a popular Wall Street magazine, he claimed that "the ensuing speculation in securities was an inevitable result, and from that orgy of speculation has come a measure of our present distress."[30] As far as he was concerned, the problem could be laid at the feet of the Fed governors' international banking connections. While the impeachment charge was extraordinary, it was nevertheless similar in tone to others made with less publicity in the 1920s, charging that the United States was falling under foreign influence with the help of the Fed. This charge was sent to the Judiciary Committee where it was allowed to die without any further fanfare. McFadden did not regain his seat in the 1934 election.

Conspiracy theorists were aroused when McFadden died on October 1, 1936. While visiting New York City with his wife and son, he was taken ill at the Lexington Hotel. He was rushed to the hospital, where he died of a coronary thrombosis. His life ended under a cloud, as did his career. He served in the House until 1935, but his later years were troubled because of the anti-Semitic statements he made on the floor during some intemperate moments. In his last term, he was investigated by the House committee on un-American activities concerning his anti-Semitic remarks. Supporters muttered privately that he had been poisoned by the international bankers whom he often attacked in Congress. They pointed to another, earlier attempt on his life in Washington, D.C. as proof of a conspiracy. The author of the McFadden Act proved to be as enigmatic in death as he was in life.

CHAIN SMOKING

Even as some of the Sons of the Wild Jackass were either denied reelection or died, the movement continued in Congress to stem the tide of change sweeping the country. Specific laws were passed to stem the power of investment bankers to fashion mergers by divorcing them from deposits at commercial banks. Then the PUHCA reduced their powers in utilities mergers. The last bastion was the chain store movement, still growing despite the Depression. Was the decade radical enough to curtail the growth of the large stores in the name of the small merchant?

The final salvo in the battle was fired in Congress by Wright Patman, a Democrat congressman from Texas. Patman, the chairman of the House Antitrust Subcommittee, was born in 1893 to poor tenant farmers in Texas. After working his way through the Cumberland Law School in Tennessee, he won a seat in the Texas legislature and his political career began. After serving as a district attorney, he won a House seat in 1928 and began a career that clearly would have aligned him with the Progressive Republicans had he been elected earlier. He served in Congress for more than 40 years until his death in 1976. Championing people's causes, he quickly adopted the anti–chain store movement.

Recognizing that Wall Street had made many bankers and merchants dizzyingly wealthy through the expansion of chain stores, Patman set out to prove that the large stores were a violation of the antitrust laws. In the 1930s, the argument found more sympathetic ears than it did in the 1920s. Bankers and store operators constantly used the argument that the large stores would lower prices to the consumer by being able to employ economies of scale. The anti–chain store contingent countered by saying that the large stores amounted to a retailing trust, being able to achieve price discrimination against consumers because of their size. The price discrimination idea became the cornerstone of a bill Patman introduced in Congress to fight the chains.

Economic conditions in East Texas during the 1930s gave Patman plenty of ammunition in his quest to stop the stores' expansion. Local radio stations and newspapers ranted against chain stores so their congressman had local support for his bill, which quickly became known as the chain store act. The Robinson-Patman Act passed Congress in 1936, partly as an attempt to plug loopholes in the Clayton Act. A speech by Louis McFadden over the radio paved the way as early as 1930. It echoed throughout rural areas where it played on antitrust sentiments, as did many other volatile issues of the decade. McFadden originally complained about the amount of profits that the chain stores reaped in the late 1920s as evidence that they must have been involved in monopoly. Citing that the chains reported sales of $395 million in 1929, he questioned the fate of the "small shopkeeper or the corner druggist. Is he permitted to be driven out of business by the chain store moving next door to him?"[31] The answer was clear to most anti–Wall Street politicians. As a result, the act sought to prevent price discrimination, which it was assumed could only be practiced by a seller of goods or services who "has market power approaching monopoly control over prices in the markets in which he operates."[32] But the law was immediately criticized for being too complicated. Unlike the Sherman and Clayton Acts, its language was difficult and its text was considered much too long and convoluted. However, it sailed through Congress and became one of the three major pieces of federal antitrust legislation.

Opponents of the chain stores claimed a victory with the act, although it did not stop store expansion. During the Depression and the war years that followed, antitrust laws were used sparingly for fear of thwarting economic recovery. After two decades of complaining, the anti–chain store forces could claim victory when the act was passed but almost no one took any serious notice. The law became one of the more obscure passed during the New Deal years and its use was limited in the years ahead. But like the securities, banking, and utility laws passed earlier, it demonstrated how deep the divisions in the country ran between bankers and the average citizen, represented by the neo-Progressives in Congress. Although their usefulness was measured in reactionary legislation rather than in a unified, orchestrated policy-making response, the fact that politicians who often behaved like loose cannons were able to pass so much seemingly radical legislation was an indication of the deep divisions in society caused by the Crash and Depression.

ONE LAST TIME

Although the Nye Committee ended tamely, another investigation was begun into the shape of American industry in 1938. President

Roosevelt created the Temporary National Economic Committee (TNEC) to look into the problem of monopoly in American industry. The committee was composed of members of both houses of Congress as well as representatives from the executive branch. It had become clear that the activities of investment bankers were ancillary to the development of big business in America on a scale that was unprecedented. The issue now was one of antitrust, not simply of regulating bankers. The committee's findings were startling, especially since many critics believed that corporate structures in the United States had changed since World War I and become somewhat smaller and more competitive.

The TNEC reported that several industries, including public utilities, life insurance, and investment banking, were dominated by a handful of leading firms that controlled between 65 and 95 percent of their industries' assets. The huge companies they represented, or created, represented a staggering amount of wealth. The assets of the Metropolitan Life Insurance Company and AT&T were larger than those of all but the 12 wealthiest states. General Motors' assets alone would have made Billy Durant smile, because they were greater than all of those of Tennessee. More damning still was the fact that the TNEC report was not written by socialist muckrakers but by a committee appointed by the president. While the late 1930s were hardly a time of robust merger activity, investment bankers, laying low since the banking, securities, and utilities acts, still seemed in command of business and industry.

Before the findings could be acted upon in any meaningful way, World War II intervened and the antitrust laws were put in abeyance so that industry could flex its muscle and help with the war effort. When the smoke cleared in the late 1940s and early 1950s, pent-up demand and a more optimistic outlook provided the basis for a bull market that would develop during the Eisenhower administration. Once a strong stock market was back on track, the merger bankers could again begin their duties as corporate justices of the peace. The war years left many companies in need of marriage partners and Wall Street recognized the trend immediately, paving the way for the first bull market in almost 30 years.

The Depression changed the dashing image of the investment banker. Long gone were the newspaper accounts of the flashy Otto Kahn of Kuhn Loeb cavorting with actresses in Hollywood or reports about Morgan's ocean crossings. Wall Street avarice now was ridiculed on the silver screen in the late 1930s, although in a light-hearted manner. The image of the corporate raider was now firmly embedded in the public imagination, where it was destined to remain for the next 20 years. In 1939, Roy Rogers and George "Gabby" Hayes appeared in *Wall Street Cowboy*, a celluloid western with a moral. Roy's ranch, endowed with a rare, valuable mineral, became the target of Wall Street bankers intent on expropriating it. Needless to say, it took less than an hour to defeat their evil plan and all ended well. The moral of the story only proved that it was becoming difficult for investment bankers to make a buck in the 1930s, even on the silver screen.

NOTES

1. United States Department of Commerce, *Historical Statistics of the United States: Colonial Times to 1957* (Washington: U.S. Government Printing Office, 1957), p. 572.
2. Ibid., pp. 508–511.
3. William Z. Ripley, *Main Street and Wall Street* (Boston: Little, Brown, 1927), p. 17.
4. Frederick Lewis Allen, *Only Yesterday: An Informal History of the 1920s* (New York: John Wiley & Sons, reprinted 1997), p. 47.
5. Marcus Gleisser, *The World of Cyrus Eaton* (New York: A.S. Barnes & Co., 1965), p. 37.
6. Gleisser, pp. 59, 64.
7. Forrest McDonald, *Insull* (Chicago: University of Chicago Press, 1962), p. 280.
8. Gleisser, p. 43.
9. McDonald, p. 287.
10. Ibid., p. 287.
11. U.S. Senate, *Stock Exchange Practices:* testimony of Samuel Insull Jr., February 16, 1933, p. 362.
12. *Stock Exchange Practices*, p. 1515.
13. According to the SEC, short sales could only be recorded if they had

been preceded by an uptick, meaning that the transaction prior to the sale had to be a buy, registering a tick up in price on the books of the specialist in the stock.

14. *Magazine of Wall Street*, March 12, 1938, p. 734.
15. *Stock Exchange Practices*, p. 115.
16. Ibid., p. 105.
17. M.L. Ramsay. *Pyramids of Power: The Story of Roosevelt, Insull, and the Utility Wars* (Indianapolis: Bobbs-Merrill, 1937), p. 277.
18. *Magazine of Wall Street*, June 27, 1931, p. 316.
19. *Stock Exchange Practices*, pp. 385–386.
20. McDonald, p. 332.
21. *Magazine of Wall Street*, June 27, 1931, p. 270.
22. *New York Times*, November 8, 1935.
23. George W. Norris, *Fighting Liberal: The Autobiography of George W. Norris* (New York: Macmillan, 1945), p. 374.
24. Ferdinand Lundberg, *America's 60 Families* (New York: Citadel Press, 1937), p. 25ff.
25. Harold Ickes, *The Inside Struggle 1936–39* (New York: Simon & Schuster, 1953), p. 284.
26. Anna Rochester, *Rulers of America: A Study of Finance Capital* (New York: International Publishers, 1936), p. 105.
27. Anonymous, *Washington Merry-Go-Round* (New York: Blue Ribbon Books, 1931), p. 184.
28. *Time*, January 20, 1936.
29. Anonymous, *The Mirrors of Wall Street* (New York: G.P. Putnam's Sons, 1933), p. 228. The book was written by journalist Clinton Gilbert, as were many others in his "Mirrors" series.
30. *Magazine of Wall Street*, January 10, 1931, p. 350.
31. *New York Times*, March 27, 1930.
32. Wright Patman, *Complete Guide to the Robinson-Patman Act* (Englewood Cliffs, NJ: Prentice Hall, 1938), p. 3.

CHAPTER 4

ROLL OVER, EUCLID

In the age when alchemy began to fall into some disrepute . . . a new delusion, based upon this power of imagination, suddenly arose, and found apostles among all the alchymists . . . and numbers its dupes by thousands.

Charles Mackay, 1841

B y 1950, mergers had transformed the American social and economic landscape. Although thousands had been accomplished since the beginning of the century, the effects of the largest still could clearly be felt. U.S. Steel was the largest company in its industry, while International Harvester, General Motors, Commonwealth Edison, and AT&T retained dominant positions, much as they had before World War I. Technology and a growing population would help many new industries break new ground and Wall Street was quick to sign up companies that would propel the economy through the second half of the century.

The general economic climate was far healthier than it had been for decades and big business was back in favor. Unemployment in 1953 was lower than in any peacetime year since 1926 and the gross national product was rising quickly. The number of business failures was smaller than it had been in decades and the number of manufacturing corporations, still the basic measure of the health of the economy, was higher than ever. Being in a management profession or in a financial services job was no longer frowned upon as in the 1930s. In the mid-1950s, the chairman of General Motors could safely tell a congressional committee that what was good for GM was good for the country. Few doubted his assessment.

Merger bankers became power brokers to companies whose grasp was international. Originally, many of the huge companies formed by J. P. Morgan in the earlier part of the century were mainly domestic. After the war, corporations spread their tentacles much wider as American overseas investment expanded dramatically. Several, notably the International Telephone & Telegraph Corporation (ITT), became emblematic of American corporate power abroad. Before World War I, the unofficial motto of American business was "In Morgan We Trust." In the 1960s, it became "The Sovereign State of ITT," named after a book of the same title by Anthony Sampson. Investment bankers would be happy to see the shift in power from themselves to corporate executives because the heat brought to bear on multinational corporations became intense, reminiscent of the pressure and scrutiny of the Pujo and Pecora hearings of earlier generations. The postwar period developed into the generation of powerful corporations, with investment bankers as their allies rather than their guiding force.

The majority of significant mergers were horizontal—that is, between two companies in the same business. Vertical mergers—those between two companies in related industries in the same food chain— were also common and were becoming increasingly popular since the Antitrust Division of the Justice Department had the most success blocking horizontal mergers. But vertical mergers suffered significant defeats in the courts, especially when the Supreme Court in 1957 ruled against the investment made by DuPont in General Motors 40 years before. The court ruled that DuPont had violated the Clayton Act by doing so because the company was buying itself favored supplier status to GM as a result. In an ideal world, corporate deal makers and their investment bankers needed a type of merger that was not proscribed by antitrust law. Logically, two totally unrelated companies merging would not violate the law. But how would the combinations be justified?

Prosperity in the 1950s brought logistical problems for Wall Street. Investors began returning to the stock market for the first time since the late 1920s, hoping to cash in their war bonds for greater rates of return. During the Eisenhower administration, the market indices began to climb again and the investment banking and brokerage businesses saw renewed business. But there was still a hangover from the Depression and the war years that would not easily abate. Big business was still not fully trusted and the hand of government was now more evident than at any time in the twentieth century.

Against this background, new ideas and strategies would have to succeed if the mergers business was to resume its 1920s pace. Business had been consolidating since the 1880s and only the Depression and World War II had broken the trend. No one expected the extraordinary measures adopted between 1930 and 1945 to continue because the war had solved the unemployment problem and the national savings had recovered since the early 1930s. But the New Deal legacy still remained. Government intervention in business was still feared and antitrust laws were still being enforced after a wartime hiatus. Active investigations into horizontal and vertical mergers suggested that business could grow individually but that marriages between large companies still needed regulatory approval.

The economy was growing but the agents of growth were still not completely trusted. A good idea was desperately needed that would be distinctly new, not evoking memories of past business practices that ended in disaster. While it could be argued that nothing new existed under the sun, the buzzwords that eventually dominated the 1950s and 1960s were as close to innovation as history could provide. True to form, the period provided its own group of corporate characters and merger bankers that looked suspiciously like the cast of an older Wall Street production playing a current reprise. The Morgans and Dillon may have departed the merger game but there would be no shortage of newer bankers to fill their shoes.

One result of World War II was the notion that superior management techniques could be applied to any business regardless of type. Efficiency in production and rational allocation of resources meant that a professionally trained manager could apply his or her skills to any sort of enterprise and make it profitable. This would be true especially if one company could acquire another and mesh it into its operations, regardless of the sort of business it was in. In order to maximize the marriage, accounting rules would have to be favorable to the acquiring company. In short, the groom needed to immediately incorporate the bride's earnings into his own income statement. If the bride was profitable, the groom gained immediately.

This type of pool accounting was avidly practiced in the 1950s and 1960s and provided a new dowry for the grooms. The term *pool* meant that the price a buyer paid for an acquired company was not reflected on its balance sheet because the assets of the two were combined, or pooled.[1] It also had another practical effect: Target companies became more desirable than ever and were actively courted by larger companies seeking to diversify their operations. Mixing apples and oranges in this manner was condoned by professional management as a rational way of blending disparate companies together for the benefit of shareholders. The terms *bride* and *groom* became standard on Wall Street when it became apparent that many of these arranged marriages required a banker to introduce them. Investment bankers would earn even more money if they stood at the altar as the best man in the proceedings.

Proclaiming that these sorts of mergers were managerially efficient did not particularly excite the new sort of investor returning to the market after being absent for decades. Securities analysts, also a rising phenomenon in the 1960s, needed something sexier to sell recommended companies to investors. They required an easy-to-understand theory that would become so popular that it actually achieved the status of standard buzzword on Wall Street. Developments in finance theory soon provided the needed language. Within a few years, a new craze had Wall Street humming and more excited than at any time since the 1920s.

A new business entity was born—the conglomerate. Unlike companies that expanded by merging with similar companies through horizontal mergers or with related companies through vertical mergers, the conglomerate was a new breed of organization: one that merged with companies in disparate types of business. The only requisite was that the companies be well managed in order to contribute to the greater profitability of the parent. The conglomerate became a basket of unrelated companies all operating under a similar assumption.

135

Those with long memories recalled the investment companies put together by Eaton and Insull that created the huge utilities pyramids of the 1920s. The new companies were similar except that their holdings could often be a bewildering array of unrelated businesses.

Conglomerates began springing up in the late 1950s and within 15 years became a fixed part of the corporate landscape. Initially they were assembled for accounting purposes and pool accounting allowed them to grow quickly. Before a theory appeared justifying them, they were already becoming investor favorites, but innovations in corporate finance and investments theory made them all the more attractive. Pool accounting made them work but portfolio theory gave them greater credence, a quality Wall Street had not witnessed for decades. Unfortunately, their growth was interpreted as an attack on the establishment in corporate America. Conglomerators expressed their dissatisfaction with the way many traditional companies were run. By the late 1960s, fear in the executive suite would have unexpected political ramifications.

In many ways the conglomerate phenomenon reflected the changes in society since the Second World War. Like the huge industrial combinations formed in the first half of the century, the conglomerates were often dominated by strong chief executives who provided the impetus for their growth. But most of these new chief executives were not from the well-trained managerial classes produced by the increasingly popular business schools. Many were from humble backgrounds and fashioned themselves into self-made successes with assumed nicknames like the "bootstrap kid." Quite often, their aggressiveness stood in stark contrast to their counterparts in more established companies, who regarded the newcomers as crass upstarts. Many times the characterization was correct but their companies made money and criticism often waned in deference to a strong bottom line.

REVOLUTIONARY THOUGHTS

Strong stock and bond markets were vital to the growth of conglomerates. Many of their acquisitions were not paid in cash but by offering stock or bonds instead. Payment in securities required a strong market because investors would not accept them in weak markets without the prospect of a capital gain. And the chief executives' compensation was also linked to their companies' share prices, proving once again that mergers are not possible without strong markets. With the SEC now well established, bear raiding in order to gain control of a company was a thing of the past so companies had to show strong bottom lines in order to appeal to investors. With good management, a little luck, and favorable accounting, many conglomerates began to achieve results that appeared to justify their investors' faith.

Contributions to finance theory also appeared to inspire investor enthusiasm. In 1952, Harry Markowitz demonstrated that a portfolio comprising many stocks was preferable to one with fewer holdings.[2] Corporate risk could be diversified to protect investors. Market risk would still remain, but one major worrying point was removed from risk/reward calculations. Quickly, analysts began pointing out that the disparate approach used by conglomerates was analogous to portfolio theory. The conglomerate was actually a diversified industrial company, less subject to swings in the business cycle than a less diversified company. Therefore, its share price should be somewhat immune to market changes as well. The idea caught on quickly in the 1950s stock market, where sound ideas were needed to offset any lingering historical doubts about equity investing.

Also in the 1950s, another contribution was made to finance literature that proved equally compelling. Franco Modigliani and Merton Miller published a paper on optimal capital structure that demonstrated how investors treated debt and equity securities of a company if its capital structure changed.[3] Their theory, known as the MM theory of capital structure, became a cornerstone of modern finance theory along with that of Markowitz. Simply put, investors were indifferent to a company's capital structure (percentage of outstanding debt versus equity) as long as it made money. The MM theory, like portfolio theory, underwent many revisions over the years but in the 1950s was considered the theoretical underpinning of a new, upward moving stock market. Theory was encouraging practice.

One bit of financial analysis that investors adopted during the conglomerate craze was the ubiquitous price/earnings ratio, or PE. Wall Street analysts began touting the ratio, or multiple, as the best way of determining a company's price relative to other companies in its industry sector. The higher the ratio, the more expensive the company, and vice versa. The calculation was simple and the PE became the investor buzzword of the 1960s. Calculated by simply dividing a company's stock price per share by its earnings per share, the ratio became firmly embedded as the best single indication of a stock's price. The problem with its popularity was that investors began to believe that all stocks should have high ratios and did not mind bidding up the prices of favored shares to the point where many conglomerate stocks were beginning to look top-heavy in the late 1960s. The waning days of the craze evoked old images of unwary investor lambs being led to slaughter by Wall Street investment bankers and brokers who needed their money to bid up the price of companies involved in takeovers. In the earlier part of the century, investors had paid attention to dividends. Now earnings became the key to wealth and investors were happy to forgo dividends if a company used its retained earnings to continue to buy other companies, which naturally would boost its earnings, keeping the cycle moving along.

Although investors were needed in large numbers if the market were to rise, memories of the past died hard. The stock markets traditionally were not known as safe havens for money and scandals often shook investor confidence. But after the securities acts of the 1930s were passed, the markets began to take on more credibility as level playing fields. Corporate financial reporting now was more transparent than ever before and the markets themselves were subject to the SEC, which governed their trading practices. And then there was the evolution of what became known as efficient market theory. First formally propounded in a 1973 book by Burton Malkiel, the theory was also known as random walk theory. Essentially, the rules made the markets accountable and, as a result, no investor had access to information that would give him or her an undue advantage over other investors. Information technology had a great deal of influence on the theory. In a world of fast communications, public

"Wall Street Bubbles-Always the Same." (Keppler, Puck, 1901)

Pierpont Morgan lending Uncle Sam a helping hand. (Keppler, Puck, 1907)

"The Magnet." (Keppler, Puck, 1911)

Small investor lambs being led to slaughter on Wall Street. (Life, 1910)

Henry Ford (left) conferring with Thomas Edison, circa 1915.

"Somebody Is Due for an Awakening." (Ding Darling, New York Herald Tribune, 1918. Reprinted courtesy of the Library of Congress.)

The first transcontinental telephone call, January 25, 1915. Alexander Graham Bell is seated beneath a picture of Theodore Vail.

Anti-chain store cartoon. (Truth, 1923)

John Raskob. (Berryman, 1928)

"Republican Insurgents." (Berryman, 1932. Reprinted courtesy of the Library of Congress.)

Samuel Insull leaving a Chicago jail after being acquitted in 1934.

"The Beginnings of a Speculative Stock Market?" (Ding Darling, May 1933. Reprinted courtesy of the Library of Congress.)

"A Chastened Wall Street." (Fred O. Siebel, 1933)

Gerald Nye, 1936.

Harold Geneen addressing an ITT shareholders' meeting, 1969.

Truth in securities sales. (Quincy Scott, 1933)

"Nixon's Problems." (Herblock, 1973. Reprinted courtesy of the Library of Congress.)

"Merger-Mania, Unabated..." (Steve Greenberg, Seattle Post-Intelligencer, 1998. Reprinted with permission of the artist.)

information is disseminated quickly and no one investor should have access to information that others do not yet have. Thus, the markets are efficient and stock price movements are random. Future prices cannot be predicted and a dartboard is as good an indicator of future performance as securities analysis.

Random walk theory was a boost for Wall Street because it implied that the playing field was level for investors. As Malkiel wrote, "The market is so efficient—prices move so quickly when new information does arise—that no one can consistently buy or sell quickly enough to benefit."[4] When insider trading problems erupted, they were viewed as aberrations rather than standard as in the case of the pre-1933 markets. But random walk theory also pulled the rug out from under the growing practice of securities analysis by implying that technical and fundamental analyses of stock prices and stocks were of no particular advantage. Investors might as well let the darts or their dogs do the securities selection, because over time the choice would be as good as any other. But that idea was overridden by the level playing field concept. The markets were now safer than they had been for years and small investors could feel comfortable investing in common stocks once again.

Inadvertently, the theory also gave the mergers business a great boost, because on level playing fields investors were always looking for events that could quickly change the turf and mergers filled the bill as well as any. Investors could buy stocks in companies suspected of having takeover potential and then wait. Random walk theory recognized risk as the major factor that differentiated investors. Those assuming more risk in their investments could expect higher potential returns. Buying a stock purely for its takeover attractiveness was certainly risky because its fundamentals may have only been appreciated by a few rather than the many. But buying a stock potentially on Jim Ling or Harold Geneen's shopping list was worth the risk because they were not miserly when buying companies they coveted. More intriguing was the question of whether the conglomerators were actually using a dartboard to select companies or whether there was a method to their shopping sprees after all. Although they were mostly finished buying when Malkiel's book appeared, the process he was describing was derived in large part from the roaring market in the 1960s.

Fusing these various theories together also brought the greatest profits that Wall Street had seen in years. Merger advising was still the most profitable single area of expertise on the Street and helping to redesign corporate America would only add more profits to Wall Street's coffers. And the corporate world was changing rapidly. New companies were springing up in new industries that had no special ties to any investment banking firm, so the playing field was level for new bankers trying to break into the ranks of Wall Street's mergers and acquisitions crowd.

The new merger trend did not begin warming up until 1955, when the number of mergers was more than double that recorded five years earlier. The total number of American corporations increased steadily during the decade, continuing a trend that began immediately after the end of World War II. But an old trend also continued. The largest companies in the country still controlled the bulk of corporate wealth. Since World War I, the largest 5 percent of companies accounted for around 80 percent of corporate profits. The trend would continue into the 1950s and 1960s as well. The greatest investment banking profits would come from merging the largest companies or merging smaller companies into the largest, which were best able to pay the banker's fees. The muckrakers of the previous generation would have had a field day with those numbers, but the cast of characters had changed since the 1930s and those holding economic power had changed somewhat. Bankers now generally kept a lower profile than they did in the 1920s and early 1930s.

Like many trends, the conglomerate craze owed much of its origins to legislation passed in 1950. Senator Estes Kefauver, a Democrat from Tennessee, and Representative Emmanuel Celler, a Democrat from New York, introduced a bill in Congress designed to plug a significant hole in the Clayton Act. The original language of the act prohibited a company from holding the stock of another company if the intent was to reduce competition in favor of the acquiring company. But the language of the act omitted the term *assets*. The loophole allowed an acquiring company to purchase assets of another, circumventing the intention of the act in the process.[5] The Celler-Kefauver Act was designed to plug the hole by specifically mentioning assets as well as stocks. As a result, companies seeking to buy other companies had to make certain that the potential merger or acquisition did not threaten competition. The best way to accomplish that was simply to purchase a company totally unrelated to the buyer. No antitrust eyebrows would be raised.

During the 1950s and 1960s, a concept that symbolized the growth of conglomerates came into existence and remained entrenched in Wall Street language. The term *synergy* was used to describe the supposedly salubrious effects of mergers on all parties concerned. When Company A merged with Company B, the resulting Company C was larger than A and B combined. The whole was greater than the sum of its parts. The concept had a quasimathematical ring to it. With apologies to Euclid, the idea proved to be something of an expansion of the original that stated the whole is greater than a part. The proof of the idea could only be found in pool accounting. The new company created by merger had to have greater profits than the old, which would not be difficult if only profitable companies were acquired by a conglomerate. Burton Malkiel described how "the trick that makes the game work is the ability of the [acquiring] electronics company to swap its high multiple stock for the stock of another company with a lower multiple . . . the faster earnings per share would grow and thus the more attractive the stock would look to justify its high multiple."[6]

Throughout the 1960s and early 1970s, conglomerates seemed to be the ideal sorts of companies in the new economic environment. When the synergy concept was added to the portfolio theory advanced by Markowitz and the work of Modigliani and Miller, it provided the bedrock of merger theory. These new companies made more money than their component parts, they were well diversified, and their financial structures were irrelevant as long as they continued to make money. This would prove important because many of them paid for their acquisitions by issuing debt securities such as convertible bonds. Investors flocked to them, convinced that they were a significant contribution to postwar finance. They were professionally run and able to make money from diversity while others had previously floundered when faced with the same set of circumstances. They indeed were a product of New Era finance.

The only problem was that the reality did not match the theory. Conglomerates were being assembled before the theory became popular and the idea of synergy was not actually used until the later years of their development. Some had professional management while others appeared to be cobbled together by larger-than-life personalities more intent on accumulating personal fortunes than introducing new concepts in finance and management. Wall Street did not make much of a distinction, however. Mergers and acquisitions specialists realized a good thing when they saw it and took full advantage of investor interest to produce a steady flow of deals until the trend finally dissipated.

The postwar era also witnessed the rise of a new version of the corporate raider. After the securities acts were passed in the early 1930s, raids on a company's stocks became more difficult to accomplish than before. Bear raids on the stock market now were proscribed. Corporate disclosure also was greater than ever because of the Securities Act of 1933, but the new regulations were a two-edged sword. Better accounting gave a clearer picture of corporate assets and liabilities, allowing those interested in buying companies with an eye toward restructuring them a better view of a company's strengths and weaknesses. Better accounting led to better raiding, a consequence of a slow move toward greater transparency in finance.

Despite the fact that the 1950s and 1960s became the era of the conglomerate, not all conglomerates were the same by any means. The one common factor among them was that they were a hodgepodge—or a mess—of companies assembled without any apparent game plan. Yet the most successful had one common element that was often overlooked: they were defense contractors to some extent. Although the early conglomerates were being assembled before 1957, the first Sputnik launched into space gave them the impetus to become hot stocks. The United States became so preoccupied with the Russian space achievement that any stocks related to defense or space were eagerly snapped up by investors since space and the national defense suggested exponential growth. The military-industrial complex had become a reality and the more successful conglomerates quickly cashed in on the trend.

The military buildup began during the Korean War and continued unabated for decades. In 1951, *The Magazine of Wall Street* listed the top defense contract awards granted to American companies, and the names on the list were familiar. The Cadillac division of GM was the largest winner of contracts, with $439 million for producing tanks. Others included Chrysler, International Harvester, Chevrolet, and Goodyear Tire & Rubber.[7] The idea of space exploration and an arms race with the Soviets was not yet reality, but the trend toward producing ordnance had already begun. When weaponry and avionics became more sophisticated, the government's appetite for new weapons would increase considerably.

Conglomerate builders recognized the trend quickly. They also realized the potential pitfalls. Big government had become more prevalent since the New Deal, but the economy was still dependent on consumer spending. As a result, the smart mix would be doing government defense business while owning consumer products companies at the same time. Any diversification beyond that simple mix proved to be truly haphazard in many cases, but the basic diversification was enough to convince investors that the conglomerates knew what they were doing and would lead the economy into a new era. Harold Geneen, the architect of ITT, would later describe diversification in soothing terms as a concept that "provides a form of security and insurance and a method of adapting to the real quickening tempo of change that we all are experiencing . . . it is a constructive influence on our economy."

The nature of Wall Street was also changing at the same time, giving deals a different tone from those of the past. New firms were pushing hard for business on the Street, challenging the older dominant M&A specialists such as Dillon Read, Kidder Peabody, Lehman Brothers, and J.P. Morgan's successor Morgan Stanley. The new entrants brought a different philosophy to the mergers game: They competed for business rather than arrange it in the traditional cozy manner of calling a fellow board member or crony. Perhaps the best example of the new game was Lazard Freres & Co., an old Wall Street firm with a new attitude under an extremely aggressive senior partner who would help rewrite the rules of the game in the 1960s.

RAIDERS OF A LOST ART

Certainly not all of the postwar merger activity was based upon applying new finance principles. Wartime developments and a belated continuation of trends established in the 1930s gave rise to the type of activities characteristic of Cyrus Eaton almost as soon as World War II ended. During the war, corporate raiding was not practiced, but in the late 1940s opportunities began appearing that no potential raider could pass up.

One of the first postwar raiders to join (or actually create) the fray in takeovers was Louis Wolfson. Born in 1912, Wolfson was the son of a Russian immigrant who was a junk merchant in Florida. Wolfson attended the University of Georgia before returning home to the family business in 1932 at the height of the Depression. One of his more memorable moments as an undergraduate came as a football player. He tackled an opponent so hard in a game against Yale that he severely injured his shoulder, causing him to retire from the team and miss the draft years later during World War II. Sensing greater opportunities in corporate junk, Wolfson embarked upon a career that was to see him make offers for some of the country's best-known companies, creating a great deal of havoc in the process. The distortions in corporate America caused by the war presented many opportunities that were enticing. Some industries were flush with cash because of excessive wartime profits, while some companies were still lagging behind others in their sectors because of overly conservative management. Whatever the cause, Wolfson saw the road paved with gold.

Using cash earned from the successful sale of a shipbuilding company bought and dismantled in the late 1940s, Wolfson took his war chest and began searching for other companies to acquire. He acquired a string of movie theaters and another shipyard before again selling out, leaving him around $10 million richer. By 1949, he had already built up a reputation for sharp deals that were highly questionable before acquiring Merritt-Chapman and Scott, a construction company that became his flagship, and then the Capital Transit Company of Washington, D.C. The latter only enhanced his reputation as unscrupulous.

The transit company ran bus and trolley service in the District of Columbia and was on the auction block. Previously, it had been owned by the North American Company, a utilities holding company run by Harrison Williams. The death sentence provision in the PUHCA required the company to divest Capital Transit and Wolfson stepped in to buy it. The company was still flush with cash in 1954 from wartime profits and Wolfson realized that the cash hoard could be paid out as dividends to a new owner. After acquiring majority control, he did just that, paying a dividend to himself and his cronies while seeking fare increases at the same time. When a union went out on strike against the company, demanding higher wages, Washington found itself without bus and trolley service for almost two months. After Congress passed a bill canceling the company's franchise in Washington, Wolfson found a buyer and sold his interest for another $10 million profit.

His greatest potential coup was with a totally different sort of company, however. In 1954, he and his allies began accumulating stock in Montgomery Ward, the mail order retail store chain founded by Aaron Montgomery Ward in 1872. Although the store began to branch out in the 1920s, it was not as successful as Sears and slipped behind the nation's leading retailer during the war. Montgomery Ward traditionally was a Morgan-run operation since its board was dominated by Morgan allies. However, the connection was to prove weak in the 1950s after the bank had lost a considerable amount of its influence since going public in the 1940s. When Wolfson announced his intention of taking over, the once powerful Morgan link proved impotent. Two Morgan officers serving as directors of the company, George Whitney and Henry Davison, resigned from the board. As Leslie Gould, who had followed Wolfson's antics as financial editor for the New York *Journal American,* wrote, "In the days of the elder Morgan any such young upstart would have been chopped down to size. Millions in support would have been thrown behind the management . . . there would have been no walking out on responsibility as the two Morgan directors did at Ward. But in 1954, the Morgan spokesmen were silent."[8]

Their reluctance stemmed from a longstanding relationship with the head of Montgomery Ward, Sewell Avery. Avery was extremely conservative and the company did not expand during his tenure, which began during the Depression. As a result, the company was vulnerable to the charge of having complacent management that was running the company down rather than moving aggressively ahead, a charge that Wolfson exploited loudly. Wolfson failed to convince the company's board that the aging Avery, who was 82, should relinquish control to him, and he eventually sold his shares for less than $1 million in profit. In the process, he established several precedents that would bode ill for corporate America in the years ahead.

The Montgomery Ward takeover attempt did underline two new trends appearing in corporate America during the mid-1950s. The influence of J.P. Morgan & Co. had waned considerably since the 1920s and 1930s and, if resurrected, would probably come from the newer Morgan Stanley & Co., created after the Glass-Steagall Act was passed. Equally clear was Wolfson's charge that companies that were not performing well should allow new management to take over. Although no one expected any potential Wolfson-appointed management to be long lasting, it did illustrate that weak companies were vulnerable to criticism from potential raiders and would have to reform or risk takeover and potential liquidation. As soon as World War II was over, hostilities transferred to the corporate battleground and would be waged constantly over the following decades. The old guard was represented as staid, ultraconservative management more interested in maintaining the company status quo than developing new markets and rewarding shareholders. New management was portrayed as better poised to unlock corporate value and forge ahead into new products and markets. The notion was compelling to investors. The corporate raiders, whatever their particular stripe, became as well followed by investors as the promoters and bankers of earlier eras. The new era market theory was simple. The market itself would eventually sort out the successful from the unsuccessful, rewarding investors for their insight.

The term *raider* came into general use, signifying someone who wanted to take over a company for its assets rather than its traditional business. In the late 1940s through the latter 1950s, it was not totally clear what the motivation was in many cases as the mergers and acquisitions trend reestablished itself after two dormant decades. Other raiders operating during the same period, notably Thomas Mellon Evans, were assumed to be genuine accumulators of companies and their assets, unlike Wolfson who was assumed to be an asset stripper or liquidator rather than a builder.[9] Clearly, the reputation hurt Wolfson badly, especially in his last attempt in the 1950s to take over American Motors. The company had just introduced the first compact American car, the Rambler, to compete with the increasing number of small imports when Wolfson tried his luck at taking over. After locking horns with company president George Romney, who would later become governor of Michigan and a presidential candidate, Wolfson again abandoned his quest after a very public battle. When signing an SEC consent decree not to malign American Motors in the press, Wolfson was discovered to be short a substantial block of the company's stock after having divested of his long positions. The reason for the position was not immediately clear unless it was being used to hedge the long in some way. When balanced against the money he and his cohorts made in the long positions, Wolfson walked away from the company about even. But failing to remain with the long position cost him a potential $38 million profit because the price of shares rose substantially after he disposed of them.[10]

The activities of the raiders in the late 1940s and 1950s permanently added the term to the Wall Street lexicon. Over time, aberrations such as war, and later inflation, would create distortions in corporate balance sheets that reorganization specialists could use to their own benefit by buying a company and splitting it up or merging it with another. Unlocking value in a company's financial statements would become another favorite expression of merger specialists and added another dimension to Euclid's axiom that the whole is greater than a part. Some companies were worth more in pieces than they were as an original whole, so asset stripping became a legitimate activity on the Street. On postwar Main Street, this was not viewed in the same genial manner, however. Often, these raider activities cost workers their jobs and caused widespread disruption in many communities. The battle that began in the postwar period would gather momentum and be a constant fixture on the business scene for the rest of the century.

NEW SHOPPING BASKETS

The conglomerates developed during the 1950s and 1960s were actually older companies that became shell vehicles for new expansion. Enterprising conglomerators used them as holding companies that would then begin buying up others in what eventually became a frenzy of acquisition. Like the raiders, the conglomerators were as different from each other as could be imagined. What they shared in common was their belief that growth could best be achieved by buying profitable companies, adding them to the holding company stable, and watching the stock price rise rapidly as a result. Yet for all of the publicity attached to the mergers craze building in the 1960s, it was notable that the total number of mergers occurring in 1963 was still less than the number consummated during the heyday of the McKinley administration in 1898.[11]

The distinction of being the first conglomerate is not entirely settled, although several companies vied for the honor. Like other trends, not all of the conglomerates would succeed and many would eventually disappear from the business scene after mediocre performances in the 1960s and 1970s. By the late 1960s, Wolfson's Merritt-Chapman was no longer a factor on the conglomerate scene. Others would make a strong impression, however, striking fear into the hearts of larger established companies that worried they would be the next takeover targets. The true test of a conglomerate's success in the 1960s was its relative size when measured against established industrial companies. Those that were included in the country's top 20 companies indeed scored a large measure of success, while others scored more on the publicity scale by being constantly mentioned in the press. But their long-term record was another matter entirely. Most of them were not able to attain longstanding success, as had been the case of the Morgan-, Durant-, or Dillon-inspired companies of previous decades.

One feature of conglomerates that made them favorites of the press and investors was the fact that most were headed by very visible executives who drove their business expansion. This was to be the last great burst of investor adulation for executives and the companies they built before the bear market of the 1970s. In many respects, it seemed somewhat out of sync with the times. The emphasis on professional management and earnings growth meant that a company's performance alone should have dictated its popularity among investors, but strong personalities became a hallmark of the conglomerate trend and could not be separated from the companies they built. Investors followed the fortunes and misfortunes of these conglomerators much as they followed Jack Morgan, Billy Durant, and Clarence Dillon in the 1920s.

The role of investment bankers changed during the conglomerate period. In the years leading to the 1970s, most mergers specialists served as matchmakers, bringing brides and grooms together for a fee. Others acted as merchant bankers to their clients, investing in their stock until they became better established and prices rose in the market. But their role began to change as the M&A market became more difficult in the late 1960s and early 1970s. When hostile takeovers became more common, the role of the banker became more visible and specialized. Rather than simply arrange acquisitions, as Lazard did for ITT, many bankers began to take sides on takeovers. Some advised the bridegrooms while others advised the brides. The rise of offensive and defensive specialists became the norm by the end of the 1970s.

In the early 1950s, most companies understood the principle of diversification and several had already employed it to cushion their operations against the risks of doing business. But conglomerating was the principle extended to the extreme. One of the first companies to employ it widely was the General Tire & Rubber Company, run by William F. O'Neil and his three sons. During World War II, the company mostly made tires but later quickly began diversifying into defense-related business. One of its first forays outside tires was the Aerojet-General Co., a manufacturer of rocket engines. In 1955, it purchased the film library of Howard Hughes' RKO. Then it sold the rights to show the films of RKO to the newly emerging television industry. Not content with aerospace and tires, it also quickly acquired chemical and plastic manufacturing facilities. But it was the defense- and space-related industries that would attract the most investor attention after the first Sputnik was put in orbit in 1957. Before that event, diversification into space- and defense-related industries was important. After 1957, it was considered vital.

The rise of Litton Industries and its mastermind, Charles "Tex" Thornton, is a vivid example of how the military-industrial complex gave strong impetus to conglomerate growth. It also gave ample evidence of how the conglomerators used people more talented than themselves to achieve their ends. Born in 1913, Thornton was a Texan who spent a few years studying at Texas Tech before going to Washington and finding work as a government statistician in 1934. He transferred to the War Department in 1941, just before the United States entered World War II. While heading an Army statistical department based at Harvard during the war, he began to accumulate experience and contacts that would serve him well in the future. He also offered a job to a young academic, Robert McNamara, who later followed Thornton to his next job at Ford, which was trying to rebuild its operations under Henry Ford II, heir to his grandfather's empire.

After being passed over by Ford for the job of chief executive, Thornton left the company in 1949 and moved to Hughes Aircraft, owned by the mysterious and mercurial Howard Hughes. Thornton spotted an opportunity for the innovative but erratic producer of military electronics in defense contracting. Within five years, he transformed a small loss maker into a profitable company. But working for Hughes did not suit the ambitious Thornton and he left to accept an offer from another small electronics company based in California, named Litton Industries after its founder Charles Litton.

This time, the move was prompted by more than just a job. Litton wanted $1 million for his company, which Thornton decided to buy. The problem was that he did not have the money and needed to finance the purchase. After two decades in government and the private sector, he now had the opportunity to run his own operation. After borrowing the down payment required by Litton, Thornton approached Wall Street for financing. One of Wall Street's success stories was about to begin.

After shopping around for the necessary capital, Thornton found two willing financiers in Lehman Brothers and Clark Dodge, both highly respected names on the Street. In order to succeed, he needed to show them how the company would prosper in the world of electronics. Clearly, the field was growing and Thornton recognized that the best way to achieve the growth rates that bankers required was to grow by acquisition. Intrigued by what they heard, the two investment banks agreed to finance Litton and created "units" of stocks and bonds to finance the purchase price. The units were highly reminiscent of those used to create the utilities holding companies of the late 1920s. They were more expensive, however. Each unit consisted of bonds, preferred stock, and common stock. They were priced at $29,000 each and the financing was complete by late 1953. The new Litton Industries was up and running. Its major weakness was that it would be totally reliant upon military expenditures by the government, which could be very cyclical.

Fortunately, Thornton encountered a fellow Texan at Lehman Brothers—Joseph Thomas, one of the firm's senior partners. After lengthy negotiations, Lehman agreed on the financing package and then created several issues of common stock ranging from 10 cents to $1 per share. Lehman took 75,000 shares of the stock for a total investment of around $50,000. Litton's progress was slow. In its first year, it produced sales of around $3 million. Then the exponential growth for which it was known began. Within 6 years, sales soared to over $100 million and the stock soared as well. Lehman's portion was worth around $750 million. In the booming postwar market, the return was astronomical but still considered a long shot at best. Thomas remarked in 1965 that "The hardest things to raise money for often turn out to be the best."[12] The remark proved to be the understatement of the year.

Thornton began acquiring electronics companies after the financing but did not begin to diversify into other lines of business immediately. Within four years, Litton's sales reached $28 million and its stock exceeded $50 per share. Thornton paid for future acquisitions with stock and quickly learned the tricks of the expanding growth company. His first acquisition outside the industry was the Monroe Calculating Machine Co., which he purchased in 1957. The old-line office machines company made calculators and check writers and was far behind its own industry leaders. However, it was still larger than Litton. After the deal was completed for stock, Monroe added a considerable amount to Litton's bottom line and the diversification had officially begun. The magic of pool accounting began to work for Litton.

Between the late 1950s and the mid-1960s, Thornton expanded Litton into other lines of defense-related electronics. He also added some ordinary companies to the mix, including Stouffer Food and the American Book Company. By 1968, the company was becoming stretched. Many units, including Monroe, never adequately revamped their product lines and remained also-rans in their respective industries. Then Litton announced a concept that sounded remarkably millenarian, even for a conglomerate. Thornton announced that the company had signed a contract with the Greek government to foster economic development on the island of Crete. In a move that traditionally was reserved for international development agencies, Litton would be in charge of attracting investment to the area, including funds for infrastructure and housing. The irony of the deal was not lost on many commentators. Litton was acting as the modern King Midas for the island. But the anticipated growth was never achieved and the company attracted so little development money that it quietly folded its operations shortly thereafter. And the handwriting was on the wall for its stock as well.

Litton's stock fell in the 1969 to 1970 market drop more precipitously than the market indices, puncturing the illusion that diversification held up under adverse market conditions. The company's fall

from grace was not unique, however: The stock prices of all conglomerates fell during the market decline in 1970, some obviously
more than others. Another poor performer was Gulf + Western
Industries, led by Charles Bludhorn. Gulf + Western was considered
one of the most publicized companies of the period that never quite
lived up to its billing as a top conglomerate. It was remembered
mostly for Bludhorn's widely publicized investment in Paramount.
Motion picture production and movie distribution had been an
industry racked by rising costs and antitrust actions over the years
since Joseph P. Kennedy and Otto Kahn were seen in Hollywood in
the 1920s, but it never lost its glamorous allure. Unlike General
Tire's incursion into distribution rights, the publicity conscious Bludhorn was attracted to it simply for the glamour.

Bludhorn's tenure at G + W began in 1957 with the intention of
transforming a small manufacturer of auto parts with revenues of
around $8 million into the country's largest producer. Within eight
years, revenues had increased to $180 million, making G + W one of
the fastest-growing companies in the country. Yet it proved to be one
of the most ephemeral, never achieving distinction in any one underlying business. Despite the flair for publicity demonstrated by Bludhorn, G + W remained a second-rate conglomerate. The top ranks
were reserved for two massive companies patched together by two
diametrically opposite personalities. The two investor favorites of the
1960s were LTV Corporation, originally known as Ling-Temco-
Vaught, and ITT, a slumbering multinational that traced its origins
to the early 1920s. More than any other conglomerate, these two
were responsible for giving the entire group its sparkling reputation
as the harbinger of a new corporate America. And both remained
on the corporate scene long after the others had faded away,
although ITT proved to be the more successful over the following
decades.

LTV had the cowboy reputation while ITT was more straitlaced
and corporate minded. The cowboy image was not without foundation. James Ling was a Texan who started his business career in 1946
as an electrical contractor in Dallas with $3,000 he raised from the
sale of his modest house. Born in 1922 in Oklahoma, near the Texas

border, to a German-American family, Ling grew up experiencing antiforeign sentiments during the xenophobic 1920s before finally dropping out of a Catholic secondary school during the Depression. He wandered the country for a while as a self-described "bum" before serving in the Navy during World War II. After being discharged he became an electrician in Dallas. He never attended college as a result. After picking up valuable technical experience as an electrician, he bought the house that he eventually sold to begin the history of LTV. By 1955, his business recorded $1.5 million in sales and Ling decided to take it public. Despite his success, it was still small potatoes as far as local investment bankers were concerned and he could not interest any local underwriters in distributing his securities. Teaching himself the basics of securities distribution, he created 800,000 shares and received permission from the Texas securities regulators to sell half to the public. His methods were hardly sophisticated, but they helped him develop a reputation for persistence that would serve him well in the years ahead. The public portion was sold by Ling and friends at the Texas State Fair and also peddled door-to-door until all the stock was subscribed at $2.25 per share.

Ling used the proceeds to buy other small companies, originally acquiring only electrical contractors and manufacturers. Within two years, sales soared to almost $7 million and then exploded exponentially to $48 million in 1959 after Ling purchased several more manufacturers. Then he expanded into the first of the two major acquisitions that would form his future conglomerate. The next year he purchased Temco Electronics & Missiles, which specialized in defense contracting, and bought a controlling interest in Chance Vaught Corporation in 1960. The new expanded company became the Ling-Temco-Vaught Corporation. The result of the acquisition put LTV in the *Fortune* 200 for the first time. About the same time, LTV lost the Wall Street firm of White Weld as its major investment banker over a dispute concerning Ling's acquisitions strategy. Lehman Brothers quickly moved in to fill the void, adding LTV to its list of clients, which also included Litton. By 1962, LTV's sales registered $325 million and Ling had become one of the undisputed masters of the 1960s financial universe. And more was to follow.

The growth of the company was not always reflected in the stock price. Knowing something about stock from his early days, Ling decided to take matters into his own hands and raise the price. In 1964, LTV made an offer to shareholders whereby they could exchange their shares for a combination of cash and preferred stock. As a result, almost 800,000 shares were taken off the market. The common was replaced by preferred stock that represented a fixed charge against after-tax earnings. Then LTV began buying its shares in the open market in a stock buyback. By the end of the year, over 1 million shares had been retired and the company's earnings naturally rose as a result. LTV added 19 cents per share to its earnings although it had done nothing more than reduce the number of shares in existence. Without the reduction, earnings would only have been $1.74, no change over the previous year.[13] The growth mantra could continue without interruption.

Other significant acquisitions followed. Lehman Brothers was now the company's principal investment banker along with Goldman Sachs. Goldman established its reputation as a top investment bank in the 1950s when it took Ford Motor Co. public, ending decades of family ownership. It regularly helped mount acquisitions by entering the market and buying stock of target companies on LTV's behalf. Gus Levy, chairman of Goldman and a legend in New York financial, cultural, and social circles, quickly became one of Ling's prime advisers and the two firms split the continuing stream of merger fees. In 1965, LTV acquired the Okonite Company, which made electrical cables, and in 1967 purchased Wilson & Company, a meat packing company that was subsequently subdivided further into Wilson Sporting Goods. The acquisition was a prime example of the financial alchemy conglomerates were practicing. The purchase price was $225 million but LTV only put up $1 million cash. The balance was either raised through debentures or by selling new preferred stock, both of which would provide a fixed charge against future earnings. But the 1960s logic was simple. Adding leverage to the company's balance sheet did not matter as long as earnings rose exponentially, which, thanks to pool accounting, they did. LTV seemed to be living proof that the Modigliani-Miller theory worked in reality.

More acquisitions followed in dizzying fashion. The Jones & Laughlin Steel Co. was added in 1968, presenting Ling with the most contentious of his acquisitions. The company was an old-line steel company with exactly the sort of management that Ling detested. He was already on record as having stated, "Today in the United States there are essentially two types of corporate management: the professional caretakers who seek prestige and job security . . . and the entrepreneurial innovators who seek challenges and increasing values for their shareholders."[14] Uncharacteristically, however, he did not purge the management ranks after buying it. In fact, he paid a high premium for the company's stock, put it in a voting trust, and agreed to allow the management to retain their jobs.[15] Commentators would always contend that he was not harsh with Jones & Laughlin because he originally came from a different social class than company management. Unfortunately for him, the acquisition did not proceed quietly. The merger was the first to fall under the scrutiny of the Antitrust Division under Richard McLaren. The investigation began in March 1969 and the steel company professed no knowledge of it, claiming it came as a total surprise. LTV, for its part, was equally shocked but quickly went on the offensive.

The same year Ling added the Greatamerica Corporation, which owned a bank, an insurance company, the National Car Rental System, and Braniff Airways. Car rental companies especially were favorites and by the late 1960s all of the major rental companies would be owned by conglomerates. By 1967, LTV's sales reached $1.7 billion and then doubled again by 1970. The growth rate was astonishing, especially for someone who had had to sell his home only 20 years before to stake his original business. Not all of the acquisitions were kept intact; shares in Braniff often were sold off to raise cash when necessary.

Despite his humble background, Ling presided over one of the decade's slickest stock offerings that proved that new math indeed was at work on Wall Street. In 1964, he announced the formation of an investment plan called Project Redeployment, a complicated scheme that followed on the heels of the stock buyback that salvaged earnings in the same year. In the spirit of synergy, he concocted an idea that split LTV into three operating divisions—LTV Aerospace, LTV Electrosystems, and LTV Ling Altec. In 1965, he planned an exchange that would offer investors cash and shares of the new subsidiaries in exchange for LTV common stock. This effectively would change the divisions into publicly traded companies. But the offer was never really intended to allow the investing public control of the three: most of the stock would be retained by the parent LTV Corporation. What the complicated deal proposed was simple. When the new shares were released for trading, they would eventually climb to prices relative to the price/earnings ratios of other conglomerates, LTV included. Thus LTV appeared to be splitting itself up when in fact it had just used investor appetite for conglomerate shares to print itself some fresh money. The assets of the parent and the subsidiaries never increased but market value certainly rose. Ling proved that new math did work after all. One plus one equaled three under the successful offerings. The first offering of the project's financing began as LTV was bidding for Okonite.

Of all the conglomerates growing rapidly in the 1960s, ITT was the most successful and proved to be the longest lasting. As its initials implied, the company was a phone company similar to AT&T except that it operated internationally rather than domestically. When AT&T received its congressionally sanctioned monopoly in the early 1920s, part of a deal engineered by Jack Morgan kept ITT out of the country so that it would not conflict with the domestic operations of AT&T. Morgan arranged an agreement that kept ITT offshore. ITT was led at the time by Sosthenes Behn, its founder, who originally wanted to tackle the domestic monopoly. Despite the agreement, ITT still maintained offices only several hundred yards from the corner of Broad and Wall, where the House of Morgan was headquartered.

ITT's rise to prominence in the 1960s was orchestrated by Harold Geneen, who remained its guiding light until the late 1970s. Born in Bournemouth, England in 1910, Geneen was sent to the United States as a young boy by his mother to attend boarding school. After graduating, he went to New York where he found a job as a runner at the NYSE and began taking business courses at night at New York University. Unfortunately, he lost his job as a result of the 1929 Crash and spent several years in near poverty until he finished his degree at night. He then took a job with an accounting firm and worked for seven years before accepting the top accounting position at the American Can Company during World War II. After a brief stint at Bell & Howell, the camera company, he took a position with Jones & Laughlin Steel, which would become the apple of James Ling's eye two decades later. He preached diversification at the camera maker, but the company was too set in its ways to pay much attention.

In 1956, Geneen accepted a job at Raytheon, the electronics engineering company that did a great deal of defense-related work. The company was run by Charles Francis Adams Jr. of the New England family that had produced presidents and writers. At first glance, it would appear that Raytheon was exactly the sort of company the conglomerators railed against. Surprisingly, Adams allowed Geneen to reorganize much of the company's structure in order to make it more efficient and profitable. During the three years he worked under Adams, Geneen made sweeping organizational changes at Raytheon, which continued making most of its money supplying defense contracts. Then in 1959, another opportunity presented itself when ITT named him president. The company was in a state of organizational disarray, having suffered from a management struggle at the top although Behn still was its chairman. When Geneen took over, the company had revenues of around $765 million and was 52nd on the *Fortune* 500 list.

When Geneen assumed the helm at ITT, the company had a history of running several telephone systems in Europe and Latin America, including the national system in Chile, but its prize possession was the unit that produced telephone and electronics equipment. It clearly was also a candidate for diversification into other lines because its agreement with AT&T still was intact and it could not compete in the phone business in the domestic U.S. market. The new chief executive recognized the opportunity and set about remaking the company into a conglomerate. He was somewhat late to the game in 1959 since many of the new diversified companies

were already on their way to fame and fortune. But Geneen began
with a stronger infrastructure than many of his competitors because
of ITT's relative size and strength. Growth proved to be rapid.

Geneen began by acquiring other electronics companies, the
business ITT knew best. After 1963, he began acquiring specialty
manufacturing companies producing things like industrial pumps,
air conditioning units, and control devices used in domestic appliances. In 1964, true diversification began when he acquired Aetna
Finance, a consumer finance company and a British insurance company, creating the foundation of ITT Financial Services. By 1965,
revenues doubled since he had taken over the helm, reaching $1.5
billion. Then Geneen caught the auto rental bug and began pursuing Avis. A large block of the company's stock was held by Lazard
Freres, the Wall Street investment banking house. Geneen began
talks with Lazard, bringing him into touch with several of its key people. Lazard's managing partner was Andre Meyer and one of its junior partners was Felix Rohatyn.

Meyer, who ruled the banking firm with an iron fist, sold
Lazard's stake to ITT, beginning the most notable corporate/invest-
ment banking relationship of the twentieth century. After 1966,
Rohatyn became the central figure in Geneen's diversification strategy, helping him to acquire a wide panoply of smaller companies.
ITT acquired companies ranging from a chain of secretarial schools
to Sheraton Hotels and William Levitt & Sons, the builders of Levit-
town, Long Island. Geneen later commented, "There were only a
few industries we stayed away from: chemicals (frankly, I didn't know
the difference between an alkaloid and a polymer and I didn't want
to find out), airlines (too unpredictable) and movies."[16] Later remarks
of that nature raised questions about the acquisitions process but it
continued unabated. While Jones & Laughlin became Ling's most
controversial acquisition, the successful bid for the Hartford Insurance Companies became Geneen's thorniest purchase and brought
out the regulators in full force. The diversification process became so
heated that ITT was adding a company per day at one point, accumulating 250 companies, having more than 2,000 operating units.

Before Rohatyn began acquiring companies for Geneen, ITT

made a bid for ABC, the television broadcast company, in a deal that severely strained ITT's budget. Originally the deal was set to cost $250 million, but Geneen finally knocked the price down to around $200 million. Then the proposed takeover set off a flurry of activity by regulators. Proposed mergers involving communications companies fell under the purview of the Federal Communications Commission (FCC), which shared jurisdiction in the matter with the Justice Department and the Federal Trade Commission (FTC). Early indications suggested that the FCC would not permit the merger without close investigation for possible effects upon competition within the industry. Geneen came to loggerheads with the sort of personalities he disdained most—bureaucrats. As far as he was concerned, ABC was a plum acquisition and he wanted to proceed, despite the relatively high purchase price.

The FCC demurred, however, citing potential threats to competition. Although it twice voted to approve the merger by votes of 4 to 3, both decisions were challenged by those in the Justice Department and elsewhere who were staunchly opposed to Geneen owning access to the airwaves. Finally, after the second decision was challenged, Geneen gave up the battle, throwing in the towel. Other acquisitions pressed for his time and he had no intention of upsetting any more regulators by pressing ahead. The deal finally was killed in 1968. Geneen remembered it later, saying, "Approval by the Federal Communications Commission seemed a sure thing—until an antibigness minority kicked up a fuss about the need to preserve ABC's 'independence.' "[17] Although the proposed acquisition raised a storm, it was nothing compared with ITT's later actions, which cast it as the ugly American corporation incarnate.

ITT acquired the Sheraton group of hotels in 1967. The hotel group possessed valuable properties but needed to be completely revamped in order to regain its appeal. Geneen proposed to infuse it with over $800,000,000 over a five-year period so that it could be refurbished and expanded properly. Critics began to openly question his methods, but they made sense on a grand scale. The public used rental cars and needed hotels when they traveled, so these two acquisitions made perfect sense. The Levitt company made less sense until

Geneen announced his most contentious potential acquistion, that of the Hartford Fire Insurance Company. As a property and casualty insurer, it became clear that Hartford's policies could be purchased by owners of Levitt homes. Although the acquisitions were not always in their ideal sequence, one acquisition seemed to breed another of related importance. The problem was that the relations were often interpreted as examples of reciprocity, a process clearly in violation of the antitrust laws.

The same idea could be found in two of ITT's other acquisitions. In 1968 Geneen acquired the Continental Baking Company, the maker of such familiar household staples as Wonder Bread, Morton pot pies, Twinkies, and Hostess cakes. It was the largest manufacturer of baked goods in the country and represented a radical departure for the pattern of acquisitions ITT was accumulating. Its margins and growth rates were behind Geneen's other purchases and no one could fathom his strategy. Then ITT also acquired the Canteen Corporation, one of the largest vending machine operators in the country. It was not much of a stretch to see the relationship between a baker and a vending machine operator, but whether the two would complement each other was another matter. Rohatyn advised on most of the acquisitions and they were all paid for using combinations of common and preferred stock. Lazard eventually acquired 68 companies for ITT. Reminiscent of corporate structures in the earlier part of the century, 27 of those companies retained at least one Lazard partner on their board of directors. Rohatyn served on the board of ITT.

By 1970, Geneen reputedly was the highest paid executive in corporate America with an annual salary of $766,000.[18] But in previous years, he was less well paid and actually trailed many of the top conglomerators in remuneration. Most of the conglomerators treated themselves extremely well. Thornton's stock in Litton was reputed to be worth over $100 million, while Armand Hammer of Occidental Petroleum held shares worth $135 million. Bludhorn was the most flamboyant, using his expense account to be seen in Hollywood while Ling was proud of his palatial, multimillion-dollar home in Dallas, replete with expensive works of art. Despite their high pay

161

at the time, most of these executives owed their fortunes, and those of their companies, to the stock market. Without high equity prices, their personal fortunes and their takeover abilities would never have materialized.

The Hartford acquisition would arouse the interest of the Nixon administration and would only be allowed when ITT agreed to divest Avis, Levitt, and Canteen Corporation. But it was the Sheraton hotel chain that would come back to haunt Geneen more than any other single acquisition, raising the specter of bribery and corruption within the Nixon administration. Was it possible that the Republicans occupying the White House were much closer to the conglomerates than their antitrust division suggested? When coupled with allegations made about ITT's interference in the government of Salvador Allende in Chile, the Republican national convention fiasco of 1972 proved highly damaging both to politics and to corporate America. Was everyone and everything for sale, or was it an incorrect perception?

The car rental business was another football being passed around among the conglomerates during the period. ITT owned Avis for a while and LTV had National Car Rental. Hertz was acquired by RCA, which became one of the less successful attempts at conglomeration. Originally, Hertz was founded by John D. Hertz, who owned the original company—the Omnibus Corporation, a bus line operator in Chicago. Hertz sold the car rental operations of Omnibus to GM during the Depression and went to work at Lehman Brothers as a partner. Later GM decided to divest itself of the car rental business and sold its interest back to Omnibus, which changed its name to Hertz. It then began buying back Hertz franchises, which had been sold by GM, and consolidated itself into the giant car rental business, all under Lehman's auspices. The operation helped Lehman maintain its uncanny reputation as an investor that could spot value in companies it helped reorganize and bring to market. In 1953, Hertz shares were worth $7 million. By 1965, Lehman's holdings were worth an estimated $100 million. A Lehman partner stated triumphantly, "The Hertz deal should help to deflate the Wall Street myth that investment banks run American industries—they *serve* America's industries."[19]

The point was well taken. Unlike previous decades, the 1960s clearly were the years of the corporate chieftain, aided by investment bankers but not dominated by them. Bankers assisted deals; they did not direct them as in the days of Jack Morgan and Clarence Dillon. But their influence was still considerable. Without investment banking assistance, the merger trend would not have developed in the manner it did. Conglomerates would always be able to find small businesses similar to their own original companies that they could acquire, but when they went shopping to diversify, they needed solid advice about which companies potentially were on the block. Since the war, a new breed of intermediary, usually known as *finders*, had arisen to act as honest brokers in many transactions, introducing brides and potential grooms. Only merger bankers could help in the buying spree because they were needed to act as justice of the peace in the transactions, in order to give them legitimacy and corporate finance advice.

REACTION

Despite their fame and fortune in the 1960s, none of the conglomerates ever were included in the Dow Jones Industrial Average, a measure of success for the largest corporations. Their flamboyant success and buccaneer tactics made them the nouveau riche of corporate America, causing a reaction in traditional executive suites around the country. Their bankers recognized the reaction and kept their heads down for fear of offending their old-line clients.

While many of the conglomerators did not understand finance theory, there was a better chance that their investment bankers did and were ready to apply some of the basics to organizing new companies from the ground up. Investment banking and loan facilities were provided by well-known Wall Street names, unlike the chain store and automobile trends of earlier decades. During the conglomerate trend, the bankers remembered the lessons from the past. They were not likely to ignore consolidations that could make them rich in the process, but neither were they likely to incur the wrath of regulators and Congress. Although some had highly recognizable names in the 1960s, several had helped finance chain store and motion picture studio and theater expansion in the 1920s—notably Lehman Brothers and Goldman Sachs.

During the latter stages of the conglomerate craze, many investment bankers adopted a low profile, hoping for less publicity than Lazard Freres was receiving for its alliance with ITT. The reason was purely political. The M&A specialists could still make their fees without showing themselves off in public. The congressional hearings of the 1930s were still vivid to some of Wall Street's old guard, and they knew that a low profile was the best defense against potential criticism. They were also keenly aware that some of the old New Dealers were still present and active in Congress. The Sons of the Wild Jackass were long gone, but critics like Emanuel Celler of New York remained. Remnants of the New Deal were still alive in Congress and occasionally made themselves heard.

One area still attracting the attention of regulators and antitrusters was bank expansion, much as had been the case in the 1920s and 1930s. Most bankers were aware that the Bank Holding Company Act of 1957 had been written with serious omissions that enabled bank holding companies to own more than one banking company and they used it to circumvent Tiny McFadden's law passed in 1927. But under pressure from strict constructionists, Congress added an amendment 10 years later that finally closed the loophole by limiting bank holding companies to owning a single bank only, highly reminiscent of the death sentence provision used in the PUHCA over 30 years before. Emanuel Celler's presence in the House provided a link between the past and the present. He was an advocate of the holding company amendment, as he had been to the original death sentence provision in the PUHCA in 1935.

The Nixon administration initially showed strong determination in dealing with conglomerates. Within two years, its zeal was questioned, however. Shortly after the 1968 election, it announced its intention to pursue LTV over the acquisition of Jones & Laughlin

Steel. The *New York Times* chimed in, "The Nixon administration, which owes much of its election success to strong support from the business community, is leaving no room for doubt that it means business on the antitrust front."[20] Richard McLaren, the head of the Antitrust Division of the Justice Department under Attorney General John Mitchell, showed surprising antipathy to conglomerates, announcing that he was willing to vigorously pursue conglomerates under the provisions of the Celler-Kefauver Act. Was it possible that a Republican administration was showing a determination to fight the new leviathans despite the fact that the election was won with business support?

By the late 1960s, many of the established companies had good reason to worry about advances from the nouveau riche conglomerates. The hostile takeover became an operative strategy on Wall Street, deployed when a takeover candidate made it clear that the acquirers' advances were unwanted. At first glance, it appeared that the large companies had little to fear; most conglomerates were smaller than the top *Fortune* list of companies and, while adept at gobbling up small companies, seemed less able to swallow a larger competitor. But the conglomerates' rise clearly was making corporate America nervous. In 1974, International Nickel Co. (Inco) of Canada would make a hostile bid for ESB Inc., an old-line Philadelphia company that was the largest battery maker in the world. Morgan Stanley assisted International Nickel in its hunting expedition, shattering the notion that mergers were arranged on a friendly, old boy basis. Morgan Stanley was aided by lawyer Joseph Flom of the then small New York law firm of Skadden, Arps, Slate, Meagher, & Flom. Inco was one of the world's largest producers of minerals but was an outsider in American industry. A warning shot had been fired at American companies. The barbarians were at the gates, regardless of where they originated. The successful takeover bid propelled the hostile takeover to the forefront and also made Flom one of the best-known M&A attorneys on Wall Street, along with Martin Lipton of Wachtell, Lipton, Rosen & Katz. Matters were only made worse by the fact that ITT and LTV had moved into the top 20 list of largest American corporations ranked by assets and their lofty stock prices meant that acquisitions could be paid for by paper alone. Fear became reality when a smaller company finally made an attempt for one of the country's older, more respected firms.

The original heart-stopper came a few years earlier. Northwest Industries was a conglomerate patched together by Ben Heineman, a Chicago lawyer attracted to the M&A game. The company, previously the Chicago and Northwestern Railroad, diversified into chemicals, steel, and clothing. Northwest had done well by diversifying, ranking around 140 on the *Fortune* 500 list. But the conglomerates had a reputation for being dé classé and the idea of one actually taking over a larger, established company was heresy in corporate circles. Then Northwest unexpectedly made a $1 billion hostile bid for tire maker B.F. Goodrich in 1968. Goodrich was ranked 82nd at the time, having a long, storied history dating back to the early days of the automobile. Clearly rattled, Goodrich mounted a defense that required all of its political connections and goodwill accumulated over the years. Its tactics would become legendary in the history of M&A.

Goodrich, led by J. Ward Keener, vigorously opposed the takeover attempt. The company turned the conglomerate game on its head by quickly beginning to diversify itself, acquiring several nondescript companies in an attempt to dilute Northwest's existing holding as well as that of Laurence Tisch of the Loew's Corporation in New York, who held a similar stake to Heineman. Goodrich placed full-page ads in the major newspapers advising shareholders to beware of the offer, saying that the takeover was certainly not in their best interests. But its best defense involved leverage. Goodrich borrowed $250 million from a syndicate of banks with the provision that the loan would be declared in default if the company were taken over. At the same time, the Antitrust Division under Richard McLaren instituted hearings into the proposed bid. When a federal judge heard of the arrangement, he gasped, "Why would Goodrich voluntarily enter into an agreement under which it threatens to commit financial suicide in the event that this transaction is consummated?"[21] The question was valid since the defense had not been employed before. Goodrich had invented the poison pill defense, stating in no uncertain terms that it was willing to drink hemlock before being dragged into an unwanted marriage. The defense proved successful by mid-1969, when Northwest abandoned its attempt. One of corporate America's old-line gems had been spared the conglomerator's harem.

A new SEC regulation was put on the books during the conglomerate craze that clearly was indicative of the reaction from conservative quarters. In the late 1960s, Senator Harrison Williams of New Jersey introduced a bill in Congress that became known as the Williams Act. The law required any company desirous of taking over another to file its intent with the SEC at least 20 days before making a cash offer if the bid would result in ownership of more than 5 percent of a company's stock, providing that company was subject to the Securities Act of 1933. Previously, Williams's father ran the North American Company, a utilities holding company that had been subject to the PUHCA of 1935. When introducing the bill, he used language that alluded to removing the "cloak of secrecy" that hostile bidders often hid behind in order to protect "proud old companies from corporate raiders."[22] The Williams Act proved not to be very effective in slowing down the takeover trend, but it did have one positive side effect for target companies: It allowed them time to fashion a defense against an unwanted takeover, something that had been lacking before. By requiring buyers to state their intentions, it also allowed investment bankers ample time to line up clients on either side of a potential deal.

Williams's interest in slowing down the merger movement was not entirely idealistic by any means. New Jersey was home to many established NYSE listed companies ranking high in the *Fortune* list. Many had been created in the glory days of the Morgan dynasty. While the new law allowed the target companies some breathing room, a change in the tax treatment of interest also helped put a damper on the intensity of the merger trend. Representative Wilbur Mills, a Democrat from Arkansas, introduced a bill in Congress seeking to limit the amount of interest that a company could write off if the proceeds of its borrowings were used to finance takeovers. When Mills introduced his bill, the *New York Times* noted the difficulty it would face given the influence of corporate America. "The road to

167

successful antitrust prosecution is hard, and even so powerful a figure as Wilbur Mills may find it difficult to deprive the merger makers of their tax glue," the paper opined, "but if the growing concern in Washington does little more than slow down the merger gold rush, the critics of conglomerates will still have scored a point."[23] Shortly thereafter, the Tax Reform Act of 1969 sought to put a limit on the amount of interest that could be deducted when borrowing for acquisitions.

In the summer of 1969, the Nixon administration, through Attorney General John Mitchell, began to sound suspiciously Democratic when announcing tough new measures to deal with conglomerate growth. In June, Nixon announced that the Justice Department would file suit against any corporation in the top 200 seeking to merge with any other company in the same group. Claiming that the country's top 200 companies accounted for 58 percent of its manufacturing assets while the top 500 controlled 75 percent, Nixon stated that further concentrations among them would be intolerable. He drew up a list that he claimed would be monitored carefully and said that any proposed mergers would be subject to the most severe scrutiny. At first glance, it appeared that he had resuscitated an old concept originally propounded by two Columbia academics decades before. Gardiner Means and Adolph Berle had made their reputations in the late 1920s by publishing a study showing that corporate America was heavily concentrated in large corporations and that shareholder wealth and control meant very little in the face of it. Was it possible that a Republican administration could be making the same claim 40 years later, after big business had helped elect it in the first place?

Quickly moving events helped dispel the theory that this was a new attempt to prevent further consolidations at the top of the corporate ladder. Critics maintained that this was simply the administration's way of placating its large corporate sponsors by protecting them from the aggressive nouveau riche conglomerates. Older, established companies now could breath some sighs of relief, not having to worry that Ling, Geneen, or other empire builders were on their trail. The newly passed Williams Act would protect them from an unwanted bid striking out of the blue, and the Justice Department promised to put further brakes on any attempt by probably forbidding it as inimical to competition. Was this a Luddite move to prevent progress in corporate management or a genuine reaction to a rapidly consolidating country?

As the administration pursued its new aggressive antitrust policy, it slowly became clear that it was acting on behest of the established companies that feared the power of the conglomerates. McLaren was dedicated to the antitrust position that the new companies stifled competition, but there was some evidence within the Nixon administration that he was not well-liked although still accepted because he would foster the administration's program of protecting established companies. The corporations' most persistent fear was that they would become targets of a hostile takeover, falling victim to the claims that many established companies had management structures vastly out of touch with modern techniques and changing markets. The administration owed much of its election support to traditional companies and pursued the conglomerates out of self-interest. However, its antitrust fervor would be tempered by events during the election of 1972 that would leave egg on the faces of many in the administration and in ITT executive suites.

The embarrassment was the greatest scandal for the administration before the Watergate affair broke several years later. It began with the ostensibly innocent choice of a site at which to hold the Republican national convention in 1972. One of the several cities actively lobbying for the convention and all of the business it could potentially generate was San Diego, but it was not a front-runner. Larger cities like Miami appeared to have a better track on gaining the convention until Harold Geneen made an appearance in San Diego in the spring of 1971 and made a pledge of $400,000 to help underwrite local merchants' subscriptions to supporting the bid. Richard Nixon had a home not far from the city and it was assumed that San Diego was his personal choice. ITT had hotel interests in San Diego that would naturally have benefited from the convention, and the city received the party's blessing shortly thereafter. The ITT hotel was quietly selected to be the one where the president would stay while attending.

Matters became even more complicated when ITT and the Justice Department settled the case the Antitrust Division had brought against the Hartford merger only nine days after the convention location was announced. It appeared that Geneen had bought a site for the convention and settled its antitrust problem with one check. Richard McLaren answered a query from an ally of Ralph Nader by stating, "There is no relationship whatsoever between the settlement of the ITT-Hartford litigation and any financial support which ITT may have offered to the City of San Diego."[24] The reply did not mollify anyone but only fueled suspicions about ITT's involvement in the convention even more. Had the conglomerate gotten so large that it was able to directly influence politics on such a large scale?

Before long, Felix Rohatyn of Lazard Freres naturally appeared in any discussions about ITT's influence peddling. It was revealed that he had had discussions with McLaren before the ITT settlement over Hartford was announced, although there appeared to be no proof that it was anything but normal discussions between a company's investment banker and a regulator. But even the small ray of light was unwanted and cast Rohatyn as a behind-the-scenes operator in the mold of an investment banker of the 1920s. Columnist Nicholas von Hoffman of the *Washington Post* began characterizing Rohatyn as an "anemic little financier" and then labeled him with the nickname "Felix the Fixer" despite the fact that no specific charges of wrongdoing were ever brought against him or attributed to him in the Hartford affair.[25]

Adding to ITT's misery in the Republican affair was a nationally syndicated columnist, Jack Anderson, who began writing about the company and its problems after the initial revelations were made. Then, just as hearings were being held in Congress about the affair, another explosive example of ITT influence hit the news. Anderson wrote in his column that secret documents, never destroyed, showed that ITT had been intimately involved in plotting to thwart the presidency of Socialist President Salvador Allende of Chile after he had been elected in 1970. Geneen and local ITT officials in Chile were fearful that Allende's government would be hostile to multinationals after the election because of its anti-imperialist Marxist hard line.

ITT's interest in Chile was substantial since it controlled the telephone system, the Chile Telephone Company, owned and operated by ITT since 1927.

Allende unofficially expropriated the phone company by placing a government manager at its helm and then claiming that it was worth about $100 million less than ITT valued it. Matters were not helped by Allende's 1972 address to the United Nations in New York when he claimed that ITT attempted to "bring about civil war" in Chile, having "driven its tentacles deep into my country."[26] He had reason to quarrel with ITT and other multinationals because it was revealed that Geneen had offered millions to the CIA to help keep Allende from power. ITT also had a former CIA director, John McCone, as one of its directors. The entire affair prompted hearings in Congress, where many of the shenanigans were revealed, but at the end of the day no legal action was taken. Unfortunately, Allende was killed in a coup later in 1973 led by Augusto Pinochet. Geneen was uncharacteristically silent about the San Diego affair as well as Chile in later years and had little to say about Emanuel Celler, whose committee hearings proved embarrassing to ITT.

IN THE LIMELIGHT

Now the Nixon administration was heavily involved in investigating antitrust, especially conglomerates that only years before had appeared invulnerable to the regulators. The new buzzword in antitrust became *reciprocity*, and McLaren used it as his rallying cry in pursuing ITT especially. The fear among antitrusters was that conglomerates forced their subsidiary companies to do exclusive business with each other, to the detriment of others. The idea was not simply theory. Conglomerates had been practicing it for some time and competitors complained loudly. The practice was something new for regulators to grapple with because it was a variation of investigating vertical relationships for exclusive dealings between related companies.

Fear of conglomerate power eventually led to a congressional investigation. The hearings, called by Emanuel Celler's Antitrust

Committee in the House, began in the summer of 1969. They began a string of adverse publicity for conglomerates even before ITT's political problems surfaced. The top conglomerates and their chief executives were called to testify, reminiscent of the Pecora hearings almost four decades before. Harold Geneen and James Ling were called to testify about their organizations, as was the ubiquitous Felix Rohatyn. Although the hearings were a corporate affair, unlike the Pecora hearings, which featured Wall Street people almost exclusively, ITT's bankers played a central role in forming the corporation and found themselves front and center. When Rohatyn appeared before Celler's committee, the chairman pointedly asked him, "If there were no Lazard Freres, would there be less mergers?" Rohatyn responded honestly by saying, "I think there would have been a few less, Mr. Chairman."

Celler reserved most of his most pointed questions for ITT and LTV. Celler expressed skepticism about the workings of an organization as large as ITT, specifically questioning whether its CEO could possibly have any idea of how it all worked. Geneen described ITT, despite its size, as a coherent operating company with a substantial operating management and stated further that "acquisition policies are not the same for all diversified or conglomerate companies."[27] He was correct in that description because ITT and LTV were quite different organizations despite their sheer size. In fact, Geneen eschewed the term *conglomerate*, preferring to think of ITT as simply a large, complex organization managed by a large team of experienced, professional managers. But size alone was not the focus of the committee's attention. Since it was an antitrust committee, violations of the antitrust laws were paramount.

Many of Celler's questions revolved around the practice of reciprocity. In conglomerates, individual companies were suspected of being forced to trade exclusively with others under the same corporate umbrella. Did Avis employees have to buy insurance from other ITT companies? The practice was proscribed, but Celler was unable to get Geneen to admit practicing it. Geneen stated categorically that the "theory of reciprocity is therefore repugnant as a basic business philosophy."[28] Although Celler cited examples of the practice, they were dismissed as simply being good business practice, not intended to violate the law. Geneen maintained that large, complex organizations that could foster internal dealings among their units were actually harmonious and would raise business and corporate life to a higher plane. Celler rebuked him by stating flatly that "human nature is different and business nature is different" from the picture Geneen painted.

While the hearings exposed many fundamental differences between the conglomerators and their inquisitors, they did not inspire much public outcry because their contents were mainly matters of corporate philosophy and antitrust, not topics that inflamed public opinion. The findings were published in 1971, a full year after the hearings concluded. Anthony Sampson noted that Celler released the findings very quietly, seeming to be embarrassed by the contents although they were highly critical of ITT and others. Perhaps it was the political implications that had the potential to cause the most stir. One commentator wrote, "As corporate concentration grows, the threat of a corporate state grows with it."[29] Not since the 1930s had the threat of corporate power presented such a distinguishable threat to the existing order. The old bugaboo about corporate America and its unaccountable generals, aided by bankers, was resurfacing after decades. But the threat that the conglomerates posed to the old order never materialized beyond the ITT escapades in San Diego and Chile. The stock market had seen enough and had decided that the leviathan newcomers had overstayed their welcome.

WHAT GOES UP . . .

The long bull market run for the conglomerates ended with the bear market of 1970. Their prices began to tumble in the market, finally proving that their high price/earnings multiples were not justified in the end. LTV stock hit its high of $136 in 1968 before plummeting to $7 in early 1970. Litton fell in similar fashion, from $90 to $14, while Gulf + Western dropped from $64 to $9. ITT fared the best, with its stock only falling from $63 to $31. The immediate cause was the poor market on Wall Street generally, which was racked at the time by a crisis involving the settling of securities accounts and the safekeeping of customer accounts although the conglomerates' earnings growth generally had stopped about a year and a half before. Other frauds also appeared, giving investors the general impression that the odds were stacked against them.

Those impressions were not helped by the performance of these companies, once touted as hedges against the economy because of their diversity. When the stock market slumped, they could not continue their acquisitions because of low stock prices, the printing press they needed to keep paying for new purchases. Then the tide began to turn because of all the debt and preferred stock the companies had accumulated during the 1960s. The most serious problem faced by the conglomerates in the early 1970s was their high degree of leverage. Most had borrowed freely to finance expansion and had also issued a large amount of preferred stock, and the dividends represented a strong drain on earnings when the economic climate turned against them. James Ling was replaced in 1970 at LTV and the company began shedding acquisitions. Harold Geneen served his last full year at ITT in 1977 when ITT was still performing well if not spectacularly. His successor, Rand Araskog, encountered a different sort of company when he took over in 1980. The company faced a new set of challenges. "He [Geneen] left behind a debt-laden corporation, one that was struggling to pay the bills for its many mergers and acquisitions," Araskog wrote. But that was only the beginning of the problem. "Worse, the company was vulnerable to corporate raiders that might come to call. And as business conditions changed, call they did," he recounted, giving some insight into the next unpleasant episode in corporate affairs.[30] The tables were about to turn on the aggressive acquisitions experts of the 1960s and 1970s.

Congress finally reacted to the conglomerate trend and the use of hostile takeovers by passing the Hart-Scott-Rodino Act in 1976. Borrowing a page from the original Securities Act of 1933, the new law required companies intending to merge to file their intent so that the FTC and the Antitrust Division of the Justice Department would have time to review the proposal. While the law seemed benign, forcing prospective marriage partners to file their intent was in keeping with the spirit of the 1930s laws and added a semblance of order to what would prove to be a wild and wooly M&A market in the years ahead.

Inflation was also a major culprit in the deconglomeration that was to follow in the late 1970s and 1980s. High interest rates and inflation persisted from the late 1970s until 1984. After Paul Volcker assumed the chairmanship of the Federal Reserve in 1979, interest rates hit their twentieth-century peak as the Fed used them aggressively to battle growth in the money supply. As a result, corporate funding began to change radically as many companies were unwilling to borrow for the long term and curtailed capital spending instead. Raising new stock issues was also difficult because the bear market certainly frightened off investors. Unable to pay for acquisitions with stock and facing high borrowing costs, the conglomerates retrenched and their profitability began to shrink. When the smoke cleared in 1984, the landscape for mergers had changed substantially.

The merger boom that was about to begin became the largest in history, making the earlier booms appear minuscule in comparison. But the trend started slowly and, much to the chagrin of conglomerators, introduced a new breed of corporate raider that set the giant, diversified companies in their sights. The logic was simple. The conglomerates possessed assets, undervalued in 1980s terms, that were worth more broken into parts than they were as a whole. If these companies could be purchased cheaply because they were poor performers in the market, their assets could be stripped and sold to pay for the cost of the acquisition. The rest would be pure profit. *Asset stripping* became a new buzzword on Wall Street. Synergy still held sway, but now it worked in reverse. The parts were greater than their sum.

After playing a major role in the conglomerate trend, accounting now aided the raiders. Many assets booked by companies in the 1970s, before inflation became a problem, were on the books at their historical cost. Both raiders and more serious buyers realized that it often was cheaper to buy these assets by taking over an existing company than to build a new one from the ground up. Declining inflation caused a fire sale among many companies as a result. Never loath to turn their back on fees, investment bankers fanned the trend by lining up on either side of the new merger trend. Some, like Goldman

Sachs, became defensive specialists, while others, like Morgan Stanley, helped buyers identify targets and design takeover bids. Lawyers also developed specialties along the same lines. Flom became the best-known lawyer advising on the acquisitions side, while Lipton became a defensive specialist.

Investors also realized that the frequent use of stock to pay for the many acquisitions had caused the conglomerates to badly dilute the value of their holdings. Before the 1929 Crash, this was known as *watering*, although now the more technically correct term was used to describe the effect on shareholders' equity. James Ling's Project Redeployment became one of the great watering episodes in financial history, although it was so shrouded in technical concepts and language that investors eventually gave up and simply bought the new shares under the assumption that the mantra of growth would continue. It was not the first time investors bought a watering story, eventually putting up cash, and it certainly would not be the last.

Bankers were no longer in the front ranks as the shapers of modern corporate America. Many of the investment banks were still partnerships until the 1970s and did not have the capital necessary to play a major part in the merger game unless they entered early on, as Lehman Brothers did on several notable occasions. In the past, mergers had been a high stakes game, with major deals reaping more than $10 million for the bankers-turned-industrialists. In the 1960s and early 1970s, merger bankers worked for substantially less in both total and real dollars. Lazard often made only about $250,000 on ITT deals, depending upon size, although when added up the sum became more substantial. Clearly bankers were not wildly profiting during the conglomerate boom, but neither were they starving. Now, the amount they made depended upon the number of deals done for a client.

The larger "killer" deals were not a thing of the past, however. In the environment of the 1980s, the rules of the merger game would change again. Mergers and acquisitions advice was still among the hottest games on Wall Street, but now a new element would enter that would change the face of the Street substantially. Investment bankers were not concerned about the new trend of dissembling what they previously helped construct. Fees could be earned either way. The main concern would be maintaining a low profile in order to avoid the inevitable political flak that followed the orgies of excess in mergers and acquisitions. Unfortunately, as the 1980s would prove, that would not be the case.

NOTES

1. The opposite of pooled interest was purchase accounting, in which any premium paid for a target company had to be booked as goodwill on the acquirers' balance sheet and amortized over time. This could result in a charge to earnings, something most conglomerators wanted to avoid at all costs in the 1960s.
2. Harry Markowitz, "Portfolio Selection," *Journal of Finance*, March 1952, pp. 77–91.
3. Franco Modigliani and Merton H. Miller, "The Cost of Capital, Corporation Finance, and the Theory of Investment," *American Economic Review*, June 1958, pp. 261–297.
4. Burton G. Malkiel, *A Random Walk Down Wall Street* (New York: W.W. Norton, 1996), p. 191.
5. Charles R. Geisst, *Monopolies in America: Empire Builders and Their Enemies from Jay Gould to Bill Gates* (New York: Oxford University Press, 2000), pp. 85, 205.
6. Malkiel, p. 64.
7. *The Magazine of Wall Street*, February 10, 1951.
8. Leslie Gould, *The Manipulators* (New York: David McKay & Co., 1966), p. 14.
9. Diana B. Henriques, *The White Sharks of Wall Street: Thomas Mellon Evans and the Original Corporate Raiders* (New York: Scribner, 2000), p. 99.
10. Gould, p. 26.
11. *Mergerstat Reports*, December 8, 2002.
12. Quoted in Joseph Wechsberg, *The Merchant Bankers* (New York: Simon & Schuster, 1966), p. 229.
13. Stanley H. Brown, *Ling: The Rise, Fall, and Return of a Texas Titan* (New York: Atheneum, 1972), p. 113.
14. Ibid, p. 155.
15. Ibid, p. 151.
16. Harold Geneen, *The Synergy Myth* (New York: St. Martin's Press, 1997), p. 32.

17. Ibid., p. 191.
18. *New York Times,* May 13, 1971.
19. Quoted in Wechsberg, p. 231.
20. *New York Times,* March 25, 1969.
21. Henriques, p. 264.
22. Quoted in Joel Seligman, *The Transformation of Wall Street: A History of the Securities and Exchange Commission and Modern Corporate Finance* (Boston: Houghton Mifflin, 1982), p. 431. The 20-day period was not chosen by accident. If a company wanted to sell new securities, the SEC mandated that the securities needed to be registered with the commission and then undergo a 20-day cooling off period before being sold to the public. The same period specified by the Williams Act would then allow companies wanting to fight off an unwanted takeover time to register new debt or preferred stock with the SEC so that they could change their debt equity structure in time to frighten off potential suitors.
23. *New York Times,* March 4, 1969.
24. Anthony Sampson, *The Sovereign State of ITT* (New York: Stein & Day, 1973), p. 198.
25. Cary Reich, *Financier: The Biography of Andre Meyer* (New York: William Morrow & Co., 1983), p. 303.
26. Sampson, p. 265. The idea of a corporate state was based on the European experience with fascism during the 1930s and 1940s. The basic premise was that legislatures represented corporate entities rather than the citizenry directly and, as a result, the state served corporate bodies rather than individuals.
27. Testimony of Harold Geneen in *Hearings before Antitrust Subcommittee of the Committee on the Judiciary, House of Representatives,* 91st Congress November 20–December 3, 1969, p. 6.
28. Geneen testimony, p. 7.
29. Sampson, p. 167.
30. Rand V. Araskog, *The ITT Wars* (New York: Henry Holt & Co., 1989), p. 3.

CHAPTER 5

VISIGOTHS VERSUS THE LEGIONS

These managements need shaking up, they're horrendous. They take money from the peasants [stockholders] and then hire mercenaries [lawyers] to protect their castle, mainly by browbeating the peasants. So we attack the castle.

Carl Icahn, *1985*

The late 1970s and early 1980s proved to be some of the darkest years for the financial markets since the Depression. The Dow Jones Industrial Average dipped below 1,000 and remained moribund until 1982. Inflation and interest rates rose to historic levels and imports increased alarmingly. The dollar hit historic highs against the other major trading currencies. *Stagflation* became a new buzzword, signifying the unpleasant combination of inflation and low levels of economic growth that produced high levels of unemployment. American industry began to be ridiculed for flat productivity levels and Japanese and European imports gained in popularity.

Against this bleak background, borrowing money became popular and the bond markets underwent something of a revival. Most corporations were not able to sell new stock because of depressed prices, so borrowing became popular out of necessity. The irony in this situation was that companies that had borrowed heavily in the past watched their stocks plummet during the 1970s and by the 1980s were close to junk bond status. Soon many of them would be targets of others, somewhat newer to the game, that would borrow heavily to finance their expansion ambitions. The problem the situation presented to

Wall Street was simple. Underwriting bonds was in demand but the fees attached were thin compared to those for common stocks or mergers. New methods needed to be found to make money or the Street would have to contract, as it did in most bear markets. Unfortunately, this bear market was the most serious since the 1930s.

What was becoming an assault on corporate America was hardly finished. In many respects, it had only begun. The corporate world and the investment banking community were changing rapidly. Previously, corporate America had emphasized long-term growth for its investors and had made capital investments accordingly. When interest rates rose into the double digits in the early 1980s, prohibitively high costs of borrowing prevented many companies from raising money for more than about five years and capital investment plunged. Analysts worried that corporate balance sheets were becoming skewed in favor of short-term debt instead of permanent capital and that this would present serious challenges to investment in the years ahead. As a result, product development slowed substantially, especially in consumer durables, and imports from Japan and Europe gained a significant toehold in the market that would be expanded in later years. When consumers wanted to buy a new car, they looked to imports for quality they could not find in domestic models. For the first time in American history, the financial markets had invaded the living rooms of consumers indirectly and set off a furious debate about what was wrong with American industry.

Management consultants analyzed problems in the labor force, trying to determine why foreign workers were more productive than their American counterparts. Others fretted over the lack of cutting-edge technology in American products. Why were Japanese automobiles better made and more efficient than the American ones? Had the American century come to a premature end? These were troublesome questions that were never adequately answered, but then they were quickly forgotten. Interest rates fell and the stock market began a rebound. Within a few years, cheaper and more abundant capital solved the problem and industry became more productive again as investment increased.

At the same time, high real rates of interest took hold and became part and parcel of the financial markets. Borrowing became more respectable for corporations and the amount of debt accumulated in the late 1970s and 1980s seemed to prove the Modigliani-Miller proposition even further. Investors apparently did not worry about the amount of debt companies piled onto their balance sheets as long as their prospects seemed bright. Once-esoteric Wall Street practices came out of the closet and became new buzzwords. Junk bonds, management buyouts, and leveraged buyouts all became accepted in corporate suites while the public tried to figure out how a handful of executives could afford to buy out their own companies, often for billions of dollars. Apparently, the world was turned upside down.

Many of the 1970s trends also reversed themselves in the 1980s, only adding to investor confusion. B.F. Goodrich, the tire maker that had savagely fought to maintain its independence from Northwest Industries, sold its tire-making business in 1986, choosing to concentrate on its specialty chemicals business instead. The Ethyl Corporation, one of the oldest manufacturers of the antiknock chemical used in gasoline, decided to diversify in the 1980s only to discover that the concept did not work well for it and reentered the ethyl business after shedding many of its newly acquired divisions. And in one of the most monumental, if not totally unexpected, announcements of the 1980s, LTV filed for Chapter 11 bankruptcy proceedings in 1986, entering the first of two prolonged periods of seeking protection from its creditors. And while these events were taking place, the idea of diversification proceeded. The only difference from the 1980s was a matter of degree. Companies still wanted to diversify, but not at the dizzying pace of the conglomerates. A little diversity was considered de rigeur in the 1980s: Too much was considered a recipe for disaster. Conglomerates were not yet out of fashion, but diversifying for its own sake in order to avoid antitrust prosecution was no longer considered a viable corporate strategy.

No one argued with the general idea that diversification could work effectively, but the realities of practicing an acquisitions strategy based upon it were a different matter. Companies often bought others when the costs of starting a similar company from scratch were considered prohibitive. It was cheaper to buy an existing company than to build one. But as more and more companies became acquisitions-minded and dozens of able investment banks lined up to aid them in their searches, the costs of entry began to rise. The cost of an acquisition could become so high that it would devour any potential return. As Michael Porter pointed out, "Philip Morris paid more than four times book value for Seven-Up Company [and] simple arithmetic meant that profits had to more than quadruple to sustain the preacquisition ROI [return on investment]. Since there proved to be little Philip Morris could add in marketing prowess to the sophisticated marketing wars in the soft-drink industry, the result was unsatisfactory financial performance of Seven-Up and ultimately the decision to divest."[1] This would prove a crucial factor as the bidding wars of the 1980s and 1990s intensified.

After the Reagan administration took office, Wall Street had reason to cheer. In order to stimulate the economy, Congress passed the Economic Recovery Tax Act in 1981. Capital gains taxes were lowered and depreciation rules were liberalized to allow for shorter write-off periods under accelerated schedules. This was particularly important because depreciation was an allowable expense under Internal Revenue Service (IRS) rules, despite the fact that no cash was laid out. Investors and corporations alike benefited from the new law and economic recovery became more important than antitrust prosecutions, which were now considered inimical to economic growth. After the last bout with high interest rates in 1984, Wall Street recognized the conditions necessary for a new round of mergers. But many companies were still suffering from the effects of six years of high interest rates. New financing techniques were necessary if a new merger trend was to develop. But the window of opportunity was short. Another tax reform in 1986 would partially close the window.

New financing techniques were aided by the deregulation of interest rates in the early 1980s. In response to severe problems within the banking industry, in 1980 Congress passed the Monetary Control Act, designed to phase in deregulation of interest rates over a six-year period.[2] Previous Fed restrictions on the amount of interest banks were allowed to pay on their savings accounts eventually would be abolished in favor of market rates. This measure would make banks more attuned to the needs of the markets and eventually would release a great deal of funds used to chase mergers deals. The new law ended 50 years of regulation of interest rates and helped foster the new, freewheeling environment of the 1980s.

Another pane in the window was opened in 1982 when Congress passed the Depository Institutions Act, better known as the Garn-St Germain Act. Thrift institutions had been faring poorly under high interest rates, and the purpose of the act was to allow them to purchase a broader array of assets to complement their traditional holdings of residential mortgages. The centerpiece of the law was to speed up the deregulation of interest rates, which now were immediately affected and essentially free of prior restrictions. The legislation also broadened savings and loans' (S&Ls') asset bases, including corporate bonds. For the first time since the 1930s, banking institutions were allowed to purchase corporate securities, under the assumption that the yields were higher than mortgages. When the bill passed Congress, it was ballyhooed by the Reagan administration as the most important piece of financial legislation to be passed in decades. In that respect, it proved correct. Savings and loans began buying junk bonds, attracted by their high yields. In less than a decade, the choice would prove disastrous for many of them.

BORROWING FROM THE JUNKMAN

As Wall Street and corporate America were suffering under the burden of high interest rates in the late 1970s, two developments occurred that would change the face of financing. In 1976, three bankers left Bear Stearns to open their own small specialty merger house that was destined to become a formidable institution on Wall Street. Then, in 1977, Lehman Brothers began helping companies' with less than investment grade quality ratings to issue new corporate bonds and was soon joined in the effort by Drexel Burnham, a distinctly second-rate investment bank. The combined effect of the two would change financing forever.

The early 1980s were primed for a takeover movement to begin again. Stock values were low and many acquisitions could be made at much lower PE multiples than in the previous decade. But values were also low for the acquiring companies, so these new financing techniques were not based upon buyers issuing more stock to pay for their purchases but on borrowing money. But buying debt from less than investment grade borrowers was not practical unless the yield was high enough to compensate for the risk involved. In the case of junk bonds and leveraged buyouts (LBOs), the potential compensation was high enough to entice many institutional investors to provide the necessary cash. Developing the market became the primary challenge.

The new tax law gave borrowing to finance corporate assets a new lease on life. In addition to the interest write-off, companies could also write off depreciating assets at an accelerated pace, and the combination of the two proved all that was necessary to start a new borrowing boom. Several years before, in 1976, a new firm specializing in buyouts was established on Wall Street by Henry Kravis, Jerome Kohlberg, and George Roberts. Kohlberg Kravis Roberts (KKR) began as a small two-office firm that purchased mainly private companies with borrowed funds, leveraging the equity to heights that only private financing would tolerate. The appropriate mix called for the company's cash flows to service the debt for a medium term—around five years—until it could be taken public at a profit. Often, the existing management was kept in place and shared in the potential profits, helping to ensure that the deal succeeded in the long run. Small operations of this sort were known on Wall Street as *boutiques.*

Henry Kravis was the driving force behind the new boutique operation. Raised in Tulsa, he attended Claremont-McKenna College in California and the Columbia Business School before taking a job at the Madison Fund, a closed-end mutual fund in New York. Unlike many other novices on Wall Street, he learned what investors on the buy side of the Street thought of securities analysis and what they looked for when making investments. This experience would be especially valuable later when he persuaded many institutional investors to join in the equity portions of many KKR buyout deals. Two years later, he went to work at Bear Stearns in New York, where he teamed up with Jerome Kohlberg, the head of corporate finance and 20 years his senior, and his cousin George Roberts.

Roberts was also a graduate of Claremont and a lawyer who had gone to work for Bear Stearns after a series of summer jobs with the firm. He went to work in Kohlberg's mergers department in New York but preferred San Francisco and was successful in getting a transfer to Bear Stearns' office in California. His replacement at the New York office was his cousin Kravis. Within a few years, Kravis and Roberts became disgusted with office politics at headquarters and with the firm's refusal to set up a separate LBO operation. All three realized that they wanted to set up their own firm and made the decision to establish KKR. After they resigned, Kravis and Roberts took the last small deal they were working on with them to their new firm. Officials at Bear Stearns became so enraged they locked the two out of their offices and stationed an armed guard outside to ensure they never entered the building again.[3]

Being small, boutique operations tended to do deals that often did not make the newspapers. But KKR was an exception. After gradually buying larger and larger companies in the 1980s, it began buying well-known companies using increasingly large amounts of debt. Institutional investors such as pension funds also contributed to the pool of money invested, although the debt raised was larger than the amounts of equity the pools provided. Many clients and banks were attracted to the deals because of the firm's reputation on Wall Street. They had good reason to cheer. Between 1976, its first year of operation, and 1984, KKR had closed 28 deals worth $12.76 billion. On average, the leverage in these companies was around 80 percent, meaning that banks financed around $10 billion. The average return was around 33 percent after appropriate fees had been deducted.[4] At a time when the stock market was still floundering, the return attracted many faithful and KKR never lacked institutional investors, now ranging from pension funds to university endowments.

The firm employed a strategy that was not totally unique but was somewhat longer-term than those practiced by other buyout specialists. Normally, it intended to keep a company for a five-year period, enough time in which to sell off assets, pay off debt, and then "flip" the company back to the market to be sold at a higher price. The deals ranged from small to very large. The smallest buyout was for $13 million, while the largest was for $2.4 billion. Some very well-known companies were represented, including Storer Communications, Motel 6, United Texas Petroleum, and AutoZone. And greater things were still to come. Deals after 1986 made KKR the best-known name in mergers and acquisitions. The first megadeal was a $6.2 billion bid for Beatrice Foods in 1986. Beatrice was a staple of the food industry and was the largest LBO recorded to date. After a failed bid for another food giant—the retailer Esmark—KKR became synonymous with retailing and consumer products although its portfolio was much more diversified. In fact, one of the criticisms leveled at the firm was that it had become a conglomerate by acquiring so many disparate types of holdings. Unlike the conglomerates, its intention was to restructure these companies and sell them off at a profit, not to hold them as operating companies any longer than necessary. "Don't congratulate us when we buy a company," Kravis once remarked, "Congratulate us when we sell it, because any fool can overpay and buy a company."

The centerpiece of the buyout trend of the 1980s was junk bonds—or, more precisely, high-yield bonds. Until the late 1970s, junk bonds were issues of borrowers that had fallen from grace. Traditionally, the bond market was reserved for companies of investment-grade standing with strong financial ratios. If the companies subsequently fell below investment grade, they were known as *fallen angels;* a limited secondary market developed among speculators who would buy them on the chance that they would rise again in the ratings. Junk had always been in the market, but it always meant a secondary market issue. The idea of a primary market developing for less than high-quality bonds was not considered before 1977 when Lehman Brothers brought issues for Zapata International, Pan American Airways, and

187

LTV to market. Admittedly not of investment quality, all three were able to borrow money by paying a high yield to investors. LTV in particular had fallen from grace in the years since conglomerate prices had begun to decline. Being junk was not a compliment, but it still was worth the foray into the market because the bonds were cheaper than borrowing from a bank.

After the three issues hit the market, Lehman backed away, leaving the incipient market to Drexel Burnham. Drexel was a second-tier Wall Street house resulting from a merger between Drexel & Co., the old J.P. Morgan ally, and Burnham & Co., a small trading house run by I.W. "Tubby" Burnham. The firm was casting around for new, profitable lines of business when one of its young members, Michael Milken, introduced it to high-yield bonds. Milken himself was the survivor of a merger. The firm he originally joined on Wall Street, Drexel Firestone, was a sleepy second-tier firm rapidly slipping in Wall Street's prestige rankings. When it was bought by Burnham, Milken was part of the deal. On the verge of resigning from the somnolent firm, Milken asked Burnham to stake some capital on a junk bond operation and Burnham readily agreed rather than lose him. The decision would result in Drexel soaring to the very heights—and then the depths—of notoriety on Wall Street.

The move proved fortuitous and Milken remained at Drexel. In the next several years Drexel made Wall Street history by becoming the largest underwriter and trader of junk on the Street. By 1984, it sat atop the Wall Street league tables as the number two underwriter, a position usually held by older investment banks with a long list of well-established companies as clients. Drexel accomplished it in unique fashion, by bringing former undesirables into the marketplace and giving them the opportunity to succeed. Technically, junk bonds were a type of what Wall Street called *mezzanine financing*. Being unsecured, they ranked between a company's senior debt and equity. In the event of a liquidation, they would be paid only after senior debt holders were compensated. As far as investors were concerned, that made them only slightly less risky than equity in a poorly rated company.

Junk bonds also benefited from favorable tax laws. Usually they were issued with low coupons attached rather than high ones, as their quality would have suggested. In order to compensate, they were issued at a discount so that their yields to maturity reflected market rates. But the low coupons saved the companies involved some valuable cash flows and the discounted amount, to be paid back at maturity, was also tax deductible. So junk companies received favorable tax treatment and investors got the opportunity to make handsome capital gains if financial performances improved. As a result, the market exploded. New issues touched $2.5 billion by 1982 and $15 billion per year by 1985. Drexel maintained an iron grip on the market and many older, established investment banks refused to enter the market. As a result, Milken and Drexel profited handsomely. With underwriting fees alone around 4 percent of issue size, the firm stood to earn around $600 million in 1985 alone. The late 1970s and early 1980s were lean years for Wall Street in general, but Drexel bucked the trend and kept bringing in heavy fees for its activities. Milken became the toast of Wall Street and his picture appeared on the cover of every major financial magazine in the country, with more than one hailing him as "the king of junk."

There was a more theoretical side to Milken that was usually overlooked in favor of the fat fees that Drexel earned. Drexel had offered him a job in 1970 when he was finishing an MBA at the Wharton School. While enrolled, he became familiar with high-yield bonds and was clearly aware of the Modigliani-Miller theory about investors and capital structure. Junk bonds fit neatly into the proposition, but Milken added a dimension of his own to the mix. Junk companies notoriously had erratic cash flows that could weaken their financial strength at any time but also had the potential to present investors with strong capital appreciation while paying out higher-than-average interest payments. In that respect, they combined the best of both stocks and bonds and soon became equated more closely with equity investments than bonds. Milken recognized that the new breed of investor emerging from the inflation-ridden 1970s wanted a combination of both and proceeded to appeal to their relatively high expectations. He sold a combination of new financing and high expectations at the same time. The idea caught on quickly and junk financing became very common in the 1980s.

In 1984, Drexel stood in second place among Wall Street corporate securities underwriters, passing legendary firms such as Morgan Stanley and Kidder Peabody. Within seven years, it doors were shuttered when an SEC fine drove the firm out of business. During its amazing 10-year reign at the top of Wall Street, the firm underwrote bonds for most of the major M&A players. It assisted KKR, Rupert Murdoch, Carl Icahn, and Boone Pickens among others in their searches for takeover targets. When Drexel decided to begin playing the M&A game in earnest, it relied on a combination of raw nerve and history in its quest to be taken seriously. Milken and company announced the existence of a $1 billion fund to assist clients in takeovers. By implication, there would be more where that amount came from, so it appeared that the war chest was well stocked. The problem was that there was no money and no fund. The fictitious fund was nicknamed the Air Fund by insiders at Drexel, who realized that they would need access to large amounts of cash if they were to play the market in an accepted way. A Drexel executive recalled, "We would announce to the world that we had raised one billion dollars for hostile takeovers. There would be no money in the fund—it was just a threat. The Air Fund stood for our not having a client with deep pockets . . . it was a substitute for that client we didn't have."[5] No one thought of it as a bluff, however, and the fund soon had a more tangible proof.

In the past, J. P. Morgan indeed had had access to vast amounts of capital for deals. Clarence Dillon had demonstrated that deals could be done and financing put in place after the fact if investors believed in the deal and the individuals involved. The conglomerators used inflated stock prices and debt to buy their sundry affiliates, but the Air Fund was something entirely new. It implied finance capital where none existed in order to lure potential clients. And it worked remarkably well, for the obscure Drexel Burnham began to succeed wildly when capital for new deals was still not abundant. Milken and his cohorts understood financial history well, but the bluff was something new on Wall Street. All deals were ultimately based on investors putting down cash. Milken was so sure of his ability to finance these deals that he was not about to let timing stand in his way of becoming the takeover financier of the 1980s.

190

One of the master deal makers of the period was the boutique firm Wasserstein Perella, named after its two principals, Bruce Wasserstein and Joseph Perella. Both were former First Boston merger specialists who finally set up their own operation after working on some of the biggest deals of the early 1980s. They established the firm in February 1988, taking some staff and clients with them in the process. Within several months, they sold a 20 percent stake in the firm to Nomura Securities for $500 million. Within a year, Wasserstein Perella opened its own LBO fund with commitments of $1 billion. Only two years after its launch, the firm known colloquially as "Wasserella" became a major adviser and already counted the mergers between Philip Morris and Kraft and between Time Inc. and Warner Communications as major coups.

Wasserstein and Perella were two different personalities that drove the firm. Wasserstein was a lawyer with a degree from Harvard who had spent time studying British mergers while on a fellowship at Cambridge. He also spent a short time as one of Ralph Nader's raiders in the late 1970s before going to work on Wall Street. He often remarked that mergers were the nexus of economics and law and that that was what attracted him to the business. During the 1980s, he acquired the nickname "bid'em up Bruce" for allegedly advising his clients to overpay for companies they eventually bought. While working for a blue-chip New York law firm, he met Perella, who at the time was the head of M&A at First Boston. After joining First Boston, the two shaped that firm into a major mergers adviser.

Perella was an accountant with an affinity for numbers, while Wasserstein was more of a negotiator. After graduating from Lehigh University, Perella attended the Harvard Business School and then worked as an accountant for several years before joining First Boston, where he was the sole member of the M&A department. Over the years, he added more staff and worked on some significant deals, perhaps the best-known being the DuPont-Conoco merger in 1981. It was the largest deal at the time and began the wave of merger deals in the energy business that followed. Lawyer Joseph Flom advised on the deal. Along the way, Perella earned the sobriquet "father of the hostile takeover." His affinity for numbers and spotting undervalued assets on corporate balance sheets, combined with Wasserstein's negotiating ability and legendary calm and patience in the midst of a potential deal, made First Boston a preeminent firm in the 1980s.

In their first two years as independents, Wasserstein and Perella earned more than $53 million advising on major deals. They advised KKR on the RJR-Nabisco deal in addition to their other coups, although their record was not unblemished. They were admonished by a Delaware court and a British takeover panel for unacceptable behavior during two highly competitive bidding deals. But slaps on the wrists by courts were not hindering the firm's ability to do deals. It considered raising the $1 billion LBO fund crucial in the event a good buying opportunity presented itself and had no problem finding subscribers. It even discussed the possibility of issuing its own junk bond to add to its war chest.

PRESCRIPTION FOR HEMLOCK

Keeping predators at bay became a well-honed art in the 1980s. Of all the known shark repellents, the poison pill was the best known and often difficult to swallow. But it was aided greatly by a little-known development at the SEC allowing pills to be prescribed to vulnerable companies with increasing speed. On Wall Street, it was equivalent to opening an all-night pharmacy.

Beginning in 1980, the SEC considered changing its registration rules to allow companies in need of capital to get to market more quickly than they could under its existing rules. Since 1933, the SEC had required a company wanting to sell new securities to file registration documents with it and then wait a mandatory 20-day cooling off period before selling securities through its investment bankers. Many companies frequently using the market complained that the process was too slow and needed to be streamlined.[6] Many had begun using the offshore market, known as the eurobond market, as an alternative. As a result, the SEC began considering what became known as *shelf registration*.

This new process, known in SEC parlance as Rule 415, allowed a company to pre-register a new bond or stock issue with the SEC and then proceed to market quickly, circumventing the traditional cooling-off period. It was first proposed in 1980 and was finally adopted in January 1984. Crucial to the junk bond market, it was introduced in temporary form in March 1982 and many borrowers took advantage of the new process. During the year and a half before it was permanently adopted, the shelf registration rule produced surprising results. About 20 to 30 percent of the companies taking advantage of it by issuing bonds or equities (including preferred stock) were rated BBB (the lowest investment grade) or less than investment grade (meaning junk).[7] The market demonstrated that an enormous appetite for capital existed in the lower rungs of the ratings. The process would help serve raiders seeking to arrange quick financing as well as companies needing to issue poison pills as quickly as possible. At the first sign of a predator filing a holding of 5 percent or more under the Williams Act, a company could now jump into action and leverage its balance sheet quickly by issuing bonds or preferred stock, providing a deterrent to would-be raiders.

Rule 415 helped many companies arrange quick financing and build quick defenses. It clearly contributed to the merger activity that was building in the early 1980s. When combined with the liberalization of assets provided by the Garn-St Germain Act, it helped change the face of investment banking from a sleepy process to one that was more streamlined and faster. There were now more securities issuers on the horizon and more investors to buy their stocks and bonds. Whether the new investors got a good deal was another matter entirely.

PREDATION

Two ideas circulated on Wall Street in the 1970s. One was generally true while the other was generally false. The concept based on reality was that corporate America was under attack, much as it had been in the 1960s from the conglomerators. Now, however, the attack came from raiders instead. The other idea was that the raiders came from a barbarian horde markedly different from their more traditional counterparts. That assumption was mainly untrue. They were no different from their predecessors, they were just more recent arrivals.

The raiders of the 1970s and 1980s differed from their predecessors in one marked respect. They were not investment bankers, nor did they have access to large pools of money like the financial capitalists of the early part of the century. By the time the bear market of the late 1970s began, all one needed was an idea and enough nerve to carry it out. Louis Wolfson set the model for this sort of activity after World War II, and by the 1980s the field was actually becoming crowded. Of all the individuals scouring corporate financial statements looking for value, none became more hated than Carl Icahn. Companies large and small came to fear his influence, much as Cyrus Eaton was feared in the 1920s. The disparate group of companies Icahn approached over the years demonstrated that conducting an effective raid depended upon the financial statements of a company and the value it contained rather than the actual business it conducted.

Icahn was born in 1936, the son of middle-class parents in New York, and attended Princeton as an undergraduate before enrolling in medical school. But the lure of Wall Street proved too strong and he left before graduating to begin his career as a trainee at Dreyfus & Co. After doing his apprenticeship, he became interested in options trading, working at several more firms before buying a seat on the NYSE in 1967 with money borrowed from an uncle. He then plunged into the then esoteric world of options and stock arbitrage years before the activity became fashionable. At the time, the options exchanges and listed options had not yet been introduced.

Having an arbitrageur's mentality would prove highly beneficial to Icahn, who became expert at spotting incorrectly priced assets and undervalued firms. He began taking an interest in buying undervalued firms in 1978 when he branched out from options and bought a real estate investment trust called Baird and Warner through a proxy fight. He changed its status to an investment company renamed Bayswater Realty and Capital Corp., and it became the company through which he would mount his future takeover attempts.[8] Within a year, he was ready to attempt a raid on an established company.

The reaction of his target was unpredictable because the tactic was relatively new and unproven.

From the beginning of his acquisitions career, Icahn adopted a different mentality than the one that dominated Wall Street at the time. Describing himself as a "catalyst of change" rather than a predator, Icahn eschewed Wall Street's typical search for companies with good earnings and instead sought those with undervalued assets. "I look at companies as businesses, while Wall Street analysts look for quarterly earnings performance," he commented. "I buy assets and potential productivity. Wall Street buys earnings. So they miss a lot of things that I see in certain situations."[9] Since the go-go years of the 1960s, Wall Street had focused closely on earnings and PE ratios. The decline of the early conglomerates was certainly a testimony to the emphasis on earnings since once they slowed the behemoth companies fell quickly out of favor. The smart raider had other methods of valuation, however.

Icahn's first trophy became the Tappan Co., the well-known but relatively small maker of stoves and kitchen appliances. It was trading well below book value. Icahn seized the company and sold it to the Swedish company Electrolux for a profit of $3 million, launching his career as a raider. His next conquest, Saxon Industries, a maker of copy machines, set the tone for many deals to come. After Icahn obtained a chunk of Saxon stock and threatened a proxy battle, the company agreed to buy out his holdings for a $2 million profit. Using his profits from the deals, he then turned to larger prey in the form of the Hammermill Paper Co. Unlike his two previous targets, Hammermill decided to put up a fight. It recognized that his methods were more harmful to smaller companies than to larger ones given his financial strength.

Hammermill decided early to call Icahn's bluff. The company would not pay a premium on its stock price to buy out his 9 percent share of the stock and was not concerned about his threat to buy a controlling interest. It demonstrated a basic defense that would affect the entire M&A business in the early 1980s. One of Hammermill's lawyers described the battle between Icahn and Albert Duval, the CEO, as a classic game of bluff and counterbluff. "You didn't have to worry that he'd make a tender offer for the company," the lawyer said of Icahn. "He didn't have the money. At 10 or 11 percent of the company's stock, he was tapped out." What angered management more than anything else was Icahn's professed ignorance of their industry. Duval recalled that Icahn confessed that he didn't "know anything about the paper business. All I care about is the money, and I want it quick."[10] Frank admissions of that nature, while true, only added to corporate America's growing distrust of, and distaste for, raiders.

A proxy fight was launched, but Icahn lost and finally agreed to settle with Hammermill. He still emerged victorious after a year, his share appreciating almost $10 million in profit when he sold his stock on the market. His shares rose in value once the market assessed the battle being waged. He again emerged victorious and his war chest was getting larger after each deal. With his newfound wealth, he then acquired almost 20 percent of the stock of Chicago retailer Marshall Field. This time he employed a tactic known as the *bear hug*. By making an offer aimed directly at the company's board, Icahn played on their fiduciary responsibility to consider his offer in the interests of the shareholders. Once that was accomplished, other interested parties such as institutional shareholders and arbitrageurs also became involved, making it difficult for the board to simply dismiss the offer. The staid retailer became so worried at the prospect of falling into Icahn's hands that it sought, and found, a white knight in a British retailer, who bought it out at almost twice what Icahn paid for his share, netting profits of almost $18 million. The store chain's quest for a white knight attested to Icahn's growing legend as a raider, but a similar tactic backfired in his face, bringing with it a host of bad publicity.

In 1982, Icahn pursued what appeared to be easier prey in Dan River Inc., a textile manufacturer located in Danville, Virginia. The company was trading at half its book value when Icahn began acquiring shares in a clear attempt to buy the company and dismember it. The book value was estimated at $35. The *New York Times* remarked that "Dan River seems an unlikely candidate to be fighting a heated battle for control of its stock."[11] When it became clear that the raider had dismemberment on his mind, the locals in Danville intervened.

Workers and management decided to take the company private in a buyout of their own. Everyone with a vested interest in the company appeared to invest their savings in the deal, which was announced in the late spring of 1983. The locals intervened to save the city's major employer, thumbing their noses at Wall Street in the process. Icahn made about $8 million on the deal, substantially less than its estimated breakup value suggested since the buyout was at $22.50.

A little local color did not deter Icahn, however. The big deals were yet to come, and even more money would be made, but by 1983 his reputation was sealed. It was revealed that Richard Tappan, the former chairman of Tappan, was so impressed with Icahn's ability during the takeover of his company that he began investing money with the raider, purportedly earning well over five times his original investment within several years. But Carl Icahn still was considered a predator by most of Wall Street as well as Main Street. His fortune was estimated at around $100 million, but the amount was not enough to mount serious operations against larger, established companies. For that, he would need access to large amounts of capital because, as the Hammermill affair demonstrated and the Dan River escapade confirmed, threats were one thing but actually buying a company was another. In order to be taken seriously as a potential buyer, much more serious capital was required.

At that juncture, Drexel Burnham and its Air Fund entered the picture. Bayswater finally acquired a company in 1984 that remained under Icahn's control. The ACF Corp., a railway car leasing company, was acquired for $410 million. Over half of the purchase price was supplied by a group of banks and the balance by selling off one of the company's profitable divisions. Later that year Drexel refinanced the bank loans using junk bonds, but the frugal financier refused to allow Drexel any equity in the company. "I don't like giving up equity," he remarked. "I've learned over the years, a dollar bill is a better partner than a partner."[12] But his next foray would take more than just a few dollars as he made a bid for Phillips Petroleum for $8.1 billion.

In December 1984, Drexel helped put the Oklahoma oil company in play by actively seeking buyers. Icahn naturally was one of the few expressing any interest. But he needed serious financial backing for the deal because it was certainly too large to be financed solely by bank loans. Phillips responded by saying that it would not consider a bid unless Icahn could show the necessary financing was in place, a tactic the oil company was sure would be both diplomatic and realistic at the same time. Icahn then asked Drexel for a firm commitment for the backing, in effect pledging the securities firm's capital to the deal. At first Drexel balked because of the risks it would be assuming, but after negotiating with Icahn, it agreed to produce a letter stating that it was "highly confident" that financing would immediately follow. The Air Fund's bluff had been called and Drexel responded with a reasonable solution. The tender offer for Phillips was made, half in cash and half in debt securities. Drexel provided the financing after the offer was made. Wall Street was agog over the offer because it was believed to be the first ever made without financing already in place. (In reality, Clarence Dillon's offer for Dodge in the 1920s actually held the distinction.)

Critics maintained that the bid was nothing more than a bluff to force up the price of the stock so that Icahn's holdings would rise in price. The chairman of Phillips, which responded to Icahn with its own reorganization plan, referred to the company's plan as a "real bird in the hand," while characterizing Icahn's as a "potentially empty bush." Drexel was pleased because it was to be paid $7.5 million for agreeing to finance the deal, regardless of the eventual outcome. Almost as soon as the potential target company was identified, politics entered the discussion as well. Fred Joseph, a Drexel executive, went out of his way to state that "virtually no savings and loan institutions are involved in this financing." He was referring to the S&Ls' ability to buy corporate securities under the Garn-St Germain Act of 1982. The Senate Banking Committee, chaired by Senator William Proxmire, a Democrat from Wisconsin, immediately asked the Federal Home Loan Bank Board to investigate to see whether Joseph's remarks were correct.[13] Politics and finance clashed many times during the 1980s, especially after the liberalization of the banking laws for S&Ls.

Phillips continued to battle and finally won the day. Icahn dropped his bid when the company offered to buy back its own shares for $4.5 billion in new securities. It then offered to compensate him for his efforts, paying him $25 million of what were described as "expenses" in order to go away. When added to the profit on his holdings, the foray netted him around $35 million, most of it in greenmail. Most commentators agreed that if Icahn had gained control of the company it probably would have been liquidated. The case for liquidating was probably stronger in the oil industry than in other industries because of the rapid growth of many of the oil companies in the 1970s and 1980s and the many structural problems in the industry as a result. Whatever problems Icahn did not emphasize would be picked up by other raiders, especially Boone Pickens, whose specialty was oil.

The Phillips deal was something of a watershed for Wall Street in that it officially proclaimed the arrival of Icahn, Drexel and Milken, and junk bonds in general. The arrival of all three parties at the same time provided a mixed message, however. Junk bonds rightly would be hailed as a new form of financing for less than investment grade companies enabling them to tap the capital markets rather than rely on bank lines of credit that proved expensive and relatively short term. But no one envisaged them being used in predatory takeovers. Previously, when a raider made overtures to a company, it was often clear that the intent was greenmail rather than an actual takeover because of the lack of deep pockets. Now, raiders were using junk bonds to refinance their bank loans and the rules of the game were changing. Buying junk bonds now allowed investors to bet on the success of a raider, something that could only be accomplished previously by speculating in stock. Regardless of the impact of junk, corporate America was not yet ready to roll over for raiders. Proxy fights would continue as they had in the past.

By 1984, the results of renewed interest in the stock market and the effects of years of inflation began to manifest themselves. The Phillips bid was the third-largest ever made for an American company. The other two also were consummated that year when DuPont acquired Conoco while Chevron and Gulf oil also merged. Oil exploration and drilling was an extremely sensitive political issue since the United States was both the world's largest importer of oil as well as one of the largest producers. If regulators attempted to block the mergers, regardless of the aims of the raiders, they could be seen as impeding the consolidation of the industry and putting the nation at risk. Against this background, raiding was easier, especially if a merger appeared to be more horizontal than vertical.

One large traditional industry was deregulated in the late 1970s, making it attractive to takeover bids. During the Carter administration, airlines had been deregulated and their routes and price structures were liberalized. Much of the deregulation was accomplished while Alfred Kahn, a former Cornell economics professor, was chairman of the Civil Aeronautics Board and later as Carter's chief inflation fighter. As a result, less price fixing was found in the industry and competition was encouraged. After the new measures began to be felt, the industry was eyed by raiders as a potential gold mine because its routes, analogous to an oil company's reserves, were worth their weight in gold, especially if they could be preserved and consolidated.

Within a few months of the Phillips bid, Icahn announced his intention to acquire TWA, one of the largest transatlantic air carriers. The company's reaction was predictable. TWA's chairman described Icahn as a threat to the company, classifying his announcement as an "extortionate greenmail scheme." In 1985, he met Icahn in the bar at the Waldorf-Astoria in New York to discuss the takeover. The session ended with the two trading insults about each other's motives and intents. TWA then mounted a counterattack. Using its status as a regulated carrier, the airline asked the Department of Transportation to launch an inquiry and to prevent Icahn from any further action until the inquiry was finished. For his part, the raider stated that he would not accept greenmail and that his offer would be all cash. That would change as the battle for control became protracted and the airline's financial position began to deteriorate. If Icahn won control, it would be the second company he actually would own.

Icahn gained control of TWA after wresting it from the hands of

Frank Lorenzo, the chairman of Texas International Airlines. Both men sought the company and at first TWA appeared to prefer Lorenzo. But the airline's unions were not fond of Lorenzo because previously he had used Chapter 11 bankruptcy proceedings at Continental Airlines to fend off union demands for higher wages and benefits. Using bankruptcy in that manner became common in the 1980s although it often incurred the wrath of workers and unions. As a result, Icahn began to look like a white knight to the unions and they eventually struck a deal with him rather than Lorenzo. TWA moved in court to block the takeover, claiming Icahn was planning to fire thousands of employees once he gained control. The bid eventually was successful after the interim battle with Lorenzo, and Icahn formally took control of TWA in January 1986, holding 52 percent of its stock. The remaining shareholders were bought out using preferred stock, deviating from the original proposal. Drexel vowed to raise an additional $750 million for future financings. Drexel again used the term "highly confident" when describing its ability to help raise the necessary cash. The additional money was clearly necessary because TWA began announcing losses, estimated to be around $150 million for the year. Icahn was quick to make a deal with the pilots' union for concessions while he agreed not to sell his own shares in the company before September 1987. However, the flight attendants' union could not reach agreement with him and began to picket the next Predators' Ball that occurred in Los Angeles. After following many TWA and Drexel executives around carrying banners, some of the attendants were finally invited to attend the festivities under the assumption that it was ungentlemanly to leave them on the street picketing when they could come to the party with everyone else. But after a year, the troublesome flight attendants were replaced en masse with new, cheaper hires. When asked if he minded being disliked, without any apparent friends in the business, Icahn once responded, "If you want a friend, buy a dog." More revealing were remarks made at his country estate as the TWA battle was nearing completion. Icahn stated that, "I'm a man of commerce, I like making money. I'm not telling you I'm Robin Hood. The poor widows of this world aren't my responsibility."[14]

Throughout the episode, Drexel represented Lorenzo while Icahn chose Paine Webber to raise the financing for the buyout. In a classic example of how the tide had changed on Wall Street over the years, Icahn required Paine Webber to place $1 million in an escrow account in the event that the firm was not able to raise the money in timely fashion. As it turned out, the firm could not sell all of the junk bonds and Drexel stepped in to fashion its own financing. Adding insult to injury, Icahn kept the deposit. Paine Webber's only consolation was that Drexel allowed it to be a co-manager of the new deal, but at much lower fees than it originally would have received.[15] The affair showed how far competition had come on Wall Street. It would have been unimaginable before World War II that deal makers would be dictating terms to investment bankers. But now that they had become separated and Wall Street had become more democratized with many investment bankers on the playing field, those who could dictate the terms of a deal were in the driver's seat. Finance capital now took a backseat to strong personalities. They were no longer joined at the hip, although they were still mentioned in the same breath.

If the change in the course of Wall Street history was not yet totally evident, Icahn's next deal certainly showed how the once mighty had fallen. Within months of cementing the TWA deal, Icahn was back in action in October 1986, making an $8 billion bid for the USX Corp., formerly U.S. Steel. The size of the deal would have made it the third-largest in U.S. history, behind DuPont-Conoco and Chevron-Gulf. The newly named company had extensive interests in both steel and oil production, although its fortunes were slipping. Steelmakers in particular were having a difficult time in the 1980s because of foreign competition, and oil prices were falling after hitting record highs several years before. U.S. Steel acquired Marathon Oil in 1982 for what was a record at the time, $6.5 billion. It later acquired Texas Oil & Gas in 1986, after which it changed its name officially to USX. Other raiders, such as Boone Pickens, had been showing some interest in the company, but Icahn's offer was the first firm one.

Attracting raiders made USX nervous and the company was

contemplating restructuring as a result. Goldman Sachs was advising on the terms and conditions of the defense. Icahn then sent a letter to USX's board in which he stated, "It appears that an alternative to a restructuring might be the optimal way to enhance shareholder value." Understanding well what that implied, USX naturally became very nervous. Drexel again stated that it was "highly confident" that it could produce the financing necessary. Icahn could have used the resources of both TWA and ACF, and he indicated his desire to renegotiate with the company's unions as soon as possible. His letter also indicated the usual political reasons necessary to keep shareholders and congressional critics at bay. It stated further that "Such arrangements . . . make US Steel and the domestic steel industry more competitive with foreign producers and provide greater opportunities for USX's employees."[16]

Still the largest steelmaker, USX decided to fight back. The company redeemed a very large number of bonds due by borrowing new notes to redeem them. Details of the borrowing gave buyers of the new notes the right to put them back to the company or to redeem them if USX were taken over by an outside party. So if Icahn was successful, the investors could immediately have demanded their money back, placing him under severe financial pressure almost immediately. USX fashioned itself an effective shark repellent and Icahn's shares did not appreciate as he hoped after his announcement to end his bid. In the early 1990s, USX divided itself into three publicly traded entities and, as a result, fell out of the Dow Industrial Average after 90 years. But its fortunes were better than those of LTV, which fashioned itself into a major steel producer using Jones & Laughlin as its engine of growth after the Ling era. The company filed for Chapter 11 bankruptcy protection in 1986, the first of what would become two filings, the other following in 2001.

After 1981, the Reagan administration made it clear that the merger boom would not be impeded by its Justice Department. In a classic laissez-faire attitude, mergers were seen as the natural outcome of efficiency and economies of scale rather than self-indulgent exercises by raiders with deep pockets supporting them. One thing that potential raiders did not have to fear was regulatory interference. They were free to threaten potential targets, and the risk arbitrageurs that made a living following their deals felt comfortable taking large simultaneous long and short positions betting on the outcomes.[17]

MORE BEAR HUGGING

Another classic greenmailer of the 1980s was T. Boone Pickens, whose forays into oil badly rattled the industry and made him a fortune. Rising oil prices in the 1970s and the accompanying inflation made many of the oil companies easy targets. They differed greatly in the amount of reserves held and the costs of producing a barrel. Inflation had made them valuable properties, but, as with all companies acquiring assets in the 1960s and early 1970s, their asset values and market prices often did not match. The oil business was capital intensive and, like many other industries that required large doses of capital investment, varied greatly in quality and efficiency. Pickens, trained as a petroleum engineer, recognized the discrepancies early and embarked on a career of raiding.

Thomas Boone Pickens was born in Oklahoma in 1928 and studied geology at Oklahoma State. After graduation, he joined Phillips Petroleum as a geologist but quickly became disenchanted with the company. During his early years at the company, he often rode a bicycle to work to save money and frequently went squirrel hunting to save money at the grocery store. He endured the company bureaucracy for a few years before realizing he did not have a geologist's temperament and left to become a wildcatter, finding several oil wells of his own. Using money made from the discoveries, in 1964 he founded his own company, Mesa Petroleum, located in Amarillo, Texas. The company became the vehicle through which he planned many of his future raids. Unfortunately, his first attempt at a takeover proved to be a personal disaster, but it was not a mistake that would be repeated.

Pickens made his first takeover attempt in 1976 when he bid $22 per share for Aztec Oil and Gas Co. The stock was currently selling at $15 per share. But Pickens blundered by not accumulating any stock before he made his offer. Aztec, about the same size as Mesa, defended itself by hiring Goldman Sachs as its investment banker, and the Wall Street firm immediately went looking for a better offer. It soon found one in Southland Royalty, another competitor whose name was not exactly a household term, even in the oil business. The new bid of $32 per share was successful. Not owning any stock, Pickens was left completely out of the deal after putting the company in play. He later remarked somewhat matter-of-factly, "We should have been more aggressive on that one."

Aggressiveness on behalf of shareholders in the oil industry became a Pickens hallmark during the 1980s. He was motivated by the fact that he believed the oil companies were sitting on what reserves they had acquired, managing them poorly. If oil consumption continued at its current pace, reserves would run dry and shareholders would be faced with bankrupt companies. Pickens often proposed breaking up the companies that were the worst managers of their assets, putting revenue from the sale of oil into a trust for the shareholders. At an investors' meeting in 1983, he told the assembled in no uncertain terms, "If companies continue to deplete reserves without replacing them, which the domestic oil industry has been doing since 1970, shareholders are facing the liquidation of their assets."[18] Given that attitude, seeking to break up a company to preserve and enhance the value of its assets seemed like an altruistic gesture rather than a raiding technique.

Aggressive bidding came much more naturally after the initial failure. Bear hugging, also practiced by Carl Icahn, became a natural for Pickens.[19] The takeover bid that made him a familiar name in the early 1980s was for oil giant Cities Service. Pickens recognized that the company was worth more in parts than it was as a whole and enlisted the help of Flom in the deal. Being an oilman by training did not carry much weight with the target company, for Cities Service realized that Pickens was interested in its assets but not in their current corporate form. Pickens had financial allies that could help him raise the necessary capital for such a large takeover, but they were not the usual Wall Street banks. Pools were used, much as they were by KKR in its acquisitions. One participant was the Southland Corporation, owner of the 7-Eleven convenience food stores and the Madison Fund, the closed-end mutual fund for which Henry Kravis once worked. But whether they could raise enough capital for Pickens in such a large venture was questionable because Cities' assets were six times larger than those of Mesa. Pickens made no mistakes this time and filed with the SEC when Mesa acquired a 5 percent interest in the company.

The next step in the takeover bid was totally unexpected. Advised by Lehman Brothers and First Boston, Cities Service in 1982 made a counterbid to take over Mesa. Pickens responded by offering $50 per share in cash for half of Cities' stock, offering to buy the rest for securities. He reckoned that he would be getting Cities' assets relatively cheap; the bid would have captured its oil reserves at $5 per barrel, $10 below the cost of exploring and drilling for it. The proceedings then turned hostile. After rejecting the bid, Pickens made another at a lower price for the other half of the Cities shares. Not to be outdone, Cities rejected the bid and raised its offer for Mesa.

Bidding and counterbidding between companies in the same line of business, suggesting horizontal combinations, did not run much risk during the early years of the Reagan administration. The administration's first head of the Antitrust Division of the Justice Department was William Baxter, formerly a professor of law and economics at Stanford, who employed economic analysis of potential mergers to determine their harm or benefits. The standard, known as *economic rationality*, considered each potential merger on its own merits rather than on a predetermined set of principles. Oil company mergers or dismemberments were not considered potentially harmful horizontal combinations because the economics of redistributing assets could easily outweigh any negative benefits.

The Mesa–Cities Service battle certainly satisfied the new criteria and regulatory issues never became prominent in the battle. Cities Service recognized that it needed a white knight to rescue it from Mesa and sent its investment bankers out to find one. Gulf Oil was approached and emerged as a logical bidder for Cities. The company bid $63 per share for Cities' stock—$13 above Mesa's bid—and won control. Pickens backed away because he could certainly not afford to match or exceed the offer. But the drama was far from over. Mesa then was informed by First Boston, Cities' investment banker, that the larger company was still thinking of taking over Mesa as a preemptive measure. Rather than sell his Cities stock at a profit, Pickens was being presented with the obstacle of being taken over himself and also paying a $35 million penalty if he chose to sell. Takeover was being used as a threat against him. The penalty suggested by Cities Service was seen as pure vindictiveness against Pickens for his temerity. But the oilman was having none of it. "The $35 million penalty was to teach me a lesson for trying to play in a league with the big boys," he said afterward, "But there was no way I was going to pay Cities a damn thing."[20]

As it turned out, Pickens kept a $30 million profit and Gulf backed away from the merger. Cities Service, after some reluctance, merged instead with Armand Hammer's Occidental Petroleum, considered financially weaker than Gulf. But Pickens was not finished. He bid for another oil company, General American Oil Co. of Texas, buying a 3 percent stake before selling it to Phillips for a reported $45 million profit. Then he turned his attention to Gulf, the erstwhile white knight. Also buying a 3 percent stake in the company, his bid seemed like a minuscule threat since Gulf had $30 billion in sales, 75 times those of Mesa. The share price was increasing rapidly at the time and a total takeover was out of the question, although the stake did put the company in play. Merging with Gulf and keeping it intact was not practical; a breakup of the company was more feasible.

Gulf attempted to defend itself by moving to Delaware, where its corporate voting structure could be changed to thwart Pickens. For his part, Pickens remained true to his original philosophy of preserving corporate value for shareholders, not management. "There has to be somebody to look after the stockholders' interest," he stated, "they make me out to be some kind of horned monster that's come in breathing fire and cause them all these troubles . . . I consider myself very much to be a stockholders' advocate."[21] While all the oil companies knew Pickens's philosophy, most considered it an elaborate populist excuse for raiding. That fear was only confirmed when he raised his offer to $65 per share in the winter of 1984 by picking up an additional 8 percent of the stock. Two months later, he persuaded the Penn Central Corp., the former railroad that declared bankruptcy in 1978, to help finance the proposed takeover. But the effort was wasted when Gulf agreed to be taken over by a friendlier rival, the Standard Oil Co. of California, or Chevron. For its part, the Penn Central would have benefited if a split-up of Gulf still occurred and it could have negotiated for some of its properties, which would have complemented its own holdings. As it turned out, the winning bid that Gulf accepted from Standard was $80 per share, which Pickens estimated to have put an extra $6.5 billion into shareholders' pockets. He recalled that he later spoke at a gathering in Louisiana where a man walked up to him and gave him a big hug. "You must be a Gulf shareholder," Pickens said to him, "How many shares did you own?" "Five thousand," was the reply. "I was glad it wasn't 10,000," Pickens recalled, "He might have kissed me."[22]

Pickens maintained his philosophy despite the detractors and the charges of unbridled greed. In 1985, *BusinessWeek* ran a cover story entitled "The Raiders," featuring the known array of suspects. It prompted a letter to the editor from Pickens, who wrote, "I believe that label is now an unshakable association. However, I don't consider it an albatross . . . this role is long overdue in American business. Growing shareholder discontent clearly reveals that."[23] At the time, he was reported to be stalking USX, not for the steel business but for Marathon Oil, which J. P. Morgan's old company had wrestled from Mobil in a separate takeover battle several years before.

Activities in the oil industry, among others, spawned several rounds of congressional hearings about the merger trend. At a hearing held in 1985, Fred Hartley, the chairman of Unocal, gave congressmen his interpretation of the trend and its potential harm. At the time, Pickens already had accumulated almost 14 percent of the company's stock but had not yet announced his intentions for the future. Hartley was very specific about what was causing the trend, especially in the oil industry. "Pickens has somehow created a speculative frenzy—his modern version of a South Sea Bubble—that has convinced many on Wall Street that there's easy money to be made in attacking oil companies, and the hell with tomorrow," Hartley said. "But this bubble—like all bubbles—will eventually collapse, leaving wreckage of ruined companies, lost jobs, reduced U.S. oil production, failed banks and S&Ls and government bailouts," he concluded, showing clearly how he felt about the trend, not to mention being a target.[24]

Regardless of opinions about Pickens' motives and usefulness, he did help restructure the oil industry after the price increases of the late 1970s and early 1980s. Although he made more money from greenmail than from actually taking over and operating companies, he remained within his orbit of expertise and did not venture outside, as did Icahn and others. But that would not mollify his detractors, who claimed that he was practicing techniques that could easily destroy an industry vital to the national economy. Could the market economy resist such blatant attempts to extort—or extract, as the case might have been—such large amounts of money simply to prove that accounting had valued many corporate assets on the low side?

OIL AND WATER

During the decade of takeover attempts on oil companies, the travails of Texaco were among the best known. The industry clearly was due for a shakeout and consolidation after Pickens made attempts on some of the less efficient companies. The company spent the better part of the decade looking over its corporate shoulder at potential takeover targets and raiders. By the time the interest finally subsided, it was becoming more clear that the raiders indeed were able to spot companies with intrinsic financial weaknesses worth exploiting.

In 1982, the Bass brothers of Fort Worth, Texas—Sid, Edward, Robert, and Lee—began accumulating stock in Texaco. Rumors abounded in the markets that they had accumulated close to 20 percent, making Texaco very nervous, because they too eyed the larger, inefficient oil companies as potential breakup candidates. Texaco was in the process of buying the Getty Oil Co. of California, a merger that would cost it dearly over the next several years. As a result, it decided to buy out the brothers' stake in 1984 for almost 10 percent more than the current market price, totaling $1.3 billion. That represented a profit of about $400 million, an amount that Boone Pickens referred to as "a whopper." Coming on top of the $10.3 billion it paid for Getty, Texaco became highly leveraged. The company was vulnerable on two counts, although anyone interested in taking it over would probably have to strip its assets almost immediately to pay off debt.

Texaco's problems began with the purchase of Getty. The Getty family decided to sell its stake in the company and first agreed to sell it to Pennzoil, a smaller company. In December 1983, Pennzoil announced an unsolicited offer to purchase up to 20 percent of the stock. Pennzoil thought it had a deal but then discovered that the Getty board had decided to sell to Texaco instead. Texaco was advised by First Boston, notably with Wasserstein and Perella spearheading the deal. Pennzoil claimed that it had been misled and filed suit against Texaco. In late 1985, a jury in Houston awarded Pennzoil a staggering $10.5 billion in damages. Texaco was put in a precarious position when it needed to post a bond while it appealed the decision. Worried that the bond could total in the billions, the company began threatening to file for Chapter 11 bankruptcy protection. In addition to the threat, the lawsuit touched off dozens of different lawsuits from both companies and shareholders, all claiming that some part of the deal caused them financial harm.

It became clear that a settlement between the two companies was in their best interests, but it did not materialize quickly. While they continued to discuss their options, the waters became murkier when Carl Icahn announced that he had purchased a sizable chunk of Texaco's stock from Australian financier Robert Holmes Court in late 1987. In filings with the SEC, Icahn disclosed that he paid $348 million for the stock and then bought another $193 million on the open market. To hedge his bet, he also bought a stake in Pennzoil. The two companies quickly realized that it was in their best interests to settle as soon as possible.

Just before Christmas 1987, the companies announced that they had reached an agreement. Texaco was to pay Pennzoil $3 billion in cash in lieu of the $10.3 billion jury price tag. The case was still being appealed at the time. Icahn reportedly was not included in the details of the settlement, although he clearly had already made millions on the stock, since he was at the time Texaco's largest shareholder. Within a few weeks, he objected to the plan, threatening to undermine it if certain conditions were not met. He filed suit to block the $3 billion agreement. After more posturing, Icahn made a formal proposal to Texaco in May 1988 to merge with TWA for $14.5 billion, which would have been the largest deal to date. As part of his takeover plans, Icahn told Texaco directors that he wanted to sell two major subsidiaries, indicating that he wanted to actually own the company as he did TWA. "We intend to maintain Texaco's core business and return it to its rightful place as a leader in its industry, just as we have done with TWA," he wrote to the directors.[25] Not everyone was convinced, however.

After months of wrangling, Icahn became more aggressive and threatened a new proxy fight if Texaco directors did not see things his way. He contemplated offering $60 per share for the stock and told institutional investors that he would have no trouble raising the $14 billion needed to complete the deal. But also involved in the deal was KKR, the second-largest shareholder in Texaco at the time, and it cast its vote for the current management, thwarting Icahn's proxy battle. Although he lost the battle, he continued to purchase stock into early 1989 so that his holdings were 16 percent. Then he signed a standstill agreement with Texaco in which he promised to leave the company alone for a seven-year period. But after several more months of infighting, he gave up his stake and sold his shares for $2.1 billion, his largest deal to date. Naturally, the amount of the sale caused endless speculation on Wall Street about his next target, since the war chest was becoming larger after each successive deal. The next consensus target was USX, which had sizable energy holdings in addition to its steel operations.

Although decades had elapsed since the days of the legendary financial capitalists, merger activity in the 1970s and 1980s still was dominated to a large extent by a cult of personality. Other large mergers were identified as deals initiated by raiders and would forever be associated with them. The second-largest deal of the 1980s was the merger between drug makers Beecham of Britain and Smithkline of the United States, valued at $16 billion in 1989. It was the best example to date of a major cross-border merger, eclipsing those between British Petroleum and Standard Oil of Ohio and between Grand Metropolitan and Pillsbury in size. But it paled in news coverage when compared to a much smaller transaction that deal maker Ronald Perelman fashioned when he successfully took over cosmetics maker Revlon in 1985. He had already acquired the Consolidated Cigar Co. and Pantry Pride, the supermarket chain, having used Drexel to raise junk bonds for his efforts. A larger junk issue led to the Revlon takeover, which brought a well-known consumer brand to the headlines.

The 1980s were not entirely about mergers, because the largest corporate breakup in history also took place in 1984. The behemoth, and much admired, AT&T finally consented to a divestiture of the regional Baby Bells that formed the basic infrastructure of its system while keeping its manufacturing and research companies. The telephone giant had lasted from the early 1920s, when the company was handed a virtual monopoly over telephone services by the government. In the 60 intervening years, Ma Bell had become something of a lumbering giant characterized by a massive bureaucracy and extremely conservative management. It also was acknowledged to produce the finest phone services but it did so in an unusually clumsy manner.

Beginning in the 1970s, AT&T's monopoly was challenged by an unlikely competitor—MCI, a small phone company that wanted access to AT&T's transmission lines. The case wound its way through the courts and became highly politicized, drawing comment from almost every conceivable quarter. *United States v. AT&T* became the best-known antitrust case since the Standard Oil and American Tobacco cases 70 years before. Finally in 1982 AT&T consented to the breakup, which had been pressed by William Baxter when he became head of the Antitrust Division of the Justice Department under Ronald Reagan.[26] After the dismemberment, the seven new phone companies, along with the new competitors in long distance, provided a new bonanza for investment bankers since they now all needed to fund their capital needs separately in the market, outside of AT&T's tutelage. As soon as AT&T announced the settlement with the Justice Department in 1982, MCI brought a junk bond to market through Milken and Drexel Burnham, raising money for the new regulation-free environment that would appear as soon as AT&T was forced to compete with others in long distance service.

THREE TIMES OVER

The "Decade of Greed" was known for big deals and ostentatious displays of wealth by Wall Street, but the biggest deal of them all made previous takeover attempts by Icahn, Pickens, and other raiders look small in comparison. Of all the buyout and takeover specialists, KKR had the best pedigree and the best track record to date. But the sheer size of its coup de grace in the takeover sweepstakes made the firm's principals Wall Street legends, without the heavy baggage acquired by Icahn and Drexel Burnham.

During the mid-1980s, KKR acquired a number of various companies in all sorts of businesses but made several acquisitions in retailing that gave it more public exposure than it normally would have anticipated. In 1986, it acquired Beatrice Foods, which had recently taken over Esmark—a retailer that KKR previously bid for unsuccessfully—and Safeway Stores. Beatrice counted familiar brands within its stable, including Tropicana Orange Juice and Avis Rent A Car, the well-traveled company that had been the apple of more than one conglomerator's eye over the years. Beatrice was its most expensive acquisition to date at $6.2 billion, while Safeway cost $4.8 billion. Both were financed in traditional KKR manner—by using a combination of equity, usually obtained from funds organized for the purpose of a deal and sold to institutional investors; bank loans; and (now) junk bonds arranged by Drexel. One of the methods KKR employed to entice bankers to loan it such large sums involved offering them a $1 million bonus pool if they signed up for a loan early. Borrowing a familiar term, KKR dubbed the bonuses "early bird specials," realizing that the prospect of earning such a large up-front fee appealed to most bankers, who could claim it as a quick source of revenue for their banks. Beatrice was bought out by combining a small amount of equity with an enormous amount of debt so that the company's new capital structure was 95 percent leveraged. As a result, it had to be pared down substantially after being acquired. If not, the heavy debt load would prove unsustainable over time. Many of its divisions were sold, often to management of subsidiaries, proving that one LBO could lead to another.

While Beatrice was dismembered with relatively little fanfare, the same could not be said for Safeway. The retail grocery chain was not as old as A&P, but it had been a familiar landmark among American shoppers since the 1920s and 1930s, when it was controlled by Charles Merrill, better known as the founder of Merrill Lynch. The 2,400-store chain, owned by a family investment group, suffered a greenmail raid in 1986 by the Haft brothers of the Dart Group while the company was in the midst of revamping many of its stores and eliminating money-losing divisions. Then KKR made its bid and gained control in 1986, again using the same package of financing that had become standard. The company was refloated in 1990 and sold for four times what KKR had invested in it, making it one of the more profitable ventures. But the public sale ignited controversy when the *Wall Street Journal* ran articles on Safeway that cast KKR in less than a flattering light. The firm was portrayed as motivated only by money and ruthless efficiency at the cost of Safeway employees and shareholders.

The new Safeway had accomplished the objectives that KKR envisaged, but the costs appeared to be great. Sixty-three thousand employees were fired, although many were rehired at lower wages with fewer benefits. The local economy in Dallas, where Safeway had its headquarters, suffered, and several suicides and deaths of longtime employees due to depression over losing their jobs were recorded as a result of the buyout. While both sides pressed their cases for or against the LBO, the deal makers did extremely well. Top Safeway executives earned $28 million after KKR took over, the Haft brothers of the Dart Company netted $100 million through their greenmail (paid by KKR), investment banks working on the deal made $65 million, and their corporate lawyers reaped another $25 million. The buyout firm also profited handsomely from up-front fees. Safeway was charged

$60 million for the restructuring and the KKR partners put up only around 1 percent, or $2 million, of the equity in return for a 20 percent share of future profits. Despite the stinging criticism, Henry Roberts maintained that the idea that many were suffering for the benefit of a few was not true. "Our 70 limited partners represent retired teachers, sanitation workers and firemen," he argued "and 80 percent of our profits go to them."[27]

Roberts was referring to the investment pools set up to invest in KKR's deals. The fact that many pension funds happened to be in the pools did not exactly mean that KKR was investing on behalf of them in more than an indirect manner. Regardless of the criticism, KKR naturally expected to find itself under scrutiny in 1990 because of the mammoth deal it had engineered to buy RJR Nabisco and take it private several years earlier. The deal was the largest in history and made the firm an international reputation almost overnight. After it was consummated, kind words for the deal would be few except in business school cases using the firm as an example of efficient corporate restructuring.

The buyout of RJR Nabisco marked a turning point for KKR because, unlike most of the firm's earlier deals, it was a hostile rather than an amicable takeover. The change in tactics forced Jerome Kohlberg to retire from the firm in the later 1980s because he disagreed with the switch although his name was retained on the letterhead. Several potential bidders were interested in the tobacco and foods company, at the time the nineteenth-largest company in the country. Many were interested for the fees charged for their services alone. KKR charged its investors a management fee of 1.5 percent on the amount of the deal and another transaction fee upon completion. That amounted to about $120 million on Beatrice, while on Safeway it came to about half that amount. Since RJR Nabisco was clearly much larger than the other two combined, the potential fees became a magnet for all sorts of offers.

Kravis first approached RJR Nabisco chairman Ross Johnson about a potential buyout. In 1986 KKR recognized that RJR Nabisco had enormous cash flow but was otherwise poorly managed and that there was great potential to reduce the scope of its operations. Over a year later in October 1988, Johnson decided to take the company private himself and signed on Shearson Lehman to help him make an offer to stockholders. Johnson assumed that the company was worth $75 per share, valuing it at $17 billion, making it the largest buyout or merger ever attempted. The bid was acknowledged to be low even by Johnson, who remarked, "My job is to negotiate the best deal I can for my people."[28] Unfortunately for him, by *people* he meant the management buyout team, not shareholders. The low bid illustrated that management buyouts were designed to be in the interests of bidders, not the owners of the company. Shortly thereafter, KKR made a counterbid at $90 per share, valuing the company at around $20 billion. RJR Nabisco now was fully in play and attracted other outside bidders, including First Boston and Ted Forstmann of Forstmann Little, a smaller buyout firm.

The bidding was dramatically played out in the press. The nineteenth-largest American company was being attacked by a small boutique firm with six partners and a handful of employees. Anyone not acquainted with the LBO trend was clearly confused. No one could remember such an agglomeration of financial power since the earlier part of the century. But this was part of KKR's mystique. Ross Johnson, by contrast, was portrayed as a greedy CEO who wanted to seize his company from long-suffering shareholders. True, his bid of $75 was above the market price but it was widely viewed as still being too low, especially in the face of KKR's $90 offer. Johnson even made the cover of *Time* under the banner "A Game of Greed." It was assumed that his bid would give him a personal fortune of $100 million, considered extreme for a CEO even during the Decade of Greed. Despite suspicions and envy about KKR, the firm began to look like something of white knight compared with Johnson and his advisers at Shearson Lehman.

Other traditional M&A advisers also played a role in the drama. Bankers from Lazard Freres and Dillon Read advised RJR's board of directors and were already familiar with KKR since they had represented Beatrice to them in the past. But in the end, KKR's reputation came to the fore and helped win the bid. The $109-per-share final bid was lower than the $112 offered by Johnson and Shearson, but the depth and strength of KKR's investors won the day. The total price of the bid was $26 billion, and KKR agreed to assume the $5 billion of debt RJR Nabisco already had outstanding. The complicated deal called for shareholders to be paid in cash and preferred stock. The cash was raised by a combination of bank lines arranged by a large syndicate of KKR lenders, the equity pools, and junk bonds issued through Drexel. Adding existing debt to the total brought the buyout to $31 billion. Ninety percent of the deal was financed by borrowed money, and it was clear from the outset that new CEO Louis Gerstner would have to begin an asset sale to reduce the company's size almost immediately.

But the fact remained that the deal proved to be the most lucrative ever for deal makers and added a new dimension to the old term *finance capitalism*. The banks that extended financing to the deal grossed $325 million, Drexel Burnham grossed $227 million, Merrill Lynch took in $109 million, Dillon Read and Lazard grossed $14 million each, and Goldman made $47 million on the restructuring while KKR itself took $75 million in up-front fees. In 1995, when common stock in Nabisco Holdings again was sold to the public, Goldman Sachs grossed $46 million in the $1 billion offering.[29]

Ironically, the biggest deal of all time also brought an end to the LBO trend of the 1980s. Many of the deals worked well because the economy improved after 1983. The lack of a recession and low interest rates helped finance many of the deals. But the 1987 stock market collapse put many future deals on hold even though many of the LBOs used debt financing almost exclusively. The prospect that the market downturn would cause a recession struck fear into the hearts of many regulators and businessmen. With a mountain of corporate debt outstanding, what would happen if many companies were finally faced with an economic downturn and less revenue with which to pay their interest? Junk companies notoriously had erratic operating incomes that could quickly put their debt service ability in doubt. The unsettling prospects were partially to blame for the market rout in October 1987, 58 years after the Crash of 1929.

NEUTRON TACTICS

The 1980s were characterized by raiders, LBOs, and big deals, but other M&A philosophies also were being practiced on a successful level. Perhaps the most successful led to the creation, or recreation, of a diversified company that became the stock market darling of the 1990s' bull market. The reshaping of General Electric in the 1980s was both a refinement of the diversification principles of previous decades and a harsh realization that property was more important than people, at least in shareholders' eyes.

The original GE was a Morgan-inspired company founded in the nineteenth century that became one of the first components of the Dow Jones Industrial Average. By the end of the twentieth century, it was the only original Dow stock still included in the index and also had the distinction of being the world's most highly capitalized company. The company's growth and relentless emphasis on efficiency were the result of the tenure of Jack Welch as its CEO. Bucking the trend of the decade, Welch concentrated on fixing his company from the inside out rather than engaging in the more popular Wall Street techniques of the day. The results were phenomenal, and Wall Street quickly embraced Welch as the most highly touted executive since Alfred Sloan at GM.

Welch assumed the helm of GE in 1981. An engineer by training, he received a PhD in chemical engineering from the University of Illinois and joined GE immediately after graduating in 1960. He steadily climbed the corporate ladder at GE over the years, succeeding at a variety of jobs before being named CEO. Within four years, he presided over one of the most dizzying acquisitions and divestiture programs in corporate history. In that period, he acquired more than 300 businesses as part of his plan to restructure the company before hard times caught up with it. An equally dizzying number of divestitures led to thousands of layoffs from the company, both from the worker and managerial ranks. Welch's reputation to critics became so harsh that he was nicknamed "Neutron Jack," after a bomb that killed people but left property intact. But the fallout may have been somewhat illusory since GE was still a giant in the mid-1980s, with sales of $28 billion generated by 300,000 employees.

In 1985, Welch began the process by which he would make perhaps his best-known acquisition. The RCA company, a competitor of GE in some areas and owner of the National Broadcasting Company, had fallen upon hard times due to a less than successful diversification strategy in the 1960s and 1970s and became the apple of Welch's eye. Welch asked Felix Rohatyn, a partner at Lazard Freres, to arrange a meeting with the head of RCA, Thornton Bradshaw. Rohatyn, more than happy to comply, asked Bradshaw to meet with Welch on the same evening the RCA chief had a dinner engagement at the Navy League. A bit of history was raising its head again, but the proposed deal, secretly dubbed "Island," would help create an even larger GE; more successful than anything Pierpont Morgan arranged almost 100 years before.

The deal itself was finally consummated in late 1985, mostly by lawyers working closely with GE. RCA was purchased for cash and the total bill was $6.28 billion, or $66.50 per share. Among all of its existing and acquired companies, GE now owned one of the country's premier broadcast companies. Sixty years before, it had also owned a part of the embryonic RCA before being forced to divest of its share in 1933 under an antitrust settlement. Now, in the face of increasing global pressures in electronics manufacturing especially, the company was better poised to face the challenges posed by international competition, mostly from Japan and Korea. But the acquisition of NBC was the better part of RCA as the broadcasting company had accounted for $248 million of RCA's $567 million earnings the previous year.[30]

Most of GE's acquisitions proved highly successful, but one clearly came to be troublesome to Welch and his senior management team. In 1986, the company purchased 80 percent of Wall Street investment bank Kidder Peabody. The old-line firm, founded in the nineteenth century, was slowly losing its grip on Wall Street although it still was something of a force to be reckoned with in some specialty fields, including M&A. GE had the most successful finance company in the country, GE Capital, already in its portfolio of highly successful

219

companies, and the addition of an investment bank in many ways presaged consolidations on Wall Street in the near future. But Kidder had problems not yet discovered that were to lead to its eventual sale and, finally, closing.

Within a year of the purchase, the insider trading scandal on Wall Street became public with the arrest of several prominent Wall Street M&A specialists and arbitrageurs, including Martin Siegel of Kidder. After lengthy negotiations with the U.S. Attorney and a thorough housecleaning of several top Kidder executives, the firm emerged from the scandal bloodied and somewhat bowed. But another scandal finally convinced GE to sell the firm in 1995, after almost 10 years of mediocre performance. When bond trader Joseph Jett was discovered to have been fabricating trading profits, earnings at Kidder had to be restated and the firm underwent another traumatic upheaval. In 1992 and 1993, Jett ostensibly was so successful that he earned a $9 million bonus, an amount that did not go unnoticed at the parent company along with other inflated Wall Street bonuses. Jett was subsequently fired and prosecuted, maintaining his innocence, but the affair left Welch bitter. "Having this reprehensible scheme, which violated everything we believe in and stand for, break our more than decade-long string of 'no surprises' has all of us damn mad," Welch commented when asked about the affair.[31]

Being one of GE's poor performers, Kidder was sold to Paine Webber in 1995 for $670 million. GE paid $600 million for the firm in 1986, so the 12 percent return was spread over almost 10 years. The return was not the sort that would enhance the GE stock price, averaging only slightly more than 1 percent per year. Paine Webber could not make a success of it either and absorbed the successful parts of its operations before shuttering it two years later.

Despite the relentless cost-cutting pursued by Welch in the 1980s and 1990s, GE remained a conglomerate at a time when the concept had fallen out of favor. However, unlike some of its 1960s predecessors, it was considered one of the most successful companies of the period, although much of its popularity was due to that of Welch, considered perhaps the country's best manager and CEO. Much of the acclaim was due to the fact that Welch was able to preside over such a disparate group of companies with great success while seemingly avoiding the pitfalls of the 1960s and 1970s conglomerators. High degrees of leverage never plagued GE as they did LTV or ITT, and as a result the company became the world's most highly capitalized during the late 1990s.

REACTION

Once a buyout was completed, the target firms were no longer public and were not required to divulge any financial information to the public, reducing the transparency that had prevailed before. The paring down of corporate structures and the troubles caused to employees devolved upon no one except current management, and the prospect did not please many regulators and legislators who saw this corporate surgery as bad press. American industry was having radical surgery performed while they simply sat on the sidelines and watched. But was it true surgery or only cosmetic?

The stream of big deals brought a torrent of criticism from labor and government. It seemed that Wall Street and management had teamed up to displace workers in the name of corporate greed. Thomas R. Donahue, secretary-treasurer of the AFL-CIO, invoked the name of KKR frequently as he recited a list of companies where, he claimed, 90,000 union jobs had been lost "because of mergers, takeovers and leveraged buyouts." He especially expressed concern about KKR's role in operating supermarkets, a trend that was emerging after the takeover of Beatrice Foods. As a result of LBOs, he said, KKR "winds up as the single largest employer of workers in the retail food industry," supervising 165,000 to 175,000 of 600,000 union workers. Donahue said he worried about "the long-term effect" of people from Wall Street pretending to run grocery stores.[32] It was not the first time the criticism had been heard. History again was repeating itself using the old chain store argument of the Depression years.

Another flag was raised in some quarters when KKR announced the acquisition of the failed Bank of New England by a bidding group it had assembled. The bid raised the troubling prospect of a nonfinancial company gaining control of what would have been one of the 10 largest banks in the country—control that was forbidden by the original Glass-Steagall Act of 1933. But not everyone was convinced of KKR's evil intentions. Its commitment of $283 million in a bid with the Fleet/Norstar Financial Group for the Boston-based bank illustrated the value of providing banking with well capitalized buyers from outside the financial system, bringing more funds to a capital-starved industry. John P. LaWare, a Fed governor, said, "All the regulators satisfied themselves that KKR was the medium for a group of investors, and their role is totally passive." The Fed was also satisfied, he continued, that "in no case, whatever the consequent options that might be exercised, would KKR control a bank."[33] Nevertheless, banking specialists were not convinced and suggested that the deal stretched the Fed's previously established guidelines for control.

A major criticism of the LBO and takeover trend was leveled at the Fed as well as the takeovers themselves. As deals became larger, critics maintained that the Fed was "monetizing" the trend by allowing banks to make loans on takeover deals without restriction. In short, it was printing money for the occasion. Since many of the takeovers were conducted through shell companies set up expressly for the purpose of buying another company's stock, many critics wanted the Fed to subject them to its usual margin requirements, the same rule that applied to investors who borrowed money to buy stocks. Since the margin requirement at the time was 50 percent, the proposal effectively would have limited buyouts to half their size.

The Fed proposal was limited to the shell companies—those simply established to do a deal without any other purpose. The margin requirements would apply to them alone. But Senator William Proxmire, a Democrat from Wisconsin, the senior member of the Senate Banking Committee, wanted to go further and include all junk bond financing in the margin requirement as well. An aide declared that the original Fed proposal did not go far enough. "All a T. Boone Pickens would have to do would be to put an oil well or a shopping center into the shell," he declared, in order to circumvent the Fed proposal since the company technically would no longer be a shell.[34] Clearly, the sheer size of the financing was beginning to bother regulators and legislators even before the truly enormous deals were announced a few years later. At the heart of the matter was the stock of the acquired company. By being placed it in a special-purpose shell company, it became the collateral for the bonds used to purchase it in the first place, creating a house of cards. As a result, the Fed originally proposed that it examine each junk financing on a case-by-case basis.

The leverage trend clearly worried Fed Chairman Paul Volcker. "We spend our days issuing debt and retiring equity, both in record volumes," he said, "and then we spend our evenings raising each other's eyebrows with gossip about signs of stress in the financial system." One of the individuals he had in mind clearly was Thomas Johnson, the president of Chemical Bank. Johnson mused, "I'm worried about what this leveraging will do . . . I don't know how all this debt will be serviced."[35] He worried publicly despite the fact that his bank was one of the major lenders to the buyout trend. Fretting about the problem revealed its dual nature: It was both troublesome and highly profitable at the same time. Henry Kravitz recognized the problem early and always ensured that his deals were kept separate from each other. Although KKR was becoming a major owner of corporate real estate in the mid-1980s, each deal stood or fell on its own merit. Their individual structures meant that one potential collapse would not endanger the others or bring KKR down with it.

The Fed enacted its proposal in January 1986. It was highly criticized by Wall Street and the Reagan administration, which saw it as interference in the free enterprise system. The rule limited junk bonds to only 50 percent of a takeover by a shell company, but the board decided late to apply the rule to hostile takeovers only. The Fed specifically cited Mesa Petroleum's raid on Unocal Corp. as an example of the sort of potential takeover financing that would be prohibited in the future, although the bid proved unsuccessful. Most critics conceded that the new rule was better than nothing, but Volcker was in a difficult position. Wall Street trends were not within the Fed's primary orbit unless they threatened the banking system, something excessive use of junk lending was capable of doing. But all agreed that the rule did help publicize regulators' fears, and that in itself was something of an accomplishment, especially in the light of the political criticism.

Two years later, after the initial bid for RJR Nabisco by KKR, Alan Greenspan, Paul Volcker's successor at the Fed, also made his fears about the takeover trend known. He asked the Senate Banking Committee to reconsider the tax laws so that corporate borrowing was not encouraged even more. Although the Tax Reform Act of 1986 cut the number of tax deductions possible, it left the corporate deduction for interest intact. As a result, corporate borrowing continued on its binge in the 1980s and showed no signs of abating. Greenspan wrote, "We do not fully understand why there has been such a large increase in the use of debt finance in the current decade, but I think it is widely recognized that the tax system provides some incentives toward leverage and it would be appropriate for the Congress to continue looking at the problem."[36]

Even some of the trend's major players were beginning to think twice about their own activities. One of the major legal advisers to the merger movement was Martin Lipton of New York law firm Wachtell, Lipton, Rosen & Katz. He specialized mostly in defense strategies rather than offense. One of his best-publicized inventions was the poison pill defense used by so many companies that were targets. While others were busy gobbling up companies, he spent the majority of his time fending off unwanted suitors. From his vantage point, he remarked in 1988 that he felt that "the nation is in great jeopardy by everything that is going on. We are forcing an unlivable amount of leverage on American business. We are forcing every business to focus on short-term results and we are depriving our future generations of research and development. One of these days we're going to have a tremendous crash."[37] He made the remark a year after the October 1987 stock market collapse.

The major acquisitions attorney, Joseph Flom of Skadden, Arps, Slate, Meagher, & Flom, saw the Fed's proposals in a different light. Commenting on the original shell company proposals in 1985, he wrote that many of the complaints about the junk bond and takeover movement "reflect more an aversion to change than a real concern for the soundness of the nation's financial system. And the couching of such complaints in pejorative language such as 'bust-up junk bond takeovers,' [referring to a comment made in a 1985 *Wall Street Journal* article] does little to inform and much to inflame. The Fed's proposed rule change, which represents a major departure from Federal policy, seems to have been inspired by this rhetoric."[38] The growing debate only underlined the fact that mergers had become a major policy issue, a phenomenon not seen since the late 1960s during the conglomerate craze.

Aside from political and regulatory developments, the junk bond and takeover craze also had its social side. Like their predecessors before them, many of the merger kings showed off their wealth and made large philanthropic donations. "If Jerome Kohlberg, Henry Kravis, and George Roberts aren't worth $1 billion apiece, they soon will be," proclaimed *BusinessWeek* in 1987. While the exact amounts certainly were not made public, Kravis was the most flamboyant and one of the most philanthropic. In addition to maintaining a regal lifestyle, he donated $10 million to the Metropolitan Museum of Art in New York so that the museum could build a new wing named after him. Another $10 million was donated to the Mt. Sinai Medical Center in New York. The Cornell Medical Center would also benefit from a large gift made by Sanford Weill. Icahn also made charitable contributions in the 1980s, although on a smaller scale initially. He contributed to Carnegie Hall for a much-needed renovation and to a home for abused children and a shelter for the homeless. Always aware of the philanthropy of their robber baron predecessors, the takeover barons continued the tradition, partially to soften their image with the public.

POSTSCRIPT TO THE 1980s

The stock market collapse of October 1987 temporarily derailed the takeover trend. Deals already in progress were not as badly affected as new proposals. Within two years, deals diminished significantly. Like many other merger trends before it, the 1980s binge slowed considerably as investors were forced to the sidelines. Although the trend owed more to debt than equity financing, it could not continue

225

unabated in the wake of significant investor losses and the recession that followed. Many of the fears about the Decade of Greed came to fruition shortly after the market drop. The first recession experienced in eight years left its toll on corporate balance sheets, the labor market, and investor psychology. Everyone agreed that the 1980s experienced a boom not seen for decades. Not everyone agreed that it was a good thing, however.

Before the trend slowed substantially, merger activity reached historic highs before slumping in 1989 and 1990. In 1988, takeovers reached a total of $311 billion, earning their advisers $1.3 billion in fees. And not all the deals were large. Over 3,300 were completed in that year alone. Goldman Sachs and First Boston were the top advisers for the year, followed by Shearson Lehman, Morgan Stanley, and Drexel Burnham. Wasserella, the only top firm operating as an independent, ranked sixth.[39] But the deals' success was offset by the deleterious effect the M&A trend had on the S&Ls. Many of the junk bonds issued through Drexel Burnham were placed with the thrifts, legally able to buy them since the Garn-St Germain Act in 1982. Most of the junk issues performed well during the mid-1980s, but after the market drop their revenues began to fall and their interest payments fell under a cloud. Within two years, the corporate bond market would suffer the greatest number of defaults in its history, due mainly to the nonperformance of junk bonds. That poor performance was not unexpected, nor was the damaging effect on the thrifts. They already had been discussed for several years by executives at Drexel and Fed officials.

The problem that seasoned issues of junk bonds presented proved daunting for the thrifts. The secondary market for the bonds was not particularly broad and Drexel mainly was responsible for quoting prices. When stock prices headed down, many investors began selling, creating more pressure than the sometimes thin market could bear. When the bonds began defaulting, they had to be marked down, causing the S&Ls' income statements to reflect the losses. Many of the institutions were small, and the loss forced them to the brink of insolvency because they relied on the higher-than-average interest payments for revenue. The final indignity came

226

when it became clear that the government would have to bail out the troubled thrifts in order to protect the entire banking system from even more serious problems. And no problem in the junk bond market would leave Drexel and Milken untouched. What affected the financier and his firm would have serious repercussions for the bond market as a whole.

The junk bond market took a serious blow when Milken was indicted in 1988 as a result of the insider trading scandal on Wall Street that had already claimed several victims, including arbitrageur Ivan Boesky and mergers specialists Dennis Levine and Martin Siegel. Although Milken finally paid a fine of $900 million personally while close associates paid an additional $400 million, the damage to Drexel was the most substantial of all. The SEC fined the firm $650 million for its part in Milken's activities. Since it was not a public company but was owned by its employees, the firm's capital was immediately depleted and it was forced to file bankruptcy proceedings. The penalty was the harshest ever handed down by the SEC against a securities firm and it helped put a serious damper on the junk market, both for new and existing issues.

The size of the fee imposed on Milken illustrated that the merger game had increased the size of the penalties imposed by the SEC against miscreants. While Milken was sentenced to a prison term, Drexel filed for bankruptcy because of the SEC fine. One Wall Street source noted, "Drexel Burnham Lambert's demise is a symbolic rather than a real end to an era—but it is an incredibly potent symbol."[40] That may have been an understatement, because the long-awaited recession soon materialized, putting a further damper on the junk bond market. Drexel would resurrect in a new form but would not engage in business on the same scale seen in its heyday. In the 1990s, just surviving would be an accomplishment because of its tarnished reputation.

The years leading to the recession of 1990 were stellar ones for mergers and acquisitions. In 1980, over 1,500 deals worth some $32 billion were done. The numbers rose steadily throughout the decade. By 1989, over 3,400 deals were announced, representing some $231 billion. Deal makers were also working on divestitures during the decade, earning even more fees. During the same period, divestitures rose from 104 deals worth $5 billion to over 1,100 worth $60 billion.[41] Wall Street had good reason to smile. Two percent fees on the total number of deals amounted to around $6 billion, split largely among the major mergers bankers on either side of the deals.

The worst fears about many junk bonds came true beginning in 1990. Large numbers defaulted—many more than Michael Milken had predicted 10 years before. Usually default rates on corporate bonds were about 3 percent of the outstanding amounts, but beginning late in 1990 and lasting until 1992, the rates were as high as 12 percent. In sheer numbers, 1991 proved to be the worst, with 91 issues worth $20 billion defaulting. Most telling was the industries the companies represented. Almost $4 billion alone came from retailing, a notoriously cyclical industry in the best of times. The recession cut deeply into the revenues of many retailers, and they found themselves short of cash. Included in the group were Robert Campeau's retail store empire, with Bloomingdale's being the best known of his holdings. Rumors persisted that Campeau had vastly overpaid for acquisitions in the 1980s, advised by Wasserella, but the firm constantly denied it. Carter Hawley Hale, Zale's, Circle K, and R.H. Macy also followed and had to reorganize. Financial institutions also suffered badly, with the Homestead Savings & Loan Association and the Executive Life Insurance Company also defaulting on outstanding issues. The defaults were the most numerous since the Depression.

Probably the best known default in the early 1990s was TWA, still under the control of Carl Icahn. Flush with almost $500 million in cash, Icahn had been pursuing Pan American as a potential merger partner when TWA was forced into Chapter 11. In late July 1991, Icahn offered $420 million for Pan Am after threatening to declare bankruptcy for several months. TWA's debt burden was extremely high at the time. According to the bankruptcy notice filed only a week after the Pan Am bid, Icahn offered equity to the bondholders to replace their bonds, a technique known as a prepackaged bankruptcy. He claimed that the reorganized airline would be more efficient, especially after winning concessions from its employees. But Icahn's tenure at the new TWA was to be short, and after a December agreement with the bankruptcy court, he agreed to step aside, ending his six-year relationship with the carrier as part of the reorganization plan.

With the fall of Drexel Burnham, easy money in the form of junk bonds would no longer be a viable option for many companies that had enjoyed the brief limelight in the 1980s. High-yield bonds did gain a serious foothold on Wall Street and continued to provide capital to less creditworthy companies in the future but would no longer be associated with the slick image projected by the takeover kings and their financiers. Takeovers in the 1990s would be even larger than those of the 1980s but would be lower profile. Drexel reorganized itself in 1992 after settling over $30 billion in past claims, something of a record for a firm involved in such complicated legal wrangling after its bankruptcy. But its name had been changed to protect the innocent. It was known thereafter as the New Street Capital Corp., named after the street behind the former Drexel Burnham where the firm used to pile its trash.

NOTES

1. Michael Porter, "From Competitive Advantage to Corporate Strategy," *Harvard Business Review,* May-June 1987, p. 7.
2. The new law was known technically as the Depository Institutions Deregulation and Monetary Control Act of 1980. It had two sides: one gave broader powers to the Fed and the other deregulated interest rates so that market rates could be offered, and charged, by banks.
3. George Anders, *Merchants of Debt: KKR and the Mortgaging of American Business.* (New York: Basic Books, 1992), p. 13.
4. George P. Baker and George David Smith, *The New Financial Capitalists: Kohlberg Kravis Roberts & the Creation of Corporate Value* (New York: Cambridge University Press, 1998), pp. 207–208.
5. Connie Bruck, *The Predators' Ball: The Inside Story of Drexel Burnham and the Rise of the Junk Bond Raiders* (New York: Penguin Books, 1989), p. 102.
6. Many companies decided to issue bonds in the eurobond market instead, where they could sell the new issue immediately without having to bother with SEC regulations. The process was perfectly legitimate but was eroding the SEC's authority over corporate debt issues. As a result, the SEC

began considering shelf registration, effectively speeding up the path to market and bringing the corporate bond issuing business back to New York from London, the center of the eurobond business.

7. Joseph Auerbach and Samuel L. Hayes III, *Investment Banking and Diligence: What Price Deregulation?* (Boston: Harvard Business School Press, 1986), p. 150.

8. In the fall of 1983, the SEC filed a complaint against Icahn for not registering Bayswater as an investment company, as required by SEC regulations. Icahn agreed to the SEC complaint without admitting guilt or innocence.

9. *New York Times,* December 12, 1983.

10. Bruck, p. 157.

11. *New York Times,* November 24, 1982.

12. Bruck, p. 163.

13. *New York Times,* February 16, 1985.

14. *Wall Street Journal,* June 20, 1985.

15. Bruck, p. 180.

16. *New York Times,* October 7, 1986.

17. Risk arbitrageurs came to prominence during the late 1970s and 1980s by taking positions in the shares of the targets and the acquiring companies. Usually, they would buy the stock of the target and sell short that of the buyer, locking in the difference between the two prices. Ivan Boesky properly defined this activity as "merger arbitrage" differing from classical arbitrage because securities of two companies were involved. See Ivan Boesky, *Merger Mania* (New York: Holt, Rinehart & Winston, 1985), p. 23.

18. *Business Wire,* December 16, 1983.

19. Bruce Wasserstein described bear hugging as "a common tactic for Icahn, Pickens and other takeover investors of the 1980s." Their tactics were deliberate, designed for maximum effect. As he put it, "These players viewed public agitation as an integral part of their investing process." See Bruce Wasserstein, *Big Deal: The Battle for Control of America's Leading Companies* (New York: Time Warner, 1998), p. 605.

20. T. Boone Pickens, *Boone* (Boston: Houghton Mifflin, 1987), p. 168.

21. *Christian Science Monitor,* December 2, 1983.

22. Pickens, p. 216.

23. *BusinessWeek,* March 25, 1985.

24. *Los Angeles Times,* April 14, 1985.

25. *Washington Post,* May 26, 1988.

26. Baxter also decided to settle another long-standing antitrust action

against IBM at the same time, maintaining that while the AT&T monopoly still dominated the market and needed to be pursued, the case against IBM did not. The company had long since lost its virtual monopoly in computers.

27. Susan C. Faludi, "The Reckoning: Safeway LBO Yields Vast Profits but Exacts a Heavy Human Toll," *Wall Street Journal*, May 16, 1990.
28. *Washington Post*, November 29, 1988.
29. *New York Times*, March 10, 1999.
30. Robert Slater, *The New GE* (New York: McGraw-Hill, 1993), p. 116.
31. Charles R. Geisst, *The Last Partnerships: Inside the Great Wall Street Money Dynasties* (New York: McGraw-Hill, 2001), p. 134.
32. *Washington Post*, February 10, 1989.
33. *New York Times*, April 24, 1991. In the 1980s, bank failures caused the Fed to loosen its interpretation of who could own banking companies, assuming that money from the outside was preferable to a bailout using public funds.
34. *The Bond Buyer*, December 10, 1985.
35. *New York Times*, December 29, 1985.
36. Ibid., October 27, 1988.
37. Ibid., October 30, 1988.
38. Ibid., December 22, 1985.
39. IDD Information Services, January 1989.
40. *Investment Dealers' Digest*, February 19, 1990.
41. *Mergers & Acquisitions*, March 1990.

CHAPTER 6

SPAWNED BY DEREGULATION

In the film Wall Street, *the star was financier Gordon Gekko. If they remade the movie today, he would be a bit player. The star would have to be the swashbuckling corporate CEO.*

Financial Times, *1998*

Following the recession of 1991, merger activity proved that constant motion was becoming a hallmark of Wall Street, replacing the peculiar logic of synergy that had been so prevalent in the 1980s. Never content to leave a stone unturned, mergers specialists seized on a new series of events to further their goal of restructuring corporate America in the quest for even greater fees. If the 1980s witnessed the siege of corporate Rome by the barbarian hordes, then the 1990s saw the city rebuilt to the Visigoths' specifications.

The 1990s also proved that merger activity had no restraints other than possible scrutiny by the antitrust regulators. Although this had always been the case, the alarm that many of the new mergers created was relatively short-lived. Part of the reaction was due to the complexity of the deals. Many new mergers were being structured in corporate suites rather than on the backs of envelopes by investment bankers and remained relatively quiet if not secret until announced. Part of this veil of anonymity was due to the fact that many corporate leaders believed that the deals were nobody's business unless they could be executed. Debate in the press, with the possibility of awakening regulators with exaggerations of a possible deal's effects, was not wanted. The new environment was characteristic of the 1990s.

The first significant merger deal of the twentieth century rained torrents of criticism on J.P. Morgan for exacting an extra $700 million on top of the asset valuation for Carnegie Steel when he brought U.S. Steel to market for $1.4 billion. Almost a hundred years later, the number would pale in comparison to the hefty premiums paid by aggressive suitors using M&A to add to their company's infrastructures and operating capacities. In the 1990s, keenly aware that time was of the essence, many high-technology companies discarded all standard valuation techniques and began paying prices based upon multiples of sales or potential sales for acquisitions with little more to recommend themselves than an idea. Regardless of the ironies between the past and the present, one fact remained clear: No deals could have been achieved without a strong stock market and an investing public willing to pay premiums to buy what they thought was a piece of the future.

As merger deals became larger in the 1990s, they became reflective of a trend that had begun during the Reagan administration. Fueled ideologically by the notion that government interference in business should be minimal, the administration began deregulating many enterprises that had witnessed the strong visible hand of government since the New Deal. The marketplace could allocate resources efficiently without a set of guidelines imposed from above. The argument had its virtues and its flaws but became the prevailing economic ideology of the decade, especially since many of the old Democratic ideas about regulation proved messy and produced less than desirable results.

While the political debate raged over the advisability of continued deregulation, investment bankers quickly spied an opportunity to cash in on the trend. If the assumption about mergers and acquisitions being at the nexus of law and economics was correct, then that intersection would witness many traffic jams, crashes, and trips to the bank over the next decade. For the first time in the twentieth century, M&A activity was not being closely monitored and attacked by government. Now it was being tolerated as a natural part of the new economy, emerging after the inflation and high oil prices of the past subsided.

The ideological bent of the Reagan administration also was extended into the early 1990s by the fall of Soviet communism. During the Bush and Clinton administrations, it became clear that communism, not capitalism as Marx once predicted, bore the seeds of its own destruction and was relegated to the historical dustbin. Finance capitalism was about to prove Leon Trotsky's Depression-era prediction correct. He wrote that "The American hegemony's future inevitable growth will signify nothing but this—the penetration of all our planet's contradictions and diseases into American capital foundations."[1] With the disintegration of the Soviet empire, American capitalism won its biggest victory without firing a shot. In the 1990s, Wall Street took up the task of proving that the capital foundations were better off without any support by government and began reorganizing American industry using the usual slogan of economies of scale while adding a new catchword—globalization.

By the end of the century, most regulated industries were technically free of their fetters. After the raids organized by Pickens and Icahn in the 1970s and 1980s, oil and the airlines had fewer players than before and larger companies dominated their industries. In the 1990s, deregulation would extend to public utilities, telecommunications, railroads, financial services companies, and banks. In addition to supplanting old regulations with new deregulatory legislation, the government also relaxed many of the rules on foreign investors owning controlling interest in American companies, paving the way for international mergers on a scale not seen before. Without the specter of the Soviets looming on the horizon, foreigners were allowed to purchase airlines, financial services companies, auto manufacturers, retail chains, and utilities companies, many of which had been off-limits to them before 1990. National security was no longer an issue in cross-border investing and Wall Street moved quickly to cash in on the new liberal political climate.

Despite the fact that the 1990s produced the largest mergers yet seen, the fanfare surrounding them was less visible than in the 1980s. After the Drexel affair and Michael Milken's imprisonment, Wall Street adopted the lowest profile possible in the new wave of merger mania after 1992. Naturally, the size of many of the deals made it impossible for their deal makers to remain invisible, but the mania was associated with fewer individual superstars than in the past. The usual investment bankers and deal makers were still at work, providing much-needed continuity to the spree that began in the early 1980s, but now they remained more in the background. Unlike Michael Milken or T. Boone Pickens, many did not make the headlines and preferred it that way. When individuals did make the news, they often came from the previous generation of deal makers, accustomed to having their names bandied about in the news media.

The sheer size of the deals in the 1990s also brought pressure on many Wall Street securities houses to beef up their operations. Merger advising was labor intensive but it proved to be even more capital intensive. Unlike deals in the past, many in the 1990s involved money provided by investment bankers, either temporarily or as an actual investment. As a result, many Wall Street houses found themselves in need of additional capital to satisfy SEC requirements. Those banks that were not traded publicly, such as Goldman Sachs, eventually succumbed to the pressure and went public or raised additional capital by selling more shares. The megadeals of the 1990s could no longer be advised solely by small boutiques that earned fees only from their efforts. Now many of the deals involved arbitrage or related operations by the banks as a service to their clients, and all of these activities required heavy doses of capital. The demise of Drexel was a clear warning to many securities houses that capital was key to remaining in the game.

Boutiques still thrived during the 1990s, but their role was limited to advisory functions for a fee. Merger banking was dominated by both commercial and investment banks working for large corporations seeking strategic merger partners. The day of the individual deal makers was not over, but the image of the lone raider radically affecting whole industries was fading quickly. The influence of Icahn, Pickens, KKR, and others was most pronounced when deals ordinarily were below the size of the RJR Nabisco deal. But when they blossomed to three or four times that amount, it was clear that M&A had returned to the corporate suite where war chests were larger. Kohlberg Kravis may have won the war for RJR Nabisco, but it was

Nabisco management that originally put the company in play. In the deals that followed in the 1990s, the amounts were simply too large for the small player. Asset stripping of an inefficient industry could be considered a noble calling in some quarters, but merging two giant automakers in a transatlantic deal was beyond the capacity of the lone raider or boutique and their ad hoc pools of takeover funds.

During the 1990s, the justification for merger deals also began to change. In the absence of strong regulation, many mergers were justified by appealing to the consumer. Deregulation in the utilities business would mean lower prices for electricity. In the airline sector, it meant lower ticket prices; in financial services, fewer bank fees. Many companies engaging in traditional horizontal or vertical mergers quickly adopted the mantra of consumerism because they realized it was a compelling argument that was difficult to refute. Whether this would prove to be genuine or just another example of Wall Street cant was difficult to determine at the time, but it often was quickly forgotten after a deal was completed. Ironically, it was in step with the political tune of the mid-to-late 1990s that played well in both Republican and Democratic quarters. Consumers and investors could be protected in the new economy by dismantling New Deal regulations, allowing the marketplace to decide what worked and what did not. Mergers that lowered prices for goods and services could not be bad. The 1930s became the starting point in rewriting law for the future. Even the suggestion that mergers could replace the guiding hand of big government by efficiently allocating resources in the private sector played well on both sides of the aisle in Congress.

As in all previous merger booms, a strong stock market was necessary to fuel equities prices. After the 1987 market rout, the rise in the markets over the next 12 years was the greatest ever recorded. Needless to say, the merger boom also was the greatest ever witnessed, with the major indices increasing by 500 percent before finally falling. Small investors played an important role in the boom, bidding up prices on many stocks, making it possible for those companies to use their stock to acquire others. What began in 1992, after the brief recession, was a cycle of bidding and counterbidding that soon acquired all the characteristics of a bubble.

Deregulation in the 1980s and 1990s was not a well-plotted script that flowed easily from Washington lawmakers, however. The term meant different things in different industries. In the airline industry, it meant loosening government control over fare structures and routes. In the case of public utilities, it meant doing away with some of the restrictions imposed by the PUHCA of 1935, mainly over ownership and activities of public utility operating companies. In banking, it meant dismantling the enforced separation of commercial and investment banking because of the Glass-Steagall Act of 1933 and further strictures found in the Bank Holding Company Act of 1957. In telecommunications, it also centered on ownership and followed on the heels of the dismemberment of AT&T, effective in 1984. Different industries were regulated in different ways, and it took time to loosen the restrictions. Often, the loosening required a champion who would doggedly pursue the issue. Frequently the champion came from within government, but on occasion he or she could be found working in the industry itself, realizing that less regulation meant greater opportunity for merger.

Harsh financial reality also helped the deregulation trend. Many utilities and airlines, as well as banks, were not in sound financial shape in the early 1990s and filed for bankruptcy. Junk bond defaults, the savings and loan crisis, and high fixed costs for utilities companies all spelled eventual doom for many companies unless a savior was found relatively quickly. In the utilities sector, El Paso Electric was the best known of the bankruptcies, with more companies rumored to be on the verge of filing Chapter 11 proceedings. Since many of these industrial sectors were still regulated in the early 1990s, government assistance eventually may have been necessary to bail them out. Rather than replay another government-inspired bailout like the one that saved Chrysler in the 1980s, Congress had a clear reason to deregulate as many industries as possible, saving the public purse in the process. Allowing mergers between previously regulated companies was a logical step, providing another opportunity for the marketplace to solve the problem rather than Congress or regulators.

The old favorite—diversification—still proved resilient after two decades. Many large companies still sought to diversify their activities, although the term had taken on a slightly different connotation since the early 1970s. Companies as different as Walt Disney and General Electric were diversified, but their activities differed. Disney diversified into lines of business such as theme parks, franchising, cruise lines, and broadcasting, which all served its original cartoon and motion picture business. It also expanded by cross-promoting its business with toy manufacturers and fast food operators. General Electric, in contrast, was diversified more in the now classical sense; it added operations that had little to do with its original business of engineering and power production. While both were diversifying, one was expanding its brand name into related fields while the other was diversifying for its own sake—that is, to protect itself from changes in the business cycle. Regardless of the type, acquisitions were still a major part of the strategy. But none of the diversified companies of the period could match the old ITT or LTV for the sheer range of their diversification. Now, reason ruled the roost rather than diversification simply for its own sake.

CESSATION OF HOSTILITIES?

While the 1980s paved the way for greater M&A success, the size and extent of the deals in the 1990s proved startling. Transborder mergers and a sweeping change of the regulatory landscape produced new institutions that would differ radically from those of the past. Companies that were once competitors were now joined at the hip. The brave new world of megacompanies spanning international borders required massive doses of capital, much as U.S. Steel had in 1901. Now many companies lined up for capital and regulatory approval. In the past, only one deal had made the news. In the 1990s, dozens of deals exceeded the original Morgan blockbuster transaction in adjusted terms, although many did not engender the same awe from the public. But their potential consequences were as far-reaching.

As the 1990s began, one of the early casualties of the new decade appeared to be the hostile takeover. New deals increasingly were becoming international in scope and the hostile takeover bid simply was not appropriate. It would be difficult to imagine a hostile bid for a previously state-owned European enterprise or a Baby Bell. When an enormous subsidiary of a state-owned holding company in Italy was spun off from its parent in 1993, the deal was won by Wasserstein Perella, which was rapidly seeking to expand its influence to planned restructurings, not simply accomplishing them by hostile takeover. Reputation was becoming more important in these sorts of deals, and the image of helping a hostile takeover bid was not in keeping with the new M&A advising that was emerging. Wasserella was most vulnerable to the new environment because of its short but stormy history. As with many of the 1980s boutique firms, its name had become legendary very quickly but the question now was whether it could retain its foothold in the market.

Many Wall Streeters thought the firm would not survive. Ever since it had been founded and expanded rapidly, it had been losing key staff and had acquired a reputation as being too sharp, even for a Wall Street M&A specialist. In its first full year of operation, the small firm ranked second in the mergers league tables, behind only Morgan Stanley. Within four years, it slipped to 30th. The decline caused some bankers to write it off. "They do pop up here and there on a deal but they're not a real competitive factor out there," remarked the head of one Wall Street firm, "Of all the things I spend my nights worrying about, Wasserstein Perella is not on the list."[2] Given the chastening of Drexel and Milken, the atmosphere certainly changed quickly. The real question was whether the hostile takeover would make a comeback or be relegated to the dustbin of outdated techniques.

One activity that was affected by the cessation of hostilities was risk arbitrage. Throughout the modern era of M&A, many securities houses had been playing the arbitrage game successfully. By buying and selling the shares of the two parties involved in a potential merger, they often profited when mergers were completed. The genuine risk element entered when a deal failed, either because of unfriendly regulators or other extraneous factors. The activity was practiced avidly by many Wall Street houses since the 1960s. In the lightning strike world of hostile takeovers, it was more profitable than in the more conservative environment when deals became enormous and the pace of takeovers a little slower as a result. In the 1970s and 1980s, arbitrageurs at houses like Salomon Brothers, Goldman Sachs, and Bache often performed their activities in as much anonymity as possible. Ivan Boesky, in contrast, actually retained a press agent to publicize his victories in the press. His reputation for publicity was well recognized and prompted another, less conspicuous arbitrageur, Guy Wyser-Pratte at Bache, to remark, "I have heard that some of his friends have been so uncourteous as to call Ivan from time to time and make piglike 'oink, oink' sounds into the telephone."[3] Within 10 years, the greedy piggy image would be underscored when Boesky was in prison for insider trading and the other legitimate arbitrageurs were taking positions in deals substantially larger than those of the 1970s and 1980s.

One inescapable fact was that the takeover firms and advisers were changing tack. Corporate restructuring now was a much more acceptable technique than it was when Icahn and Pickens threatened a hostile takeover in order to force changes on a company, all in the name of greater efficiencies. In the 1990s, restructuring required hiring an adviser well before a deal was announced, not doing so only after being threatened with extinction. Companies realized that it was better to hire someone to help before it was forced upon them. That realization naturally led to the decline of the hostile bid. Repositioning or selling assets and enhancing shareholder value had gone mainstream. The fortunes of General Electric and a host of other traditional corporate names depended upon acquisitions and exit strategies that were carefully planned, not dictated solely by ad hoc circumstances and aggressive investment bankers eager to sell a deal.

After the massive bond defaults of the early 1990s, debt became less fashionable in financing takeovers. The days of the LBO receded but certainly did not disappear. While LBOs by corporate managers or buyout firms became less popular, those by employees became the rage, especially at smaller companies. These were known as employee stock ownership plans (ESOPs) and had been touted for years as a viable method by which employees could own part or the whole of their company. By owning the stock, employees could have a greater voice in the running of a company. A derivative benefit was that firms owned by employees were more difficult to take over by an outsider, as Carl Icahn discovered with the attempted takeover of Dan River. The ESOP was the closest thing to capitalist democracy that finance had to offer, and when faced with the uglier side of takeovers, it made an attractive alternative to workers and middle management.

The best-known employee buyout of the decade occurred at United Air Lines (UAL), the airline that rivaled Pan Am and TWA in sheer size. In the late 1980s, discussions began at the airline about employee ownership and Lazard Freres acted as investment banker to several unsuccessful attempts by various employee groups to buy the stock. A failed attempt to structure a deal in 1989 led to a widespread stock market drop, indicating how closely the market had become intertwined with potential merger deals as bellwethers of its own performance. By 1990, Lazard already made $6 million in fees simply by advising various unions, although it would take another four years before a successful ESOP at UAL would be consummated. In restructurings of this nature, the advisers' role was significant because of the logistics of the deal. The potential payout for restructuring in 1990 made the successful outcome important because the potential pot of fees amounted to almost $60 million. The prize was so great that two senior Lazard bankers, dubbed "union bankers," left the firm to set up their own boutique just to reap the rewards. Despite the potential, dealing with unions was not something that investment bankers relished. A Lazard specialist commented, "Excluding this deal, Lazard really hasn't seen union representation as a terribly profitable line of business."[4]

One of the first highly regulated sectors to be deregulated in the 1990s was public utilities. Congress passed the Energy Policy Act in 1992, effectively deregulating sales of power between the utilities companies. In theory, allowing free sales would lower rates to consumers and provide more competition in the monopoly-ridden industry. Many states followed suit, notably California, allowing easier sales across state lines. Many utilities companies then began actively seeking merger partners in the new environment. In 1991, before the Energy Policy Act was passed, over 50 potential utilities mergers were announced, two of them international. Even the prospect of deregulation before the ink was dry on proposed laws was motivation for merging. In addition, many utilities companies began opening offices overseas in search of cheaper energy and potential merger partners. Britain's policy of selling off previously owned state assets to the private sector put many of its own companies in play and raised billions for the U.K. Treasury. One of the most notable privatizations took place when Margaret Thatcher's Conservative government sold off British Telecom (BT) in an enormous stock offering on both sides of the Atlantic. Thatcher was able to claim, "The consequences of privatization for BT were seen in a doubling of its level of investment, now no longer constrained by the Treasury rules applying in the public sector. The consequences for customers were just as good. Prices fell sharply in real terms, the waiting list for telephones shrank and the number of telephone boxes in operation at any particular time increased. It was a convincing demonstration that utilities were better run in the private sector."[5] The privatization plan also triggered a subsequent takeover attempt of an American company by the newly independent BT that would rattle Wall Street in a few years.

BEGGING TO DIFFER

After the stock market recovered from the early 1990s recession, mergers again went on a binge not seen since the mid-1980s. Business picked up in 1993 and 1994, soaring to new highs each year. That is not to say that business was bad during the previous years. Between 1991 and 1993, Goldman Sachs earned $167 million in mergers fees while Morgan Stanley earned $112 million.[6] Both deal sizes and fees earned were set to explode as the stock market climbed.

In previous decades, mergers had often provoked congressional hearings. In the 1990s, the new type of corporate merger did not engender the same sorts of fears, but criticisms rose to the surface nevertheless. During the Clinton administration, a more benign attitude was adopted as long as prospective merger candidates convinced the administration that mergers would not cause an undue amount of unemployment. "The climate has certainly changed," remarked Clinton labor secretary Robert Reich in 1996, "and perhaps we have contributed to that."[7] But the relentless restructuring was viewed in many quarters as nothing more than change for its own sake—and a bonanza for executives and bankers. The larger question being posed was loaded with implications. Were mergers adding value to corporate America or simply lining the pockets of anonymous bankers and executives?

Much of the evidence suggested that most mergers were simply done for their own sake, not for value or the benefit of shareholders. As early as 1995, *BusinessWeek* concluded that the 1990s deals fared better than those in the 1980s, many of which it characterized as financially driven. Many of the deals did not seem to make good operational sense or to hold the prospect of enhanced business results for the companies involved. One of the reasons that they were ineffective was because of a rush "in search of synergies that don't exist. To make matters worse, they often pay outlandish premiums that can't be recovered even if everything goes right."[8] The case could certainly be made on the basis of the evidence on hand at the time. Deals such as Quaker Oats' expensive acquisition of Snapple Beverages, Time Inc.'s acquisition of Warner Communications, and Kmart's relentless expansion by buying specialty stores were only a few examples. The next several years proved the characterization correct, since most of the deals produced less than stellar results. Others naturally succeeded. There was still a hint of history behind some of the deals. *Business Week* criticized First Chicago Corporation's acquisition of the National Bank of Detroit as being motivated by fear. The Chicago bank wanted to grow larger in order to fend off a possible bid by NationsBank, which was actively seeking merger partners at the time. Adding the Detroit bank to its stable would be one way for First Chicago to defend itself as well as serve its primary motivation— "[the] goal was to keep a Chicago bank in Chicago."[9] The goal was reminiscent of Samuel Insull and Harold Stuart, both of whom had preached a similar philosophy in banking and utilities 70 years before. After decades, it was still possible to appeal to geography when fighting off the barbarian hordes with great ambitions in mind.

By the middle of the 1990s, merger activity was frantic but paled when compared to the numbers recorded by the end of the century. In 1995, 3,500 deals were recorded worth a collective, and historic, $356 billion. Within four years, the number recorded was over 11,000, worth $1.387 trillion.[10] With so many deals looming on the horizon, the terminology surrounding them was bound to change. Terms such as *horizontal* and *vertical merger*, once the mainstays of antitrust and merger language, were becoming rapidly outdated and now were useful only as generic categories. In a world dominated by information technology, the old categories were inadequate when describing the multitude of new mergers constantly being announced. With securities prices now available in real time and company valuations changing to reflect future projections rather than current value, more flexible terms were needed to describe merger strategies. Terms such as *overcapacity, geographic roll-up, market extension,* and *industry convergence M&A* began to be used widely to more adequately categorize the thousands of new deals being done each year.[11] The complexity was adding to the confusion in the marketplace. With growth concepts occupying center stage and the past relegated to the dustbin, new mergers being announced looked suspiciously like older ones dressed up in lamb's clothing. Regulators and antitrusters now allowed mergers that would have been strictly forbidden 20 years before.

FUNNY MONEY

Not since the days of the conglomerates had companies used mergers and acquisitions as such a deliberate part of their corporate strategies. Most companies employed them in order to diversify their operations, but certainly not as widely as James Ling or Harold Geneen did with their behemoth companies in the 1960s. There were notable exceptions, however. New, complicated technologies sprang up quickly that in many ways resembled the railroad industry in the nineteenth century. Some of the infrastructure needed to be built initially, but much could also be purchased from others whose niche businesses fit well in the larger companies' game plans.

In this latter respect, there was no shortage of smaller companies across the board that could be purchased by a buyer with deep pockets. Since the nineteenth century, many entrepreneurs had realized that building competing operations often resulted in a buyout from a larger competitor, netting handsome results for the smaller company only too happy to sell for an inflated price. In the long run, many of the smaller competitors could not have provided significant competition, but their presence crowded industries that in some cases were begging for some order if not outright consolidation. Russell Sage and others had recognized that fact before the Civil War in the railroad industry and had made significant fortunes selling out to those with even larger ambitions. The old Nickel Plate strategy had never been forgotten and was about to emerge again in a new context. The same proved true of many smaller technology companies in the 1990s that avidly hoped for a larger buyer.

There was a distinct difference between the way that General Electric or Cisco employed mergers compared with the Daimler-Chrysler or MCI/WorldCom deals. Cisco acquired 62 companies between 1996 and 2002 alone and developed specific methodologies through which it could assess another company's potential for becoming integrated into its own corporate culture and operations. Investment bankers were useful in the process but not vital in all cases. In many respects, investment banking M&A specialists were better equipped to deal with traditional mergers on a macro level. In order to service specialty industries located in Silicon Valley, they often had to develop specialty boutiques within their own banks. Boutique specialists could fill the niche better since they knew about an industry and where to find compatible companies suitable for acquisition. Many Wall Street firms began searching for northern California real estate to keep abreast of developments in dot-com land. As early as 1987, investment bankers had already held a meeting en masse on Alcatraz Island to celebrate the opening of the new Internet investment banking market. While on the island, they dined in prison cells, where tables were set with fine china. Few thought that several Wall Street figures would follow in their footsteps—without the fine china—within a year.

The strategy was simple and also broke many Wall Street hearts in the process. Cisco identified a company it wanted to buy, using its own pricey stock to pay a hefty premium. As the Dow reached new highs each year from 1995 to 2000, Cisco found itself with more and more merger money to play with, dubbed "Cisco money." As with the conglomerates, the stock was crucial to the company's expansion plans and the market provided a rich source. Chief executive John Chambers paid $4.1 billion in 1996 for StrataCom, a manufacturer of computer networking technology. At the time, the acquired company had sales of $335 million, meaning that Cisco paid a multiple of 12 times sales for the company. Paying multiples of sales or potential sales definitely was a sign of the new economy, in which all tried and tested techniques of valuation were overlooked. Three years later, Chambers announced that Cisco was paying $7 billion for the privately owned Cerent Corporation, a small network equipment company that had only been in the marketplace for two years. The deal was packaged by Frank Quattrone, head of the CSFB Technology Group, one of the leading investment bankers for the technology sector. Credit Suisse First Boston also advised on the much larger Lucent Technologies' $21 billion acquisition of Ascend Communications at the same time. Although many of the Silicon Valley acquisitions were small—somewhere between $5 million and $30 million—others proved to be blockbusters, mainly because of the value of the stocks involved rather than any traditional asset valuation.

Chambers joined Cisco in 1991 when it was already becoming known as a hot stock to watch. The company had had a quirky beginning. It was founded in 1977 by two Stanford computer afficianados who invented the Internet router because they could not communicate with each other using the current technology. From that point, Cisco began to grow exponentially along with the use of the Internet, first in academic use and then later in general commercial use. Chambers became CEO in 1995 and continued the aggressive strategy that made the company a phenomenally rising star. Cisco's game plan was simple. If it needed technology and did not have the expertise or the time to develop it, it would buy others who did. Time was of the essence in the burgeoning industry, where developments took place in months rather than years. The practical side of acquisitions was the domain of Michelangelo Volpi, an Italian educated at Stanford who joined the company in 1994 after graduating from business school. Volpi noted that his strongest weapon in the acquisitions battle was the company's stock, "which I think is considered a very good currency."[12] High-ranking employees of acquired companies were given jobs with Cisco and paid in stock, which made many of them very content new hires. In 1997, Cisco acquired the software maker Lightspeed International for $194 million, a relative bargain in its own terms. But the sellers, who went to work for Cisco, had reason to smile. A year later, their stock increased to $320 million as the market continued to rise. The strategy was not unlike the one practiced by Harold Geneen at ITT 30 years before.

Cisco used many investment bankers as advisers but always drove the direction of its deals from its home base rather than Wall Street West. CSFB, William Blair & Co., Warburg Dillon Read, and Merrill Lynch were all used as advisers, among others. A San Francisco location served many of them well because many of the companies acquired by Cisco were from the immediate area. Unknown at the time was the short-term nature of the dot-com boom. Alcatraz would not be hosting any more elegant luncheon parties by the time the decade ended.

BABIES GROW UP

In the years following the AT&T breakup, the telecommunications market was thrown wide open to competition. No longer in the local phone business through the Baby Bells, AT&T had to content itself with long-distance services but was being challenged on that front by other new companies, many of which were founded specifically to access existing AT&T lines. Soon developments would occur in the regional market that made many wonder whether the old monopolistic structure was about to be reinvented by some familiar corporate names.

Any suggestion of merger in the telecommunications industry would have to originate from the companies themselves. Raiders, predators, and aggressive investment bankers were not welcome in the field, where most old Bell companies were still considered quasi-public utilities. The sector was also dotted with regulators at all governmental levels and it is doubtful whether any marriages would be approved unless they adhered to strict guidelines. An attempt to strip assets or restructure them would not be tolerated, regardless of the economic argument. Telephones were still a vital public service. The U.S. telephone industry was in private hands but under strict guidelines. ITT may once have operated Chile's phone system, but that sort of influence was not tolerated in the United States.

The opening salvo in the new telecommunications war was fired when the Telecommunications Act of 1996 passed Congress. The new law allowed the traditional distinction between long-distance and local telephone calls to fall. Now local Bell companies could enter the long-distance market while AT&T could enter the local market. Other companies that had sprung up to challenge AT&T also entered the fray, and competition was rife in an industry that 15 years before was characterized by a "natural monopoly."[13] Ironically, many of the local Bell companies claimed that they needed to merge in order to provide competitive services. They did not see that claim as a tacit admission that the old AT&T provided the best services possible at cheap prices. The urge to merge struck several of them just as the new law was signed.

The first of two major mergers that followed was between SBC Communications and Pacific Telesis. The two announced plans to merge in a $17 billion deal that clearly would have benefited Pacific Telesis more than SBC. The California company was suffering cash flow problems at the time and had recently announced a dividend cut due to competition in its home market. The two combined would create a huge company offering services from the Mississippi to the Pacific. But the announcement had its critics, many of whom did not favor mergers between Baby Bells. Many feared that allowing them to merge would only turn back the clock and augur the return of another telephone giant. "The deal eliminates two potential competitors from each other's local markets," countered a spokesman from a major consumer advocacy group, "It's a blow to competition."[14] But the competition argument was now producing some strange economic and regulatory math. Merging two companies was not seen as a throwback to the old AT&T monopoly, although the clear implication was that a combination of more than two participants could cause regulatory problems.

Before the law became effective, other Baby Bells also got the urge. NYNEX and Bell Atlantic began exploratory talks to determine whether a merger would be beneficial and pass regulatory muster. But the scarred, and scared, history of the past two decades seemed to be ever present. Even as NYNEX and Bell Atlantic were examining each other's books, Bell Atlantic arranged a $140 million bank line of credit to fund executive golden parachutes in the event of a takeover. The parachutes, used to give senior executives who may have been made redundant by a takeover a lucrative going-away gift, traditionally were used as poison pill defenses by a company to discourage unwanted suitors. The sheer size of the bank line certainly might have discouraged outsiders, but the companies proceeded with their talks. The clear implication was that executives were arranging lines of defense that may have been inappropriate to companies that were still practically in an oligopoly industry. The real question raised by such traditional antitakeover tactics was almost rhetorical. Who were these Baby Bells afraid of? Was it simply a matter of hoping for a regional accommodation between two companies that knew each other well and did not want outsiders from other regions intervening? Regardless of apparent motive, the companies made their merger plans public in April 1996, citing the proposed marriage as a "merger of equals." In a press release made public shortly after the SBC–Pacific Telesis deal was approved by the Justice Department, NYNEX and Bell Atlantic stated, "We're encouraged that the Justice Department has approved the merger of SBC and Pacific Telesis and we see no reason why they won't do the same for Bell Atlantic and NYNEX." The bandwagon was clearly rolling toward consolidation.

Almost immediately, the companies announced that the merger would eliminate some 3,000 jobs at a savings to the new company of $300 million. Both were in the midst of job cuts individually, so the new numbers were not startling but caused misgivings. "Mergers are synonymous with job loss," remarked one union official. "On the other hand, it could be a good opportunity . . . if they want us to be a player, then we will work with them. If not, then we will be a detriment."[15] One major bone of contention that emerged later and was challenged in court was a "breakup agreement" that the two companies signed worth $550 million. According to its terms, either company would have to pay $200 million if its shareholders failed to ratify the agreement and $350 million if another party sabotaged the deal by making a successful bid for either. Questions were raised by both the size of the breakup agreement and the golden parachutes. What harm would be caused if two former Baby Bells merged? Why employ a shark repellent defense? If this deal was so beneficial to both sides, why bother with details that made it sound like the companies were fighting off Carl Icahn rather than another Bell?

Both companies were sensitive to the issue of corporate downsizing. NYNEX's chairman called Secretary of Labor Robert Reich to assure him that the 3,000 job losses would be offset by future growth. He termed the losses a matter of "consolidation" rather than cuts, borrowing a traditional M&A term. In the heady years of the mid-1990s, the explanation was considered standard since many mergers, despite the fact that they appeared to be traditionally horizontal, were portrayed as between equals or matters of industry convergence. The merged company had a value of $50 billion at prevailing market prices.

Before the deal was consummated, the two Bells changed tack, citing the deal as a takeover of NYNEX by Bell Atlantic. Bell Atlantic had operations in the District of Columbia, and, as a result, Congress had to vote on any merger that affected utility service in the district. Calling the deal a takeover meant that a vote was not necessary. Bell Atlantic was the stronger of the two financially, so the merger of equals concept was abandoned, although the deal still had to face a bevy of state and federal regulators before it could be sealed. The new structure cost Bell Atlantic $22 billion for NYNEX. The new company quickly announced that it was eager to enter the long-distance market to challenge AT&T and cited economies of scale as a result of the successful merger, which passed the Federal

Communications Commission (FCC) in the late summer. When the smoke cleared, the final bill was $25.6 billion (excluding debt assumption), the largest in U.S. history. The new company serviced over 26 million customers in 13 states, changing its name to Bell Atlantic. Another change several years later, after Bell Atlantic acquired GTE, renamed the combined companies Verizon.

Needless to say, the deal also benefited investment bankers. The main marriage broker for the two companies was Merrill Lynch, not a traditionally strong name in M&A until that time. Merrill scored another significant deal victory at the same time when it arranged Cisco's acquisition of Stratacom Inc. for $4 billion, occurring on the same day as the Bell-NYNEX deal. For years Merrill had been actively pursuing M&A in order to compete with Morgan Stanley and Goldman Sachs as a top M&A banker but had fallen short. But the two deals helped vault it into the big leagues, where it remained. The value of the two deals put Merrill in number one spot for 1996, helping the one-time retail brokerage chain complete its ascent to the top of Wall Street's league tables in many categories. "We have gotten to the promised land," quipped the head of Merrill Lynch's M&A department. The deal was the largest to date, although in real terms it still lagged behind the RJR-Nabisco deal.

While Merrill was in the land of milk and honey, the size of the deals contained a note of warning. As Mark Sirower noted, the previous year over $400 billion had been spent on M&A and the $27 billion was noteworthy as a daily record. But when compared with the average $500 billion that managers spent on new plants and equipment over the preceding years and only $130 billion on research and development (R&D) during the same time, the M&A numbers seemed out of proportion.[16] Clearly, M&A was the major expenditure during the 1990s. The new economy relegated traditional capital spending to a distant second place and the comparatively small amount spent on R&D showed that it was easier to buy entry into a business than it was to develop it from the ground up.

The Bells were not the only phone companies with consolidation on their minds. The deal that bore the seeds of its own destruction in the telecommunications sector in the 1990s brought together phone companies MCI and WorldCom. Earlier deals in the sector showed that consolidation was thought necessary in order to provide competitive services both in long-distance and local phone services. The emergence of wireless services complicated matters further and the Internet also played a large role in long-range planning as companies experimented with ways to make the service faster and more efficient. Ironically, it would be newcomers to the business rather than the older Bell companies or AT&T that would fashion the huge merger that would have a profound impact upon the stock market and investor psychology several years later.

MCI got its start in the 1960s as a start-up provider of long-distance services for business customers. In the 1970s, it began the challenge that eventually brought AT&T to its knees. Then in 1983, shortly after AT&T finally agreed to its own dissolution, a group of local businessmen in Mississippi founded a long-distance company that would purchase wholesale long-distance service from AT&T and resell it, mostly to the small business community. One of the founders was Bernard Ebbers. Born in 1941 in Alberta, Ebbers migrated south to college in Mississippi. His first listed job was as a milkman. He later coached in high school before buying a motel and expanding it into a chain. The company founded humbly in a motel restaurant in 1983 would later be renamed WorldCom. Through a series of acquisitions, Ebbers built the company into a major long-distance provider. He acquired 68 phone companies after 1983, beginning by offering long-distance services mostly to small businesses. He then branched into the local markets with the $12 billion acquisition of MFS Communications in 1996. WorldCom stock soared on the prospects and Ebbers was presented with a golden opportunity to use it to expand even further. The apple of his eye was MCI, better known than his own company but cheaper in market terms. Clearly an acquirer of other companies rather than a long-range planner, Ebbers once remarked, "We spend so much dang time planning things, and not getting much done." The planning side would have revealed that the price of long-distance services was falling throughout the decade, casting a shadow over the strategy. But Wall Street initially was impressed.

Bruce Wasserstein described the potential deal between World-Com and MCI in familiar terms: "As a result, WorldCom could play the old 1960s merger game. By merging with MCI . . . WorldCom would see its earnings per share increase approximately 20 percent. This positive impact was helped by the fact that the deal as proposed would be structured as a pooling of interests for accounting purposes. There would be no goodwill recognized from the deal on WorldCom's balance sheet, and no annual amortization."[17] But in order to capture the prize, WorldCom would have to defeat BT (the new name for British Telecom, the former state-owned enterprise that had been privatized by the Conservative government). BT already had an agreement in place to purchase MCI in another example of the cross-border mergers that had become so popular in the 1990s.

Another competitor was GTE, which made an all-cash bid for MCI worth $28 billion. WorldCom prevailed, however, with an all-stock bid valued at $37 billion, proving that 1960s techniques could still be practiced successfully. The sheer size of the all-stock deal dumbfounded many on Wall Street. WorldCom issued an additional 760 million shares to pay for it, with MCI shareholders receiving 1.2439 shares of new stock for each share they held. BT also received $51 in cash for each of the MCI shares it held as compensation. The day the deal was originally announced, shock was obvious on Wall Street. "That is it, the world has finally gone mad," one investment banker remarked after hearing the terms. Another remarked, "I literally thought that the WorldCom deal was the deal that would end all, or at least most, deals." Arbitragers especially were hard hit, having bet millions on the successful outcome of the BT bid. But in traditional Wall Street fashion, after the dismay was shaken off, most investment bankers went in search of the next deal.

MCI WorldCom was a giant in telecommunications, with combined revenue of $30 billion and operations in 65 countries, including 75,000 employees and 22 million customers. Regulators in Europe and the United States insisted on certain divestitures, including Internet service, so that the new company would not have undue influence in emerging communications. The new entity remained the brainchild of Ebbers, and investment bankers from Lazard Freres and Salomon Smith Barney among others advised on the deal but remained discreetly in the background. True to the tone of the 1990s, the bankers were happy to collect their fees while letting the CEOs who had dreamed up the deals bask in the public spotlight. Within four years, they would be happy with the decision, especially after WorldCom unraveled under massive accounting irregularities.

The investment world quickly sang WorldCom's praises. A technology magazine, *Network World,* named it one of the 10 most powerful companies, behind only Cisco and Microsoft. After listing its virtues, the magazine went on to conclude, "MCI WorldCom will probably be a keeper on this list."[18] As for its investment virtues, they were impeccable according to technology analyst Jack Grubman at Salomon Smith Barney. Based partially upon his recommendations, *Fortune* listed WorldCom as one of its 10 safe harbor stocks—those that should protect value in good times and bad. "There are few, if any, companies anywhere in the S&P 500 that are as large as World-Com . . . that have [its] growth potential . . . this company remains the must-own large-cap stock for anyone's portfolio," Grubman glowed.[19] Based upon projections, the company indeed seemed to justify the hyperbole. Revenues for 2000 were projected to be $42 billion and earnings were expected to reach $5.5 billion. The enormous deal proved the overcapacity thesis in some respects, however. Phone services were falling in price and customers expected better services for less. Only consolidation could help some companies that otherwise may not have survived. Following the merger, MCI WorldCom quickly announced job losses amounting to almost 3 percent of its workforce.

ROCKEFELLER'S REVENGE

The first great merger trend emerged in the United States between 1880 and 1890. The trusts were born during this period and the holding company was devised in order to consolidate corporate holdings under one umbrella. One of the major reasons for the phenomenon was the direction of wholesale and retail prices. Many prices, both agricultural and industrial, remained flat. As a result, many of the existing firms had little choice but to merge with others or eventually go out of business. Some commentators saw the same trend emerging during the 1990s, especially in the oil and telecommunications industries. As a result, oil mergers were expected and several large consolidations eventually were announced that quickly broke the records for the size of deals.

One of the most significant brought together Exxon and Mobil, two of the companies created when the original Standard Oil Company was broken up after the monumental Supreme Court decision in 1911. During the mid-1990s, oil prices were flat and were actually less in real terms than they were 15 years before. Many international oil companies were counting on expanding drilling and exploration in Russia and other former Soviet states where reserves were still largely unexplored. But their plans were shaken when the Russian economic crisis erupted in the summer of 1998, precipitating a debt default and bringing about the collapse of the American hedge fund Long-Term Capital Management. Suddenly, many of the oil companies looked to domestic mergers or mergers with friendly foreigners to fuel their expansion and desire to cut costs. Companies once too proud to merge were now willing to consider marriages forced by necessity.

The bandwagon effect began after British Petroleum agreed to buy Amoco in the summer of 1998 in a deal worth $48 billion. The result was the world's third-largest oil company. Unknown at the time, two other oil giants were also discussing a possible merger. The Exxon Corporation and Mobil began preliminary talks to discuss a possible merger of two old Standard Oil offspring, which had grown to become keen competitors over the years. But their talks, which lasted for several months before a deal was announced, were not prompted by bankers but by the chief executives of the companies. It was almost inconceivable that any investment banker would have the economic clout or reputation to suggest that a deal that large could be consummated. The impetus would have to come from the companies themselves.

The Russian crisis quickly convinced oil executives that fewer risks were attached to deals done closer to home. The CEOs of both companies—Lee Raymond at Exxon and Lucio Noto at Mobil—kept their discussions very quiet until they were ready to announce a deal and then invite investment bankers and lawyers to participate. The main bankers were Goldman Sachs for Mobil, in its usual role of representing the bride, and J.P. Morgan & Co. for the groom. Morgan was chosen in part because Raymond sat on its board of directors, although its inclusion seemed ironic based on history. When establishing Standard Oil, John D. Rockefeller steered clear of J.P. Morgan & Co. He was originally afraid of the high price that Pierpont Morgan could exact from companies he advised. Almost 90 years later, it was not the bankers who were directing the deal but the companies themselves.

The sheer size of the merger made it the largest in history. Exxon had a market value of about $177 billion while Mobil was worth about $61 billion. The deal itself was worth $81 billion, and, when announced, made investment bankers and merger lawyers salivate at the prospect of the fees. Costs associated with the deal were $2 billion, of which around $100 million went to securities specialists and lawyers. Goldman and Morgan each received $100,000 per month for their efforts as the talks continued and a lump sum at the closing, while the lawyers also did well by tying up loose ends and defending the combination to regulators who took a hard, but eventually friendly, look at the potential repercussions of the deal.[20] The new company was known as ExxonMobil. Although originally greeted with some skepticism, the new company was touted as a merger that would improve competition in an industry that, while dominated by large companies, had become less efficient over the years and was in serious need of restructuring. Boone Pickens' original warning about the companies eventually running out of reserves appeared to be incorrect, although the merger, in a sense, did acknowledge that domestic and existing reserves would have to be managed more efficiently in the wake of international economic crisis.[21]

But some of the other predictions made about the new combined company proved to be wrong. Some analysts suggested that the new company would benefit consumers by lowering prices, but the argument was a bit odd since it was falling prices that prompted the large oil mergers in the first place. Amoco, BP, Exxon, and Mobil were all familiar names at the gas pump and while the regulators did insist that some restructuring occur among the companies' gas stations, lower prices were not what the companies had in mind. The merger was a classic horizontal merger designed to shore up the combined companies' costs and market share. In the lax atmosphere of the 1990s, it passed regulatory muster and was allowed to proceed. While the economics of the situation could be debated, an even greater debate was building on the political front.

Energy was not confined to the traditional oil industry, however. The crucial part of the Energy Policy Act allowed sales of power between utility companies and liberalized rules for mergers. As a result, mergers also began to occur between energy companies and utilities. On the surface, this seemed perfectly logical but it also smacked of vertical combinations; that is, allowing suppliers and users to merge in what was still a controlled industry. Despite appearances, the industry was being shaken by the new competitive environment. Many states were now threatening to allow consumers to choose their own utility suppliers. In the new environment, merger appeared to be a valid way to achieve economies of scale and produce cheaper prices.

One of the most aggressive energy companies in the 1990s was the Houston-based Enron Corporation. Originally a natural gas producing company, it began to expand into electrical utilities in 1997 with the acquisition of the Portland General Corporation, the Oregon-based electrical utility. The merger was the first of its kind, although it was almost blocked by Oregon regulators until Enron agreed to provide $140 million of merger-related benefits to consumers. It also introduced the Texas company to electricity trading in addition to its traditional gas trading. "The proposed merger with Portland General represents an outstanding opportunity for us to create the leading energy company of the future in the North American energy markets," said Kenneth Lay, its chairman and CEO.[22]

Enron was one of the most aggressive companies in the merger market in the 1990s. One management consulting company referred to the company, along with WorldCom and Conseco, the insurance company, as "serial acquirers." Their main avenue of growth was through acquisition and, if necessary, divestiture. They used merger as their chief method of research and development, preferring to buy the expertise they needed rather than develop it internally. Enron in particular hired its own mergers specialists from Wall Street and employed them rather than pay fat fees to the usual merger specialists for their expertise. "The company is one of the most transaction-oriented non–investment bank companies in the world," one of its directors remarked. "Acquisitions are a part of the daily life of the company."[23] Operating like an investment banking trader, the company began moving away from its core businesses toward the end of the 1990s and began shopping for a buyer for Portland General. The utility was not returning the 20 percent annual return that Enron required. The quest for higher and higher returns finally led to fraud and the demise of the company in 2002. But it was not alone. Both WorldCom and Conseco, the other two serial acquirers, also found themselves in bankruptcy at the same time, providing a chilling final chapter to the strategy that had allowed them to grow exponentially in the previous decade.

Since the 1970s, regulators at both the Antitrust Division of the Justice Department and at the FCC had been employing more economic analysis than at any other time in trying to assess the economic impact of potential mergers. Size no longer dictated whether a merger would be approved, but the potential impact upon competition did merit close scrutiny. Such studies opened a whole new field of study—antitrust economics—originally attributed to earlier studies coming from the University of Chicago. The Chicago School of antitrust was prevailing over what was traditionally known as the Harvard School, which emphasized political and social factors in classifying mergers. Although the Chicago School clearly was in the ascendancy, the noneconomic argument was still heard, but mostly in opposition.

Was the sheer size of these new combined, and in many cases international, entities a sign of the rise of a new political order? Did the new companies exercise a political and economic clout out of all proportion for the private sector? Writing in the *New York Times*, Yale School of Management Dean Jeffrey Garten argued, "Companies like ExxonMobil Corp. will deal with oil-producing countries almost as equals, conducting the most powerful private diplomacy since the British East India Company wielded near-sovereign clout throughout Asia."[24] Their sheer sizes made them the equal of many smaller nation-states. One fact was becoming clear as the M&A trend continued: The old mercantile trading companies had given way to the private bankers in the nineteenth century, who in turn had given way to the conglomerators of the 1960s and 1970s. In the 1990s, the pendulum had swung again, this time in favor of the leviathan global companies caused by several generations of previous merger and acquisition activity. The results of the influence were suspected but were sometimes hard to prove. Corporate influence could be detected in American campaign financing, Social Security issues, and the health care debate, to name but a few. But, as Garten and others noted, corporations' war chests were so large that they were capable of defending themselves with litigation so dense and drawn out that only the most courageous regulator would confront them with any hope of a clear-cut victory. Without hope of a successful outcome, many regulators preferred not to bother since an unsuccessful attempt could cost their agency serious erosion of muscle. And the giant corporations had deep legal defense pockets that could drag any litigation through the courts for years.

DRIVEN TO DISTRACTION

In the seventeenth and eighteenth centuries, Dutch capitalists began sending capital abroad in search of better returns than those that could be found at home. The small country had all but exhausted its own domestic investment sources and needed new outlets for its excess cash, earned by trading during the Mercantilist Age. One of its favorite investment sites was North America, where it became one of the largest investors in the American economy along with Britain. At the end of the twentieth century, the same could be said of automobile companies. Overcapacity at home sent them in search of new territories to conquer and the United States still was considered one of those fertile territories because of its huge consumer base. Globalization gave many car companies the excuse needed to forge expensive alliances and mergers with foreign manufacturers.

The largest international merger deal to date was a combination of the old and the new. The early stages of the merger were dominated by a corporate raider from an earlier period, while the latter stages were characterized more by business school topics such as merging corporate cultures, product lines, and synergies. The Daimler-Benz–Chrysler deal was welcomed on one level as an example of international economic cooperation and decried on another as the best example of a sweeping leviathan with the potential to create significant job losses internationally.

Since its founding in the 1920s, Chrysler had occupied third place among American auto manufacturers and had gone through a wrenching series of changes, including a government-led bailout and later absorbing American Motors, the fourth major manufacturer. Chrysler's main irritant in the 1990s was investor Kirk Kerkorian. The 77-year-old Kerkorian first began buying Chrysler stock in 1990 through his investment company Tracinda. He originally bought 22 million shares for $12.37 per share before adding substantially to his holdings over the next four years. Chrysler had become known as one of the great turnaround stocks of the 1980s since its bailout by the federal government. However, by the mid-1990s its earnings were growing at a faster pace than its stock price, suggesting that investors were still wary about the company's long-term prospects, especially during the 1991–1992 recession. Kerkorian adopted a typical raider's approach, claiming with some justification that the company was not managed well enough and was being too conservative in its corporate philosophy. He wanted to see the stock price advance in line with earnings and finally decided to make a takeover bid to prove his point.

Chrysler had reason to worry about Kerkorian's presence, because his business background was akin to that of Pickens or Carl Icahn. Listed as one of the country's richest men, he was a high school dropout and former boxer who had made his first fortune flying military and commercial air flights from Las Vegas during the 1950s. One of his reputed passengers was Bugsy Siegel, the gangster who also invested heavily in the resort city during its early years. Kerkorian added to his reputation by buying and quickly selling land in the city profitably and more recently built one of the city's largest hotels. He was also involved in gambling. Using Las Vegas as his base, he owned the MGM Grand Hotel in addition to his holdings in Chrysler. Frustrated by its phlegmatic stock price, he announced in April 1995 an offer for all of Chrysler at $55 per share. The bid valued the company at $22.8 billion and was joined by former Chrysler chairman Lee Iaococca. A Tracinda spokesman emphasized that the deal was "not a leveraged buyout, where assets need to be sold to help finance the transaction. The buyers are principals who are investing their own money."[25] At that price tag, they needed much more than their combined net worth. Twenty years before, the market had been skeptical of Carl Icahn's ability to raise financing in his early days. Now, the same questions were raised about Kerkorian at a later stage in his career.

The tender offer failed because Kerkorian failed to win the crucial support of bankers and other car manufacturers, many of whom saw it as nothing more than an inappropriate bid by someone totally unfamiliar with the industry. The market remained somewhat skeptical of Kerkorian's ability to raise the necessary funds for the transaction without borrowing. The stock price of Chrysler never reached the potential tender price, reflecting the skepticism. The automobile industry was one of the last bastions of traditional corporate America and did not welcome outsiders easily, especially one with Kerkorian's exotic and nontraditional background. For his part, the CEO of Chrysler, Robert Eaton, blasted Kerkorian publicly at an investors' conference, accusing him of "trashing our company, its management and its products."[26] As far as Eaton was concerned, Kerkorian was more interested in Chrysler's cash hoard at the time than he was in its products or reputation. But Chrysler was forced to take notice. It raised its dividend twice during the takeover threats and also split the stock. Eaton eventually mended his fences with his largest shareholder and the stage was set for a takeover with another auto company.

The DaimlerChrysler deal, similar to that of ExxonMobil, was engineered primarily by the two CEOs of the carmakers. Robert Eaton of Chrysler and Jurgen Schrempp of Daimler met privately over a period of months beginning in 1998 to ensure that the deal would be structured properly and kept under wraps at all costs. In its planning stages, the deal was referred to as Project Gamma. Eaton, who joined Chrysler from rival General Motors in 1992, viewed Daimler as an ideal partner because its line of luxury automobiles complemented his own lines rather than competing with them. Chrysler made most of its money selling vans and utility vehicles and was flush with cash at the time, making it an ideal target for the larger Daimler-Benz, eagerly seeking to expand its product line and influence without having to develop more products from the ground up.

Emphasizing the relatively successful picture on the surface, both companies claimed that the merger was in their best long-term interests. Europe was not a good market for Chrysler vehicles because they were too large for the most part, but the markets that Daimler dominated in South America and elsewhere proved attractive. Similarly, competition for luxury cars had increased dramatically over the previous decade. The German company realized it needed to diversify its base of operations, however, since demand for high-end cars could drop with a slowdown in economic activity. But at the heart of the matter was overcapacity. The automobile industry in general was saturating certain segments of the market, especially for the ordinary American sedan, and needed to find new markets where it could flex its excess muscle. Competition for utility vehicles was increasing as dramatically in the United States as it was for luxury cars in Europe, so the two companies decided to join in order to exploit each other's strengths. The deal was cast as a merger of equals, although the term would come home to haunt the combined entity several years later.[27]

The merger proved to be a bonanza for investment bankers and securities lawyers. Goldman Sachs advised Daimler-Benz along with Deutsche Bank, the German company's largest shareholder and major banker, while CSFB advised Chrysler. As the deal was announced, bankers were estimated to split around $100 million while another $25 million would be spent on legal fees. The usual array of merger lawyers also worked on the deal, including Skadden Arps, Shearman Sterling, and Cleary Gottlieb. Ironically, the amount of investment banking fees was similar to what Clarence Dillon had reputedly made when he had sold Dodge Brothers to Walter Chrysler 70 years before.

Lost in the maze of details surrounding the deal was the fact that one of the traditional big three U.S. automakers had been purchased by a foreign company and technically was no longer American. The same had happened to DuPont some years before when it was bought by Canadian interests, turning the chemical company into a foreign entity for U.S. statistical purposes. The merger market had truly become global, raising the ante and the arguments justifying the deals to a much higher level. Despite the torrent of press releases and favorable reviews surrounding the Daimler-Chrysler deal, not everyone believed that it was as good, or rational, a deal as the two companies professed. As Jeffrey Garten of Yale put it succinctly; "Announcing a big global merger is nothing compared to making it succeed."[28] In the years that followed, domestic troubles at Chrysler and consumer comments about Daimler's poor quality began to haunt the company as it worked to make the merger effective.

LEVIATHAN

As corporate America continued to be restructured in the 1990s, the old companies were continually being overtaken and absorbed by the new. Fears about the trend originally surfaced in the 1960s and had continued over the years. The most audacious merger between a new upstart and an old respected media company occurred in 1999 when America Online (AOL), the Internet service provider, used its market capitalization to capture one of the entertainment and communications industry's prizes, Time Warner.

The amazement and incredulity surrounding the MCI-Worldcom deal soon evaporated when the largest deal ever consummated was announced in 1999. Time-tested terms like *synergy* once again were used to describe and justify the combination that would be the new economy version of combining the old and the new. But the 1990s were waning quickly. Even before the ink was dry on the deal, questions were raised about its feasibility. Was it a well-conceived merger or was it nothing more than the stock bubble gone amok?

Part of the environment of the late 1990s was permeated by fear. Many companies and regulators, worried that the trend in cross-border mergers would finally propel a foreign company to take over an innovative American technology company like AOL, especially one that was highly visible. A telecommunications company in Britain, Vodaphone, had already completed a successful takeover of German company Mannesmann, and it appeared only a matter of time before an American Internet or telecommunications company fell prey to a foreign bidder. Similar fears were found in the banking sector, where large foreign banks were on the prowl for America acquisitions.

The largest deal of the twentieth century, and the only one initially worth in excess of $150 billion, meshed two companies with entirely different business cultures into what appeared to be a media powerhouse. The deal was initiated by AOL chairman Steve Case, who was actively searching for a merger partner outside his own Internet industry. Receptive to his overtures was Gerald Levin, his counterpart at Time Warner, who had been hoping to integrate new Internet technology into his traditional communications company for some time. The potential merged entity would have created the world's largest communications and entertainment company, with services running from AOL's Internet empire to Time Warner's publishing, cable, and broadcasting facilities. On paper the deal appeared to be a coup for both sides, but the details left Wall Street as well as Time Warner shareholders and employees less than enthusiastic.

Time Warner began as *Time* magazine, founded by Henry Luce in 1923. The company added *Fortune* several years later and over the years gained respect as a well-run mainline company known for its evenhanded news coverage and conservative management. In addition to *Time*, the company published over 30 other magazines and owned recording companies and book publishers. It also was the second-largest provider of cable TV operations, including Home Box Office and CNN. Its merger partner had something of a different reputation. AOL was founded in 1983 as an Internet provider and game company and had witnessed spectacular growth under Case's aegis. He joined the company soon after its inception and became CEO in 1993. By the late 1990s, when it began adding advertising to its web pages, AOL had 26 million paying subscribers and was the world's preeminent online service. Although its tangible assets were much smaller than Time Warner's, its stock market valuation was more than twice that of the older company. AOL was portrayed as the company of the future while Time Warner was depicted as a stodgy old media company in need of new blood. Its image was aided by Levin's intense desire to add New Economy communications to his company.

The deal was arranged by the two chairmen, with an army of investment bankers and lawyers supplying technical advice. AOL was represented by Salomon Smith Barney, Merrill Lynch, and Goldman Sachs, while Time Warner was represented by Morgan Stanley and Wasserstein Perella. Even by previous standards, the size of the deal was staggering, valued at $156 billion. It would be the largest all-stock deal ever. When news first broke on Wall Street, AOL stock declined as investors realized that the deal was moving into unknown territory. Steve Case commented, "This is a historic moment in which media truly has come of age." Even more shocking to some observers was the fact that Case, not Levin, would become chairman of the new company. Levin, clearly with more experience in media, became CEO of the new company.

Given the potential obstacles, the deal sailed through the marketplace relatively quickly. Media mogul Ted Turner, the founder of CNN and Time Warner's largest shareholder, agreed to the deal quickly, his stake amounting to 4 percent of the new company. Regulators in Europe and Washington did not provide much resistance despite original fears that the new company would be able to block competitors from its Internet and cable services, especially where new interactive technologies were concerned. The new company was expensive in traditional terms. Its market value originally was about $350 billion, representing a multiple of almost 12 times combined revenue. Market veterans, still accustomed to valuing companies by

PE ratios, were left wondering whether the new valuations were a bit ambitious for companies of this size although they certainly were used on smaller Internet companies. The market soon would pronounce its judgment: The valuation was too high by a considerable margin.

When the deal was first announced, the terms called for AOL to exchange 1.5 of its shares for each share of Time Warner. At current prices, that would have meant $110 per share, a 70 percent premium to its current value. Within six months, prices had begun falling and the deal looked much less attractive. AOL's price fell by over 25 percent and the premium for Time Warner had fallen to only 20 percent. Steve Case blamed the market in general for the problem. "What's happening really has less to do with AOL and less to do with the merger and more to do with what's happening in the sector," he stated confidently. "Almost every company that we compete with, ranging from Yahoo to Amazon to Microsoft to AT&T, [is] down substantially more than we are in that period."[29] Critics of the deal, and of the Internet bubble in general, disagreed. The major factor behind the decline in the markets *was* the deal, which showed the trend and all of its hyperbole in the harsh light of day. One year after the deal was announced, the value had dropped to $103.5 billion when finally it was approved by the FCC.

The subsequent collapse in the price of AOL to less than $10 per share at one point bolstered the critics. The nature of the biggest deal raised some disturbing questions about the deal itself and the merger trend in general. In the nineteenth and early twentieth centuries, deals were often arranged by bankers or industrialists without much consultation, as the original deal between Morgan and Carnegie illustrated. In the days of the robber barons and industrial trusts, corporate governance was not a working concept, so deals could be arranged between individuals regardless of how large the deals were or the potential negative effects they might cause. Oddly, a hundred years later, the same seemed to be true. A minnow had swallowed a large fish and no one objected effectively since the price was right, at least to Time Warner shareholders. Enormously overvalued stock was used to pay a healthy premium for the acquired company by a buyer that could not have raised even one-quarter the purchase price in cash. After 100 years of securities legislation and market development, the ultimate high stakes game of M&A was still being played by a small coterie of individuals who, despite their supposed obeisance to corporate rules of governance and modern financial analysis, still behaved much like kingmakers if not monarchs in their own right. Unfortunately for the AOL Time Warner deal, just one such modern development was lurking around the corner that would give it another, unwanted distinction within a year of being consummated.

The deal was one of the last for Wasserella. The firm was sold in early 2001 for $1.37 billion to Dresdner Bank of Germany, which merged it into its own investment banking division Dresdner Kleinwort Benson. Dresdner raised the cash by selling 5 million shares of its stock to institutional investors and used it to purchase the 20 percent of Wasserella owned by Nomura Securities. Wasserstein's own stake was around $600 million, which the *Wall Street Journal* said "[gave] his old moniker of "bid-'em-up-Bruce new meaning." Within a year, the deal turned sour over internal management problems at Dresdner and Wasserstein left to become CEO of Lazard Freres, since renamed simply Lazard. With the demise of the firm, the hostile takeover had lost one of its most avid adherents.

Takeover deals used to create conglomerates were still employed in the 1990s, although the results of some eventually were obscured by corporate misdeeds. One example was Tyco, the New Hampshire–based conglomerate that began an ambitious expansion under CEO Dennis Kozlowski. Kozlowski ranked high on the list of buyers of other companies and was an avid admirer of Jack Welch and his performance at GE. Like most other conglomerates on a long buying binge, Tyco owed its reputation to Kozlowski and his classic buy-and-trim techniques.

Kozlowski was born in 1946 in Newark and attended local public schools and college. He then went to work as an accountant and was eventually lured to Tyco in 1975. The company was founded in 1960 as a research laboratory and already had begun an acquisitions strategy in order to diversify. In 1989, Kozlowski was made president and chief operating officer and gained the top jobs as chairman and CEO in 1992. During the intervening years, he already had played a crucial role in the company's acquisition plans. In its constant quest to expand, Tyco acquired Kendall International, ADT, US Surgical Corporation, AMP Inc., and CIT Financial among almost 200 other companies during Kozlowski's tenure. His record for acquisitions was unmatched during the 1990s. The company's main businesses were fire protection systems, electronic security devices, telecommunications systems, and disposable medical products. By 1995, the company's revenues began to rise dramatically—from $3 billion to $30 billion by 2000. Its stock followed, rising from around $6 per share to more than $55 in the same time period. From all appearances, Tyco was merely following in the footsteps of Jack Welch and Harold Geneen and apparently becoming a huge success in the process.

Like his predecessors in the 1960s and 1970s, Kozlowski paid for the acquisitions with stock swaps. As the market was rising in the 1990s, paying for purchases was not a problem, and pool accounting helped smooth the road. Yet problems began to arise in the late 1990s as some outsiders questioned Tyco's accounting practices. One problem centered around US Surgical taking a large write-off days before the deal closed, making it look cheaper on the books and having a potentially beneficial effect on future results. Kozlowski defended his company, stating, "There is no risk that investors will wake up one day and find there is something wrong."[30] But investors were not assuaged. A class action suit was filed against Tyco by an investor group alleging that the company was employing unorthodox methods to inflate its results, artificially enhancing its performance after acquisitions.

Accounting problems would continue to plague the company for the next several years until Kozlowski's ouster and subsequent indictment for fraud and looting the company. In a sign of the heady days of the merger era, Kozlowski and several other executives designed a Web site that would offer companies and subsidiaries for sale, available to subscribers only for a fee of $20,000 per year. Mergers and acquisitions were entering the virtual world where targets could be identified online and initial contacts made without the traditional services of investment bankers or finders. Kozlowski obviously had parts of Tyco in mind when he helped initiate the idea. "No one is going to buy all of Tyco," he commented, "but some people who are interested in buying or selling a division are more comfortable appealing to me directly. If I can approach someone directly on the site, I can do it in own time. I can lay out a case better."[31]

Accounting problems were not a passing fad that would disappear. By the late 1990s, it was recognized that pool accounting had helped create a runaway merger trend and the stock market bubble that always accompanies it. Tackling the accounting problem came at the same time the market bubble began to burst, but only the bubble received public attention at the time. The quiet introduction of purchase accounting as the only standard for mergers accounting was one of the most anonymous significant market forces of the century. Because of the lack of publicity accompanying purchase accounting, it was safe to assume that most market professionals were not even aware of its existence until the effects were felt. The ruminations of accounting board practitioners, never a popular topic, would finally seal the fate of the last great merger trend of the twentieth century.

THE X FACTORS

Mergers and acquisitions activity began to taper off as the stock market retreated from its historic highs after 2000. As in all periods of intense activity, investor psychology fueled the market, allowing companies like Cisco and WorldCom to virtually print money in order to expand. Although the same phenomenon had been seen in the 1920s and 1960s, the 1990s version prompted the largest stock market bubble in American market history and with it the largest M&A boom ever witnessed.

The $1.3 trillion worth of M&A activity recorded in 1999 was not equaled in the years that followed. In 2000, activity was still resilient, with over 8,500 deals recorded totaling $1.268 trillion. Then activity drastically dropped in 2001 and 2002 to half and then one-third the amount.[32] The drop paralleled the drop in the major market indices but was more akin to the drop in the NASDAQ indices than the other major indicators. Matters were exacerbated by a quarterly loss announced by AOL Time Warner, which had only recently merged. In the first quarter of 2001, the new merged company lost a staggering $54 billion, the largest loss of its type for an American company. This loss was not attributed to the usual slowdown in revenues or even extraordinary losses in the traditional sense. Rather, AOL's loss was caused by the introduction of a new accounting rule destined to play havoc with the market.

In response to complaints about accounting methods used in takeovers and mergers, the Financial Accounting Standards Board (FASB) issued a new statement, number 141, better known as FAS 141. The new ruling confronted the decades old debate over which method of accounting to use for merged entities—pool accounting or the purchase method. The issue had been hotly debated since the 1960s with no resolution. But the FASB finally acted and M&A specialists did not like the outcome. The new rule required the use of the purchase method only after June 30, 2001. The older, softer way of pooling interests finally was put to sleep in favor of a more stringent method of accounting for the premiums paid by many firms when they acquired others. The results were dramatic.

Now firms were required to record the premiums paid for acquisitions as goodwill above market value and the difference was to be amortized, resulting in losses to income in many cases. Many companies accustomed to paying premiums, such as Cisco, felt the reverberations from the new method quickly, but the AOL Time Warner results struck the market like a thunderbolt. The cochairman of the mergers department at CSFB, Steven Koch, remarked in an interview that the "most influenced sectors will be those with meaningful amounts of intangibles that will need to be written down; those will ultimately affect the economics of transactions. That can happen in a variety of different sectors—any company in which intangibles will become a meaningful part of the balance sheet. Given the diversification of most large companies today, we could see this occur in many areas."[33] This was a bit of an understatement since intangibles had become standard in many high-tech and dot-com companies in the 1990s. Their stocks already had collapsed and many companies had gone out of business.

Even more mature, diversified international companies could not escape the new ruling. Not since the FASB changed its rules to account for overseas assets and liabilities of U.S. companies in the mid-1980s had such a potential mess hit the stock market. But one implication was already clear: Future M&A activity had to take the new rule into account because pool accounting was no longer permitted. And the notion that the problem was ephemeral because it was only an accounting technicality was no longer valid because the rule recognized that too many high prices paid for acquisitions were being ignored in the original pool accounting method, seeking to incorporate earnings immediately into the acquiring company while ignoring the goodwill problem. Goodwill was poised to usher in a bad period for the merger trend.

Another problem posed by the phenomenal merger trend was the serious strains put upon the due diligence process on Wall Street. Due diligence was the homework that investment bankers and securities lawyers were expected to do when packaging a deal to ensure that legal and financial problems were not present. The degree to which it was pursued depended to a great extent upon the urgency and speed with which a deal was generated. When deals were suggested by their CEOs—a characteristic of the 1990s—due diligence could often be taken for granted by bankers, accountants, and lawyers working on a deal. When presented with the facts, investment bankers in particular were faced with either double-checking information presented by CEOs and CFOs or taking it at face value. In the case of a hostile takeover, facts were more often checked than not since the hostile bidder needed to be armed with complete and accurate information. In the 1990s, some faith prevailed in the process, leading to less than favorable results after 2001 when accounting frauds were discovered, much to the chagrin of Wall Street as well as investors.

The accounting problem was accompanied by a financial engineering concept that had both its bright and dark sides. As the Enron collapse in 2002 proved, off–balance sheet items were a bane that many professionals and investors never considered when assessing corporate risk. The problem with these contingent liabilities and assets was that they were created over a period of years and were ad hoc in nature. As a result, no one was quite sure of their effect on corporate balance sheets and income statements, except their creators, who in many cases were not talking.

The use of off–balance sheet liabilities in particular had been practiced for decades by government-sponsored enterprises. A special purpose vehicle was created and assets were deposited within it, so that the assets became the property of the owners of the vehicle. The assets themselves, formerly owned by the corporation that created the vehicle, were swept off the company's balance sheet although it would normally be required to make up any difference if they should drop in value. In such a manner, federally sponsored agencies were able to buy mortgages from banks and then put them in special vehicles, which were purchased by bondholders. The only remaining obligation of the enterprise was to service the bondholders if something should happen to the mortgages themselves.

When the process worked well, assets could be shifted from one owner to others with only the residual risk remaining with the original owners in case of a default. Many utilities companies used special purpose vehicles to assume debt they wanted to sweep off their balance sheets in the wake of deregulation, partly to make themselves attractive to merger partners. But when practiced surreptitiously, the specially created vehicles could be hiding places for all sorts of financial shenanigans that the asset owners wanted to conceal. In the most egregious examples of chicanery, the assets would be posted to the vehicle and any downstream revenue they were estimated to produce was booked immediately to the parent's income statement, inflating earnings and making the parent appear more profitable than it actually was. The shell vehicles were not the problem; it was the motives of those who created them in the first place.

Special purpose vehicles also created problems for M&A activity. Before a merger, buyers would have to be certain that they were not assuming hidden liabilities by buying a company that created these vehicles, especially if they were offshore and their structures were opaque. Although accounting standards and SEC requirements mandated transparency in financial statements, these vehicles could be used with some stealth to mask the true financial condition of a company, misleading investors and regulators alike.

The 1990s also were the decade of the financial merger. Many of the most notable deals of the decade were among financial service companies, once forbidden from operating under the same roof. Banks, investment banks, and insurance companies began merging in a frenzy to create the next financial powerhouse that would embrace all sorts of financial services under one roof. Furious activity of this sort had not been seen since the pre-Crash days of the 1920s, when National City Bank and others fashioned themselves into financial department stores. In their rush to the altar, many of the modern companies were in direct conflict with the existing banking and securities laws, passed during the Depression, forbidding marriages between them. Their hastily arranged weddings and the justice of the peace who presided are the subject of the next chapter.

NOTES

1. In an interview published in the *New York Times*, March 18, 1933.
2. *Investment Dealers' Digest*, April 26, 1993.
3. Quoted in Richard Phalon, *The Takeover Barons of Wall Street* (New York: Putnam, 1981), p. 130.
4. *Investment Dealers' Digest*, January 8, 1990.
5. Margaret Thatcher, *The Downing Street Years* (New York: HarperCollins, 1993), p. 681.
6. Charles R. Geisst, *Investment Banking in the Financial System* (Englewood Cliffs, NJ: Prentice Hall, 1995), p. 200.
7. *BusinessWeek*, May 6, 1996.
8. Phillip L. Zweig, "The Case Against Mergers," *BusinessWeek*, October 30, 1995.
9. Ibid.
10. *Mergerstat Reports*, December 2002.
11. See for instance Joseph L. Bower, "Not All M&As Are Alike—and That Matters," *Harvard Business Review*, March 2001.

12. David Bunnell, *Making the Cisco Connection* (New York: John Wiley & Sons, 2000), p. 101.
13. AT&T's monopoly began in 1921 when Congress passed the Willis-Graham bill, allowing AT&T to purchase competing exchanges, subject to approval. At the same time, its number of competitors was decreasing after World War I and the company entered the stage of government-sanctioned monopoly that was to last until 1984.
14. *New York Times,* April 3, 1996.
15. *Boston Globe,* April 23, 1996.
16. Mark L. Sirower, *The Synergy Trap* (New York: Free Press, 1997), p. 5.
17. Bruce Wasserstein, *Big Deal: The Battle for Control of America's Leading Corporations* (New York: Warner Books, 1998), p. 343.
18. *Network World,* December 28, 1998.
19. *Fortune,* December 21, 1998.
20. *New York Times,* April 6, 1999.
21. Pickens finally lost control of Mesa Petroleum in a boardroom coup in 1997. The company was merged with a rival and renamed Pioneer Energy Resources.
22. *Financial Times,* July 23, 1996.
23. *Merger & Acquisitions Report,* September 9, 1996.
24. *New York Times,* October 26, 1999.
25. *PR Newswire* release, April 12, 1995.
26. *Washington Post,* October 4, 1995.
27. Kerkorian later filed a suit for $8 billion against DaimlerChrysler, claiming that the merger of equals concept was a ruse by Daimler-Benz to acquire Chrysler and then dismantle it, eroding the value of his holdings. See *Die Welt,* June 21, 2001.
28. *BusinessWeek,* July 20, 1998.
29. *New York Times,* June 24, 2000.
30. Ibid., October 29, 1999.
31. Ibid., December 5, 1999.
32. *Mergerstat Reports,* December 2002.
33. *Financial Executive,* March/April 2002.

CHAPTER 7

OLD BEDFELLOWS

Not since the Age of Morgan have so many people been able to convince so many others that they are not only larger than life, but also have more than one trick up their sleeves.

The Daily Deal, *2001*

During the merger mania of the 1990s, deal makers on Wall Street scored their biggest victory. After thousands of deals that changed the faces of many industries, finally they were able to change the structure of their own industry in the name of efficiency and improved competition. Although they were successful in the process, many questions began to be raised about the efficacy and intent of the changes. Were the deck chairs rearranged simply to charge more fees or would they prove to give a better view of the surroundings?

Deal making in the 1990s included combinations of many institutions in the financial sector. As banking and securities laws were slowly dismantled, mergers between institutions that had not shared the same roof since the early 1930s were sanctioned, showing that the new economy was as much institutional as it was technologically advanced. In the old economy, banks and investment banks were separated in order to protect bank depositors from the vagaries and risk of the securities markets. In the new economy, walls of separation were not needed because proponents claimed efficiency and modern risk management techniques could adequately handle the job.

The lateness of the trend in financial services attested to the importance regulators attributed to the sector. Unlike airlines, public utilities, or oil companies, banks and savings institutions were considered to operate as a sort of public trust. Their purpose was to protect the savings of their depositors, not to assume risk that the depositors themselves would not have taken if left to their own devices. The original banking laws passed during the first year of the New Deal in 1933 recognized the principle and enshrined it in the Banking Act of 1933, universally known as the Glass-Steagall Act. The law proved remarkably resilient for over 50 years before finally being challenged on a wide front by bankers and the Fed itself. By that time the original intent had faded far into the background.

Separating commercial from investment banking in the 1930s was clearly designed to keep the poachers out of the henhouse—or, more specifically, to keep Morgan and his cronies from using other people's money for their own purposes. The divorce lasted for 66 years, but intense lobbying pressure began to reintegrate the two sides in the 1980s and continued relentlessly until the late 1990s. Life insurance was separated from banking by the Holding Company Act and state insurance regulations, dating back to insurance company problems arising before World War I. When the New Deal legislation was passed, the problem of life insurance company ownership was not forgotten and was included in the 1933 legislation. But it was not an act of Congress alone that rolled back Glass-Steagall. The movement also had substantial help from the Federal Reserve, which paved the way for the giant combinations that occurred late in the century despite the fact that the old law was still on the books. By the end of the century, American banking took on the characteristics of European "universal" banking, a goal of many deal makers for some time.[1] As in many other industries, the question naturally arose whether these new behemoth financial companies offered anything special or were just bigger than their predecessors.

Deal makers scored a first in many of these financial mergers by arranging combinations within their own industries. The deals also broke a long series of precedents and changed American business culture in the process. Pressure was brought upon Congress and the Fed to change the laws, considered to be arcane and out of date, especially in light of the new economy. As with all deregulatory legislation, the final barriers were not all abolished in one swoop but were dismantled over time. By the time the Financial Services Modernization Act, or Graham-Leach-Bliley Act, was passed in late 1999, the new financial environment already was a fait accompli. Little argument was offered in defense of the old regime, especially since bankers and the Fed seemed intent on revamping the system despite substantial foot-dragging by Congress.

The regulations surrounding banking and Wall Street were the last vestiges of the New Deal. Not all banking regulation could be traced to the 1930s. Congress had passed a bank holding company law and amendments to it in the 1950s and 1960s, designed to prevent loopholes in the original law from allowing bank holding companies from owning more than one bank. If they were able to do so, they could then effectively circumvent the prohibition against banks branching across state lines, something that had been prohibited since the days of Tiny McFadden. In the early 1970s, the lines of demarcation were clearly in place. Banks could not open new branches across state lines, commercial banks could not merge with investment banks, and life insurance companies were separate from banking in general. Investment banks favored the status quo because it protected them from the larger, better-capitalized commercial banks. For their part, the commercial banks desperately wanted to enter the securities business because of the potential fees involved, especially in corporate securities. The twain would only meet again when Wall Street deal makers entered commercial banking and then brought about a merger of the two sectors with substantial government assistance.

The merger binge that occurred in the financial services sector resulted in a new concentration of financial power not seen since the days of Pierpont Morgan. The Financial Services Modernization Act passed through Congress with relative ease. But the 15 years preceding its official demise illustrated the influence of Wall Street deal makers and the growing belief that New Deal regulations could be discarded in the New Era of the 1980s and 1990s. Part of the argument in favor of its demise was that too many banks existed in the country and that the number could effectively be reduced without doing any harm. But even after the law was passed and some consolidations occurred, there were still thousands of banks remaining. The deal-making frenzy of the 1990s in particular infected financial institutions as well as their customers. Among commercial banks alone, over $310 billion worth of mergers among the larger banks was completed in the 1990s. A broad historical argument was used to argue for change from the New Deal regulations, which found a willing ear in Congress when control switched to the Republicans in the mid-1990s. The arguments made for consolidation within the financial services industry convinced many on both sides of the congressional aisle that history need not be heeded as the new century approached.

As the stock market continued to rise in the mid-1990s, many senior bankers felt that modern risk management techniques and forecasting tools could protect them from catastrophe. And the past would be of little use in a bull market because the popular market philosophy on Wall Street—the efficient markets hypothesis or random walk method—suggested that the past history of securities prices gave no indication of their future movement. As far as Wall Street was concerned, what was true of securities prices was true of market developments. History was of little use except to relate the accounts of robber barons or past scandals as an example of how far the market had developed. Was there not a safety net in place to prevent banking crises from developing? And was it not the Fed's responsibility to preside over a rising market, applying cautionary remarks when appropriate?

The actual history of deregulation of the banks and Wall Street did not actually belie these sorts of comments, but the unraveling of most New Deal regulations was accomplished by a gradual method of dismemberment that nevertheless raised some serious questions. The McFadden Act (1927), the Glass-Steagall Act (1933), the Eccles Act (1935), and the Bank Holding Company Act (1957), were the foundations of the financial system and gave American banking its peculiar flavor. Over the course of the late 1980s and 1990s, two of these acts would be declawed so that the banking system could become more competitive, with foreign banks in particular. In order to achieve this, a new law replacing the McFadden Act would be needed while the Holding Company Act would be used by the Fed to dismantle Glass-Steagall de facto before Congress finally addressed the task in 1999. The increasing power of the Fed during the bull market played a major role in the process because no one appeared willing to challenge the leadership of the central bank while the good times rolled along.

Alan Greenspan was fully behind the modernization act, also known as HR 10. Regarding the de facto dismantling of Glass-Steagall since 1989, he told the Senate Banking Committee that "only the Congress has the ability to fashion rules that are comprehensive and equitable to all participants and that guard the public interest . . . What is most important is that for the first time there is an extraordinary amount of agreement on nearly all of the key principles in the bill. There is no disagreement—and there has been no disagreement for many years—that the Glass-Steagall Act must be repealed."[2] The tenor of the remarks may have been true but it depended upon where the agreement came from. In light of the opposition of local community groups and consumer groups, Greenspan's words could only be taken to mean that there was no serious disagreement over the intention of the bill from those in the financial services industry.

The manner in which these changes occurred was not unprecedented, but since they came about during a period of close regulation of the markets, their de facto erosion was somewhat surprising. When Pierpont Morgan created U.S. Steel, he did so in a time when the Sherman Antitrust Act was still relatively new. The act had not yet been successfully tested and McKinley's administration showed no willingness to constrain big business in the slightest. Still, the creation of the huge company seemed a gamble since Congress could have acted during a period of intensifying trust busting. The Roosevelt administration would not challenge the consolidation until the deal was finished, however, since the government did not yet have the apparatus in place to block a deal before it was done. The same attitude prevailed in the late 1990s. The dismantling of the Glass-Steagall Act, arguably the most effective (and inadvertent) antitrust act ever enacted in the country, was done with the assent of Congress, which obliged by passing the deregulatory legislation of 1999.[3]

Supporting the relaxed attitude were arguments that sudden changes in the banking system were often accompanied by scandal and financial losses in their wake. If sudden change could be avoided, then so too could the usual problems accompanying it. Gradualism would be the best solution to changes. The Depository Institutions Act, passed in 1982, was still remembered. Rescinding one of the basic prohibitions of the Glass-Steagall Act, that law allowed savings institutions to purchase corporate bonds (within certain limits) so that they would have high-yielding assets on their books. The results were disastrous for many, as they purchased junk bonds only to see their values decline sharply in the wake of the stock market decline in October 1987. A more gradual change would have allowed bankers to become more comfortable with purchasing corporate securities rather than be led into believing that junk bonds were the panacea for all of their problems. What were known as "Big Bang" financial events in the financial world had never proved successful, and dismantling over time was viewed as preferable to dismantling in one fell swoop.[4]

When the Glass-Steagall Act was written, separating investment and commercial banking was a tricky proposition. It was achieved with some fairly arcane language that did not forbid the two from joining but did forbid them from jointly profiting. According to Section 20 of the act, a commercial bank could not engage in securities markets activities. "Securities" excluded Treasuries and was confined to corporate bonds and stock, the bread and butter of investment banks' underwriting and trading activities. Banks like J.P. Morgan & Co. and other members of the money trust were put at a disadvantage by being forced to choose one type of banking or the other. The decision had to be made by 1934.

Many of the dual capacity banks chose investment banking, the most lucrative part of their business. As a result, they stepped away from taking deposits and making loans. Morgan, for its part, chose commercial banking and spun off the securities side to the newly created Morgan Stanley & Co., which had mostly partners from the bank as its preferred shareholders. It was, however, a separate company, and did not violate the act. As a result, the modern American investment banking industry was born. The new American banking community was not created from theory but from crisis. Investment bankers were considered too predatory to be allowed access to bank deposits. The spirit of Louis Brandeis and his view of other people's money was alive and well in the 1930s.

The gradual approach was supported by the fact that many top regulators were not clear about the original intent of the Glass-Steagall Act. Banks first began attacking the law in the 1960s, when they wanted the authority to underwrite certain types of municipal bonds, notably revenue bonds that the SEC had maintained since 1933 were none of their business. By the early 1970s, they were pushing the law hard to enter businesses that the investment banks considered their sole preserve. When they did, the investment banks howled that the law was being violated. Ellmore Patterson, chairman of J.P. Morgan (then known as Morgan Guaranty Trust) in 1973, complained about a revival of "an ancient sport known as 'Blame the Banks.' Banks are likely to encounter opposition whenever they show innovative enterprise and initiative." Besides municipal bonds, banks were pushing for entry into other forbidden areas, such as stock exchange membership, investment management, and mutual funds. The lines of demarcation were not that clear once they were put under a microscope. In the early 1970s, Ray Garrett Jr., chairman of the SEC, frankly told the Chicago Bond Club, "I really don't know whether the Glass-Steagall Act was intended to, or in fact does, prohibit banks from offering these particular securities investment programs."[5] By the end of the decade, the confusion still reigned on Wall Street. Representative Henry S. Reuss of Wisconsin, chairman of the House Banking Committee, remarked that as late as 1979, the new Congress would be faced with the revenue bond issue again. "We will also have hearings on whether banks should be allowed to underwrite municipal revenue bonds. Under Glass-Steagall, they cannot."[6] If the experts were not sure about the intent, it was vulnerable to official interpretation.

Fifty years later, the Fed was able to relax the Glass-Steagall restrictions by liberally interpreting the securities activities of banks prohibited by Section 20. Through its authority to oversee bank activities through the Holding Company Act, the Fed relaxed the rule and allowed banks to derive greater and greater percentages of their income from corporate securities underwriting and trading. J.P. Morgan & Co. had been actively lobbying against Glass-Steagall since 1984, when it entered the fray with a publication supporting the act's repeal. At the same time, the bank was planning to change its core commercial banking business to investment banking. The Fed obliged when it began allowing commercial banks to underwrite, on a limited basis, corporate bonds and then stocks, beginning in 1987. A small crack in Glass-Steagall was about to turn into a fissure.

The investment banks did not welcome the intrusion of commercial banks into their preserve and began lobbying against the move. Their protests were only of limited value because the Fed was not their regulator and they did not possess the lobbying power of the commercial banks. Additionally, many of the major money center banks were members of the Fed and their CEOs sat on the boards of directors of the regional Fed banks. As a result, the investment banks were put on the defensive and began losing their independence as they were snapped up by commercial banks with securities aspirations. Those that had once been the agents of change now were becoming prey. In the first stage of the acquisitions cycle, commercial banks acquired only smaller, regional investment houses whose revenues would not violate the relaxed Fed rules when consolidated into their own.

Problems on Wall Street were developing that would leave some of the Street's better-known names vulnerable to consolidation. Salomon Brothers' problems in the Treasury bond market in 1991 left the powerful investment bank with a host of internal troubles that would require large doses of capital to rectify. Its tarnished image did not make it less attractive to a buyer since its reputation in bonds and arbitrage was considerable. But the perception problem, combined with a sharp reputation, suggested that it would eventually need a larger parent that would help reconstruct its image. Before the mid-1990s, the only logical suitors would have been other investment banks. Almost no one could have foreseen Salomon being bought by an insurance company. When it was, the handwriting was on the wall for Glass-Steagall.

Beyond scandal and image problems, the investment banks were facing a crisis that led some to the conclusion that only a merger with a larger, better capitalized partner would allow them to succeed in the future. The size of new underwriting deals was becoming larger all the time, and although many of the investment banks had already gone public in the 1970s and 1980s, many were still short of the capital required by regulators. By the mid-1990s, only Goldman Sachs and Lazard Freres remained as partnerships among the major Wall Street houses. All of the others had gone public, with Merrill Lynch having the most capital and occupying most of the top spots in the league tables by which the Street measured itself. Given the situation, investment banks were on the verge of their own revolution in ownership and the way they did business. When the big banks came courting, many acceded to marriages that 10 years before would have been unacceptable. Recognizing this, Goldman eventually went public in 1999, leaving Lazard with the distinction of being the last partnership. Still acting as an M&A boutique under Bruce Wasserstein, the firm continued on its way as adviser.

Providing encouragement to the commercial banks was the demise of the McFadden Act in 1994. When Congress passed the Interstate Banking Act, the prospect of a truly national bank finally was a reality. Since the Depression, American bankers had pointed to the Canadian banking system, showing that commercial banks that stretched from coast to coast in Canada had survived the Depression and flourished through the years. If the Canadians could do it, so could the Americans, went the logic. How was it possible that the world's strongest economy had a balkanized banking system that reflected 1920s pork barrel politics more than the economic realities of the 1990s? The McFadden Act finally was gone and many banks scrambled to make their coast-to-coast dreams a reality. Ironically, the old act prohibited commercial banks from establishing new branches across state lines. In the 1990s, establishing a new branch was out of the question because of the expense involved in building a new bank from the ground up. Consolidation was the only way to achieve it. Needless to say, the consolidation began before the ink on the new law was dry.

MORE WEDDING BELLS

Mergers in the financial sector in the 1990s were of all types—horizontal, vertical, conglomerate, and many others falling somewhere in between. The Fed began the process with its relaxation of Bank Holding Company Act provisions after 1989, and the new interstate banking law in 1994 added to the trend. In the process, many old venerable names in finance would disappear. Tradition was finally beginning to break down among Wall Street securities houses as demands for greater capital and market flexibility took precedence over prestige and prior market position.

The deregulation of interest rates, beginning in the early 1980s, added fuel to the latest merger trend among financial services companies. The deregulation brought pressure on financial institutions to become more competitive, although the changes were not complete until banks were allowed to merge across state lines and with investment banks. Only then did the potential of the changes become clear. For the first time in decades, banks were able to offer customers across the country a myriad of banking services that had not been available under one roof since the 1920s. Most startling about the trend was the participants. Big commercial banks were always in the vanguard of the movement to expand, but observers were surprised to find that old-line firms like Morgan Stanley, Bankers Trust, and Alex. Brown were also more than willing to join the party, either as brides or grooms.

As the Fed relaxed Section 20 of Glass-Steagall, many large banks began acquiring medium-size securities firms that fell within the guidelines. Some of the oldest names in investment banking were absorbed as a result. Alex. Brown, originally bought by Bankers

Trust, became part of Deutsche Bank when the German bank bought Bankers in 1998. Dillon Read was bought by S.G. Warburg & Co. and Roberston, Stephens was absorbed by Bank of America in 1997. Of the group, Warburg's purchase of Dillon Read was the most important for the M&A trend since both firms were extremely strong as M&A advisers and would record significant merger fees in the late 1990s.

The commercial banks used the Interstate Banking Act as a launching pad to fulfill their ambitions for expansion within their own spheres. Even by the mid-1990s, it was still widely acknowledged that the United States was overbanked; in short, too many banks existed. In the mid-1980s, there were about 14,000 banking companies. Ten years later, the number declined to around 10,000 but still was considered too large. By 1999, it declined to 8,675. That was an average of approximately 173 different banks per state, and the inefficiency implied by the numbers sparked a major banking mergers boom. But the numbers were somewhat misleading when examined by the distribution of assets. In the mid-1990s, the 25 largest banks controlled more than 50 percent of all banking assets. By 1999, the largest controlled 66 percent of the assets.[7] And the numbers were even more concentrated, with the top 10 accounting for over one-third of all assets. The first significant bank merger after 1994 was not destined to provide the first truly nationwide branching system but more closely resembled a classic horizontal merger. In the summer of 1995, two of the largest banking companies agreed to a merger among equals. Chase Manhattan and Chemical Bank announced their intention to create the largest banking company in the country and the fourth-largest in the world. They were based in New York and provided services that were not materially different.

Both banks were traditional large money center banks with a large number of branches in the metropolitan area. But retail was not their forte; both were mainly corporate banks providing a range of services to large business clients. After the merger, a number of duplicate retail branches were shut and other redundant services were eliminated. Ordinarily, a merger admittedly between equals would have raised the scrutiny of regulators, but this merger was allowed without much fanfare. Since both banks were adept at corporate finance advising, investment bankers played less of a role than they might have in a nonbanking merger. Goldman Sachs advised Chase and Morgan Stanley advised Chemical. Chase was also advised by a mergers boutique named after James D. Wolfensohn, the president of the World Bank, who had taken a leave of absence from Wall Street to go to Washington. In Wolfensohn's absence, the firm was headed by Paul Volcker, so the deal was given additional credence. But on both sides, the investment bankers were merely advisors. The deal remained driven from the top by Chase and Chemical officials who knew each other well.

The resulting bank was a behemoth with $297 billion in assets. The merger itself was valued at $10 billion. Part of the deal involved sacking up to 12,000 employees, an acceptable number on the part of the cost-cutters but a major blow to employment, especially in New York City. But the potential benefits caused elation among senior management. "Our size allows us to be a market leader in every business we're in," proclaimed Walter Shipley, the Chemical CEO who chaired the new company.[8] The comment would have drawn the ire of the Antitrust Division a generation earlier, but large banking companies were better poised for international competition, or so went the prevailing argument in banking and regulatory circles. New York City public advocate Mark Green did not necessarily agree. "This merger is certainly good news for shareholders, but for consumers and neighborhoods, it is questionable," he declared after the deal was announced.[9] The new bank would disagree. Some parts of the city had Chase and Chemical bank branches across the street from each other. Little would be lost if some could now be closed. Although consumer advocates often complained about the potential effects on local consumers, they usually lost the battle.

The first attempt at a truly nationwide banking company came in 1998 when the Bank of America agreed to merge with the ever aggressive NationsBank, headquartered in North Carolina. Like Chase and Chemical, Bank of America was considered a venerable bastion of American banking, although it was not as old as its two New York counterparts. Founded by A.P. Giannini in San Francisco in 1904, the bank became one of the largest, originally specializing in retail banking. Its extensive branching operation in California was the source of envy for many retail bankers and the bank had long-established roots in the state. But the original McFadden Act meant that when Bank of America wanted to open offices outside the state it had to open limited subsidiaries or exploit other loopholes to expand on a limited basis.[10] A merger with NationsBank would allow both banks to establish the first coast-to-coast operation ever seen in the country. The opportunity to expand was too great for either to ignore.

The merger immediately made the new banking company the largest in the country. While federal regulators did not raise any objections to the deal, the California Reinvestment Committee, a coalition of community groups, objected to the deal until its effects could be studied. The committee called upon Alan Greenspan to hold hearings on the potential impact on California since NationsBank was located in North Carolina. "The new dominant bank in California will not be headquartered here, does not know California's community needs and, in fact, its record in its own home state of North Carolina raises serious questions as to its meeting California's diverse needs," stated committee director Alan Fisher.[11] The group was interested in the North Carolina bank's poor record of loans made to low-income groups in the South and feared the same policy would be pursued in California. The argument was easily supported by the numbers. The new bank was indeed a giant. Combined revenues would be almost $37 billion, assets totaled $571 billion, and employees numbered 180,000. The combined bank would also have 14,000 automated teller machines, 14 million accounts serving 29 million households, and 2 million business customers in 22 states. With that size came costs to California that consumers groups feared. Hugh McColl of NationsBank would become the new bank's chairman and CEO and would be based in Charlotte, while David Coulter of Bank of America would be president, based in San Francisco. When combined, the estimated cost savings inspired by the deal would be $1.3 billion and required the firing of around 8,000 employees.[12] The threat to California's liberal community investment policies was perceived as very real. "NationsBank is famous for cookie-cutter loans," said Fisher. "Will the new bank reach out to California communities, or only to Ozzie and Harriet?"[13]

The new Bank of America began trimming jobs after the deal was complete, only confirming the fears of the consumer advocates about the negative impact of the mega-deal. By mid-2000, the company announced the cutting of 34,000 jobs within a two-year period after the deal was sealed. The number of employees was still large (150,000), but the bank's president acknowledged, "Our days of growth by merger and acquisition are behind us. For the most part, our merger transition work also is behind us."[14] As with all bank deals, the years following would provide the actual numbers that would confirm whether the deal was as successful as its proponents originally hoped.

With the field clear for mergers, banks also began expanding into previously forbidden territory. A Morgan Stanley banker described the process in familiar but operational terms. "Historically, banks have offered certain services, insurance companies offered different ones, and investment banks still others. But now that the regulatory barriers are down, we're able to see pressures on people in the business to restructure and focus not on products, but on a customer segment."[15] While corporations and middle-class consumers had little to fear, the major worry still was the impact that the mergers would have on low-income groups. As the number of branches declined and banks consolidated, the fees charged for banking services were increasing, according to Mark Green. Earlier bank mergers in New York had already forced up the costs of Chase's monthly checking account fees by $2.00 per month. "This may seem like nickel and dime stuff," Green said, "but it is costing consumers millions of dollars."[16] Clearly, those with less in their accounts eventually paid more for the services than others. But serving lower-income groups had never been an aim of bankers unless they were loaned money through subprime lending units, which could charge much higher rates of interest to their customers for mortgages and personal loans.

ROLL OVER, PIERPONT

The merger boom affected almost every bank and investment bank, but none more than the two successors to the legendary House of Morgan tradition. J.P. Morgan & Co. was still the most influential commercial bank in the country, although it had been switching its business back to investment banking since the Fed's relaxation of Glass-Steagall in 1989. Morgan Stanley was considered by most to be one of the two top investment banks on Wall Street since the 1930s. Could they survive the trend unscathed? More intriguingly, would they reunite to create a new House of Morgan after their long separation?

Traditionalists on Wall Street may have logically concluded that the two would eventually merge, bringing their expertise to bear in investment banking. J.P. Morgan & Co. was especially keen on seeing Glass-Steagall repealed so that the financial sector would be free to consolidate. But it was Morgan Stanley that jumped the gun by agreeing to merge with a large retail brokerage that was once owned by Sears Roebuck. The news did not startle Wall Street since Morgan Stanley had been discussing the matter with Dean Witter for several years, but many thought that the two corporate cultures could never successfully be merged. In early 1997, the two companies surprised many by announcing their intention to join, in what they billed as a merger of equals.

The two firms were not strangers. Dean Witter had been a subsidiary of Sears Roebuck since the giant retailer had bought it in 1981 hoping to gain entry into the world of financial services. Like Merrill Lynch, Paine Webber, and E.F. Hutton, it was predominantly a wire house, selling securities to the retail investing public. Sears hoped to station some of those brokers in its stores so that its customers could purchase securities in addition to traditional Sears products. But the experiment did not work as well as hoped. After 12 unsuccessful years, the firm was spun off from Sears and Morgan Stanley managed its public offering. Dean Witter had a solid, volume retail business but was not a trendsetter in any respect. However, when it became independent again, it took along a valuable asset—the Discover credit card business. The card business earned over $500 million per year on a pretax basis and, when combined with the firm's 9,000 stockbrokers, proved an alluring target to a firm seeking to expand into retail and gain a valuable cash earner.

Morgan Stanley did not seem to be a good fit at first glance because of its heritage and its preeminent position in investment banking services, which distinctly were not retail oriented. If combined, however, the two would be the major presence on Wall Street, eclipsing Merrill Lynch as the top broker in market capitalization. The proposed deal was worth $23 billion in market cap, versus only $14 billion for Merrill at the time. The actual terms of the $10 billion merger called for a stock swap, with Morgan Stanley shareholders receiving 1.65 shares of Dean Witter for each share they held. Dean Witter was the larger of the two companies, and its CEO, Philip Purcell, was named CEO of the combined company, with the top Morgan Stanley executives, John Mack and Richard Fisher, taking the number two and three spots. Wall Street was impressed by the size and breadth of the new company but wary of the difference in the component corporate cultures. "One firm is white shoe and the other is white socks," commented one Wall Streeter. "They may both have the same philosophy but they are very different."[17] The cultural differences between the two would resurface for a few years after the merger, but the firm took great strides to recognize and accommodate them, notably the differences in pay and product emphasis. In order to have a fresh start, Morgan Stanley Dean Witter moved into new headquarters in Times Square.

The motivation for the merger came from the changing face of investors in the 1990s. Retail investors were increasing rapidly during the bull market, and Morgan Stanley had almost no access to them without linking up with a retail-oriented firm. Since the late 1980s, when 401K pension plans had become the rage, the number of investors owning stocks and mutual funds had exploded. In the period 1990 to 1997, the amount of money invested in mutual funds increased 10-fold and the number of investors buying them almost doubled. The number of 401K accounts had increased 15-fold since the mid-1980s and the defined contribution industry as a whole totaled almost $1.5 trillion. Numbers of that sort lured Morgan Stanley into retail and breaking with its own tradition. A year after its merger, Morgan Stanley Dean Witter had a profitable year, showing balanced revenues across the board from its various activities. But there was still a note of apprehension about pronouncing any new securities firm an instant winner. "There is no such thing as insta-firm," remarked Joseph Perella, the head of investment banking at Morgan Stanley since breaking with Bruce Wasserstein. "History shows it takes three generations to build a top business. You cannot buy your way to the top league."[18] But the Morgan Stanley name still proved strong. Several years after the merger, the Dean Witter name was dropped from the company's letterhead.

Morgan Stanley found its match in a retail broker, but J.P. Morgan & Co. would find a merger partner in a commercial bank, ironically the same sort of business it had all but abandoned by the mid-1990s. Its move back to investment banking had been so successful that by the mid-1990s it ranked high on the Wall Street underwriting league tables for bonds and equities. On the surface, its new partner appeared to be a good match, since both were old American banking names with established franchises. But the similarities stopped there. Chase Manhattan was a large amalgam of banking interests that had the advantage of diversity and sought Morgan for its investment banking prowess rather than as an addition to its commercial banking operations.

The Chase bid for Morgan came in the wake of the Travelers-Citibank deal (discussed later) and was seen in the same light. The deal was the first major bank merger after the Financial Services Modernization Act was passed, so it was not under any deadline as the Travelers-Citibank deal had been. Unlike the Chase–Chemical Bank deal a few years before, the merger was not horizontal in nature. The two banks did have certain similarities but their core businesses were different. Chase wanted Morgan in order to make an imprint in investment banking. Morgan needed a wider capital base in order to expand and increasingly was being viewed as a takeover candidate. If a foreign suitor like Deutsche Bank emerged with a bid, it would cause problems in regulatory circles and shatter the bank's distinctly American image. A domestic partner certainly was prefer-able to one from abroad. And hostile bids were not out of the ques-tion: Wells Fargo had made a successful hostile bid for First Interstate in 1995.

In 2000, the deal was announced, creating a full-service bank roughly equal to the Bank of America in terms of assets. Previously, Chase and Morgan were the third- and fifth-largest banks in the country. The new J.P. Morgan Chase Bank had assets of $660 billion, presence in almost two dozen foreign countries, and a substantial retail banking operation, including the Chase branch network and extensive credit card services. The combined operation had over 30 million customers. The deal itself was worth $36 billion, paid for by a stock swap of 3.7 Chase shares for each Morgan share. The deal was quickly approved by the boards of both banks. The Chase name became affiliated with the retail side of the merger, while the Mor-gan name was used for investment banking purposes.

Despite the benefits and drawbacks of the deal, executives closely involved in the merger did very well after the fact. The CEO of the new bank, William Harrison, was paid $17.1 million in salary and bonuses plus another $4.8 million in stock options a year after the deal closed. The payment came as the stock price was falling and remuneration generally on Wall Street was declining because of the slowing economy. The bank also lost $4 billion between 2000 and 2001. The performance was in stark contrast to Harrison's remarks when the deal was completed. He claimed, "It's a very fair deal and most importantly, when we look at the overall transaction two years from now, it should be accretive to the shareholders."[19] And Harrison was not alone. Chairman Sandy Warner received almost $14 million in bonuses in 2000 and three subordinates of Harrison—one of whom had joined the bank only four months earlier—received spe-cial bonuses of $10 million each. Harrison admitted that the deal had taken only around three weeks to complete.

The deal also created the world's sixth-largest investment man-ager. Both banks had extensive money management capabilities, and the fit was widely viewed as the best part of the deal. The two had $576 billion in total assets under management when the deal was completed. Expertise in fund management also attracted customers to the bank's other fiduciary services and was viewed as crucial to its long-term success. But the merger also had its potential pitfalls. As in all financial mergers, the all-stock exchange was used although it would prove thorny because of corporate culture problems between the two banks and Chase's habit of lending money to potential Morgan investment banking clients. The practice of providing short-term loans to eventual securities customers came under closer examination after scandal erupted when Enron, WorldCom, and Tyco announced financial problems in 2001 and 2002. Regulators began to question whether the marriage of both sides of banking was as efficient as they had thought several years before.

TRAILER PARK

Although the limelight in financial service mergers was taken by commercial and investment banks, insurance was also a key part of the industry. Ever since the days when J.P. Morgan's extensive control over the New York insurance industry was headline news, insurance was considered a key variable in any equation that also included banking. Like its better-publicized counterparts, the industry was changing rapidly in the 1990s. It was only a matter of time before one company emerged from the news shadows to embarrass its industry.

Most takeovers and mergers in the financial services industry continued to employ pool accounting until the FAS 141 ruling. By 2001, the results began to manifest themselves and did not inspire confidence. The two largest bankruptcies ever recorded were those of WorldCom and Enron, both serial acquirers. The third largest was that of Conseco, a large Indiana-based insurance company that filed for Chapter 11 in 2002. Similar to WorldCom and Enron, Conseco was another relatively new company that had taken Wall Street by storm in the 1990s. By adding smaller companies to its portfolio, it had become a major insurance company that seemed to exemplify the growth-oriented attitude of the 1990s.

Conseco was founded in 1982 in Carmel, Indiana by Stephen Hilbert, a college dropout and former encyclopedia salesman. Hilbert bought smaller insurance companies, employing familiar accounting techniques and radically cutting costs after the acquisitions. Earnings soared as a result, sometimes exceeding 40 percent per year, and the company became one of the high-flying stocks on the NYSE. The growth-by-acquisitions strategy in the insurance industry certainly had its critics, especially during the late 1980s and early 1990s when the merger boom was taking a breather. When the market was high and the earnings numbers strong, critics of the tactic were rarely heard. Asked about Conseco's acquisitions strategy, Hilbert remarked that "When you're going with the beat of a different drummer, and you've been successful, it's just human nature to say, 'Hey, this is a flash in the pan,' or this can't last.' "[20] He clearly attempted to paint his company's growth as innovative. And he did not react well to criticism from the outside. When Moody's downgraded Conseco debt to B2 (junk status), Hilbert reacted strongly, claiming that the rating agencies did not understand how to rate insurance company debt. It would not be the last time that he would come to loggerheads with Wall Street, but the stock continued to perform well. Hilbert also treated himself well, earning over $119 million in 1997 alone.

Another skirmish with Wall Street in 1994 provided more unwanted publicity and raised some ethical questions that would resonate again within several years. In 1994, Conseco attempted a takeover bid for the much better known Kemper Insurance. Conseco was in the process of raising a large convertible bond issue to help finance the deal through Merrill Lynch when, unexpectedly, a Merrill analyst issued an unfavorable report on the company. As a result, Hilbert immediately fired Merrill as his lead underwriter and instead installed Morgan Stanley to run the deal. Hilbert claimed that Morgan Stanley was better for the deal than Merrill and that the two incidents were unrelated. Merrill lost a potential $1 million in fees in the fiasco, but questions were being raised again about Conseco that the CEO tried to quash. The incident shed some light into the sometimes uneasy relationship between analysts and investment bankers operating under the same roof. Within a few years, that relationship would change on Wall Street as analysts became much more sympathetic with firms with which their firms had, or wanted to establish, an investment banking relationship. It also demonstrated the means that some companies would pursue to keep their images shiny.

Hilbert continued with his plan to acquire other companies and then streamline operations, but in 1998 made a blunder that would cost Conseco its future. The company agreed to purchase another financial services company, Green Tree Financial, in a deal worth $5.8 billion, paid in stock. The price was about seven times book value. Green Tree had been founded in 1975 by Lawrence M. Coss. As its main business was lending to buyers of "manufactured housing," a euphemism for mobile homes, it made most of its money outside urban areas. At the time of the merger, Hilbert called Coss "a legendary figure in the financial services industry. Starting with uncommon vision and $25,000 of capital in 1975, he built one of the true franchises in the consumer finance business."[21] Like Hilbert, Goss was also well paid for his efforts, earning $65 million in 1995, followed by $102 million in 1996. On top of that, the acquisition provided him with another $30 million as a golden parachute if he retired shortly after it was completed, which he did. The reputation and remuneration of the two executives led many on Wall Street to begin viewing Conseco more skeptically than before.

Hilbert suggested that his strategy in the later 1990s ultimately was to be acquired by a larger financial services company due to the relaxed regulatory environment. After the Green Tree deal was complete, Conseco stock plunged 15 percent as Wall Street remained skeptical of the new line of business Conseco had acquired. Added to the company's woes was a $498 million charge it absorbed as a result of prepayments by many of Green Tree's borrowers as interest rates were dropping and they repaid their loans. Others went into default, compounding the situation. Still optimistic, Hilbert told *Institutional Investor*, "I think the insurance industry is going to have a viable role from now on. And I also think that when you take a look at what's going on with Glass-Steagall and HR10 and all those different regulatory changes that you're going to see that banks really come after the insurance industry. The financial services industry is absolutely changing. And I think we're just in round two of a 15-round bout as far as consolidation goes. Over the next five to ten years, you're going to see an awful lot of action."[22] It appeared that the Nickel Plate strategy was being employed again, with banks viewed as the ultimate buyers of insurance companies. Fortunately, Conseco never made it to the altar.

The deal proved to be the unraveling of Conseco. The high price paid for Green Tree plus a slowing economy finally pushed the company into bankruptcy proceedings. Its stock, once trading at almost $60 per share, fell to less than 40 cents. It listed $52.3 billion in assets at the filing and $51.2 billion in liabilities. Adding to the company's woes, its new chief executive, Gary Wendt, hired from GE to turn the company around, abandoned his plans to rescue Conseco and agreed to file for bankruptcy. He was another controversial CEO for the company since he had been paid a $45 million signing bonus when succeeding Hilbert. The previous year, he had forecast a total turn-around for the company, which had lost $3.69 per share in 2000, predicting it would earn $3.30 by 2004. After the filing, few kind remarks could be made about the company and its past indulgences. "It's a history of excess. After Hilbert, Coss, and Wendt got such munificent packages, there was nothing left for shareholders," remarked one news service.[23] Conseco proved that success ultimately relied on the quality of choices made by the acquiring company rather than the acquisition strategy itself. It also proved that Wall Street knew little about less than highly desirable finance companies, preferring to simply look at their financial statements rather than go out and kick the tires of an aggressive but distinctly second-rate company.

GOODBYE, GLASS-STEAGALL

Despite all of the large mergers of the 1990s, one stood out as the deal marking the end of the twentieth century much as the U.S. Steel deal marked its beginning. In many ways, the last big deal was as important as the first because it helped revolutionize an industry and galvanize opinions about its potential efficacy and repercussions. It also marked the high water point for deal makers who, like their early 1900s predecessors, had things mostly their own way in the marketplace.

After two decades of consolidation and takeovers in the banking industry, the final blow for the vestiges of New Deal regulation came with the largest merger of the twentieth century before AOL Time Warner. When the Travelers Insurance Company merged with Citibank, the largest bank in the country, more than one wall of separation fell. Suddenly, life insurance, brokerage, and commercial and investment banking were all being practiced under the same roof, a phenomenon never seen before in American finance.

The creation of the largest financial institution in the country was an example of pure deal making in the classic sense. Without a strong figure willing to propose the merger, the new behemoth institution would never have been created. Growing through merger was the forte of the master deal maker of the 1990s, who owed more to the tradition of Pierpont Morgan than casual observers might have guessed. Even precedent was there. Seventy years earlier, the largest financial institution in the country practicing the 1920s version of supermarket banking was National City Bank, the predecessor of Citibank.

The transaction was engineered by Sanford "Sandy" Weill, the CEO of Travelers Insurance. By background, he was almost the exact opposite of the Morgans. Weill was born in 1933 and lived with his family of modest means in Brooklyn before attending military school and Cornell. After graduating, he embarked on a long and varied Wall Street career. He got his start in 1958 when I.W. "Tubby" Burnham gave him a job at Burnham & Co., a brokerage founded in 1935. The same firm would later give Michael Milken his first job on the Street. Weill started ambitiously and within several years began his own brokerage, leasing space from Burnham. His small firm grew rapidly and he spied his first opportunity to expand in the wake of the backroom crisis that plagued Wall Street in the early 1970s.

In 1970, Hayden Stone, an old retail brokerage 10 times the size of Weill's firm, was on the auction block because of solvency problems. Weill purchased Hayden Stone, adopted its name, and eventually became its CEO three years later. The acquisition began a pattern for Hayden Stone and the ambitious Weill. After the purchase of another firm in 1974, the name was again changed to Shearson Hayden Stone. In 1979, the company became significantly larger by buying the ailing small investment bank Loeb Rhoades & Co., becoming Shearson Loeb Rhoades. After purchasing more than a dozen small and medium-size firms, Weill then sold Shearson to American Express in 1981, staying on at the well-known firm but only as third in line to the chairman.

Despite being named president in 1983, Weill quit American Express in 1985. A year later, he emerged as the CEO of the distinctly second-rate Commercial Credit Corp., a consumer credit company that financially was on its knees. Relegated to obscurity by many on Wall Street, Weill employed a familiar tactic and began a series of mergers using Commercial as his acquisitions vehicle. In 1988, he acquired another financial services company, Primerica, which owned the old-line securities house Smith Barney. He then purchased Shearson back from American Express and also acquired the Travelers insurance company. Finally, he purchased the jewel in his Wall Street crown by acquiring Salomon Brothers in 1997 for a hefty $9 billion on top of his already substantial stable of companies. Smith Barney was an old retail firm that traced its history back to the Civil War period, while Salomon was one of the top institutional houses on Wall Street, especially strong in arbitrage and bonds. Despite the dazzling list of purchases, Weill and Travelers were still not in major danger of bumping into the provisions of Glass-Steagall. Technically, Weill had not yet crossed into the forbidden zone by acquiring a commercial bank.

In the year following the acquisition of Salomon Brothers, Weill was forced to close the firm's previously successful equities arbitrage unit because of huge losses. Ironically, betting on the prospect of a merger was no longer allowed at one of the firms that had made money on some of Weill's own deals in the past. Even as Travelers was absorbing Salomon into its culture, the company was in the early stages of a deal that would leave Wall Street gasping. Unknown to most, Weill was in secret discussions with John Reed, the CEO of

Citibank, about a potential merger that would make the venerable Citibank the target of the largest acquisition to date. Even by Wall Street standards, the idea of an insurance company and an investment bank acquiring one of the largest and best-known commercial banks while the old banking laws were still on the books was audacious, to say the least.

The deal would be proclaimed a merger of equals, but Travelers clearly was the buyer. For its part, Citibank would not have been in a position to make overtures to an insurance company because of existing legal restraints and a conservative management style, but Weill was under no such constraints. He was not bothered by the Holding Company Act and certainly was not as conservative as Citibank senior management. But the legal situation was still sticky. As Weill and Reed worked out the details of the merger, time was of the essence. Would regulators finally sanction the mammoth deal while HR 10 was still on the table but not yet passed? The only possible stumbling block would be the Fed, but the central bank under Alan Greenspan had already shown its willingness to change policy quietly behind the scenes.

The general consensus at the time was that the merger would not put the bank or the financial system at risk. Accordingly, regulators were sophisticated enough not to allow problems to brew at a bank that would undermine its viability. The *New York Times* opined, "In one stroke, Mr. Reed and Mr. Weill will have temporarily demolished the increasingly unnecessary walls built during the Depression to separate commercial banks from investment banks and insurance companies. . . . A collapse in [Citigroup's] securities and insurance operations could drag down the commercial bank. But that will happen only if Federal regulators fall sound asleep."[24] The assumption that the collapse of the walls of separation erected by Glass-Steagall would do no harm was not shared by all banking experts, many of whom argued about what sorts of controls would be left in the wake of the merger. The question turned to the nature of the firewalls between subsidiaries of the bank and whether they were sufficient to prevent a fire from sweeping from one subsidiary to other parts of the holding company, threatening the entire structure.

Opposition to HR 10 arose from several quarters, including the Clinton administration. The administration feared that such a huge bank holding company could easily circumvent the objectives of the Community Reinvestment Act (CRA), which required banks to make loans to their neighborhoods as a way of supporting local economies, especially in the inner cities and minority neighborhoods. The administration clearly was influenced by the consumer groups. "We are concerned that the bill would diminish the effectiveness of the Community Reinvestment Act," claimed one consumer advocate. "Financial conglomerates envisioned under the bill would shift activities to holding company affiliates, where the CRA does not apply." This was one of the first times mergers were actively being attacked on a proconsumer basis. One of the best-known consumer advocates pulled no punches in his critique of the bill in progress. "If Congress stampedes this legislation, as the giants in the financial industry demand they do, the day will come when the corruption or speculative risks facilitated by the bill will materialize into gigantic taxpayer obligations to bail out these debacles," Ralph Nader posited, alluding to the phenomenon in banking known as the "too big to fail" doctrine.[25] When financial institutions became too big and ran into financial problems, they would have to be bailed out by the Fed with considerable public money. Although Nader's comments were taken as rhetorical at the time, several months later the giant Connecticut-based hedge fund Long-Term Capital Management failed and required a substantial support operation by the Fed and a consortium of investment and commercial banks.

Consumer groups could not slow the tide of deregulatory fever, however. Hundreds of community organizations joined forces to plead with members of the House and Senate banking committees to oppose the bill but went unheeded. Then the three other regulators of the banking system also publicly stated that HR 10 was not in the public interest. In a letter to Senators Alphonse D'Amato, a Republican from New York, and Paul Sarbanes, a Democrat from Maryland, Acting Comptroller of the Currency Julie Williams and Director of the Office of Thrift Supervision Ellen Seidman stated that parts of the legislation "would undermine the safety and soundness of the insured institutions regulated by our two agencies," referring mainly to thrift institutions.[26] They also complained that the language of the bill affected their two agencies specifically but did not affect the Fed or the Federal Deposit Insurance Corporation (FDIC). By implication, the complaint suggested that the bill was written for the Fed and the FDIC specifically, leaving them out of the loop.

In the months that followed the Citigroup merger, competing groups continued to do battle over the nature of the modernization bill. Senator Phil Gramm, a Republican from Texas, the primary supporter of the bill, did not see HR 10 as a threat to the CRA. Rather, he considered the bill so important that the administration would be forced to concede and sign it in it original form, acquiescing to the demands of the industry and modernization. In 1998, his sole opposition to the bill, originally containing references to the CRA, killed it in the 1998 Congressional session. But Nader persisted in his objections. "The bills before Congress have been cobbled together from wish lists of the various industry groups," he complained, and "in the process, the rights of consumers have been trampled, or more often, ignored."[27] The battle between various interest groups was shrill. The *Christian Science Monitor* noted in 1998 that "there are many, many cats in this legislative fight and the squeals are loud." The squeals continued for another six months and then began to diminish as the momentum for the bill gained strength in the second half of 1999.

Securities firms as well as banks also actively lobbied for the passage of HR 10. Merrill Lynch took the position that it should be allowed to acquire a bank because if the power was not extended to it as well as banks, then the securities firms might disappear entirely. "Within a few years there will be a handful of players doing financial services and Merrill Lynch wants to be one of them," stated a Merrill official. "Banks can buy us but we can't buy a bank," added another, noting that the arrangement that Travelers and Weill had worked out with the Fed before the Citibank bid would do securities firms harm since they did not have the same access to the Fed as the banks.[28] Regardless of the position, HR 10 proved a bonanza for lobbying firms. In 1998, it was estimated that financial services companies spent over $177 million on lobbying efforts and $100 million on congressional elections in the 1998 campaign, supporting legislators friendly to the bill. It was the largest amount spent by any sector of the economy to support candidates.[29]

The combined institution created by the merger was huge by any standard. The newly created Citigroup had assets in excess of $1.5 trillion, 250,000 employees, and revenues of $84 billion. The deal also helped bring Weill's personal wealth close to the $1 billion mark.[30] But the deal still was at risk. While it conformed to the Fed's interim measures for merging banks with other financial companies, deregulatory legislation was needed if it were to stand. The Fed did its part by approving the merger in October 1998, but the ink was not entirely dry: The Fed approved the deal on the condition that Travelers and Citigroup conform to all the requirements of the Holding Company Act within two years of approval. But that was not the difficult part. The Fed's approval also stated that, "The Board's approval is also subject to the condition that [Citigroup] conform the activities of its companies to the requirements of the Glass-Steagall Act . . ."[31] Only hard lobbying by Citigroup would put the necessary pressure on Congress to repeal the relevant sections of Glass-Steagall. Otherwise, divestiture would be on the horizon within a few years—a prospect unthinkable in M&A terms.

Skeptics were a bit more blunt. Did larger necessarily mean better? Not in all cases. The logistics and economics of the deal escaped many commentators as they focused on personalities and short-term financial results. In a clear reference to the impetus of many deals, *Newsday* put it plainly: "John Reed and Sanford Weill, proud fathers of this deal, may have egos the size of aircraft carriers. But it is hard to imagine they have gone into it on a vanity trip without convincing themselves they can create greater shareholder value and profits."[32] And Citigroup's financial results in the immediate aftermath of the deal were strong, alleviating many of the worries about the size of the deal and its immediate effects. Weill saw the deal as nothing more than another move in the chess game of creating a truly international financial powerhouse. As he stated in the company's 2000 annual report, "Few companies that have led the world in earnings would be described as a work in progress. The fact is, we are."[33] By implication, Weill was not about to abandon his traditional tactics with the formation of Citigroup.

A year later HR 10 passed Congress and it was clear that the Financial Services Modernization Act (the Gramm-Leach-Bliley Act) was ready to be signed. Citigroup then announced the hiring of Robert Rubin, the former treasury secretary in the Clinton administration who had resigned his post in 1999. While in office, Rubin favored the dismantling of Glass-Steagall. Rumblings were heard from consumers groups almost immediately after the announcement. They only became louder when Rubin's first-year compensation, including salary, bonuses and stock options, was reported to be around $45 million. Although he favored HR 10 in principle, Rubin had not endorsed it without reservation at times while it was still on the table. In another move that would have left muckrakers from an earlier era howling, Weill was named to a three-year term on the Board of Directors of the Federal Reserve Bank of New York beginning in 2001. It was natural that the CEO of the country's largest financial institution sit on the board, but it seemed to critics that the gamekeepers and the poachers had all joined the same club.

Consumer groups did not agree with the Clinton administration's idea of progress, especially after the administration signed on to HR 10 and put its weight behind it. Ralph Nader took exception to Robert Rubin's handling of HR 10 while he was still Treasury Secretary. Claiming that Rubin had attempted to work out a compromise between treasury officials and Congressmen working on the bill, Nader charged in a complaint to the government that Rubin had improperly influenced the legislation, especially since he subsequently took a job at Citigroup upon leaving office. The justice department concluded that no criminal investigation was warranted after receiving Nader's original complaint in January 2000. The response did not satisfy him, however. Writing to the treasury, he claimed, "It is impossible to determine what facts were investigated or what witnesses were interviewed, on the basis for the conclusions by either your office or the Department of Justice."[34] But the marketplace was not interested in hearing complaints by consumer groups. The new economy was still moving along at great speed and the idea of one-stop shopping for financial services was one of its greatest institutional developments. Providing corporate and retail customers with a wide range of services from under one roof was considered part of the future. The past had been defeated and criticisms mostly fell on deaf ears.

The demise of Glass-Steagall and the official opening of a new era occurred in the late fall of 1999. As President Clinton signed the new law, he stated, "This legislation is truly historic, we have done right by the American people." Senator Phil Gramm, chairman of the Senate banking committee, added a note of progress by adding that "the world changes, and Congress and the laws have to change with it."[35] Gramm was a staunch supporter of HR 10 (without the references to the CRA) and was one of the authors of the Financial Services Modernization Act that eventually passed. Like Rubin, he benefited from the new legislation when he was offered a job with the investment banking unit of UBS Warburg as its vice chairman in 2002. The bank, which specialized in M&A, was an amalgam of the Union Bank of Switzerland and S.G. Warburg & Co., which earlier had merged with Dillon Read. The job was seen by many as payback because it was the Gramm-Leach-Bliley Act that had allowed UBS to buy securities house Paine Webber for $12 billion in 2000 in a smaller yet significant product of the new deregulated environment.

Gramm later joked about his new job, commenting that he would have to take the appropriate securities licensing tests along with "a group of 30-year-olds" before he could settle down to work. Critics were not in so jovial a mood, however. A writer at the ever watchful *San Francisco Chronicle* commented that the paper was "glad to see Wall Street is serious about cleaning up its act . . . the man holds a doctorate in economics from the University of Georgia, awarded during the Harding administration, I believe."[36] It seemed that memories of the Teapot Dome scandal, like the Glass-Steagall Act, died hard.

THE RESULTS

Mergers in the financial sector were applauded in the 1990s as signs of modernization in the financial system. American banks would now be more efficient, offer a better range of products to customers, and be free from takeovers by foreign institutions. The apparent success of Citigroup in the first few years after its merger gave heart to advocates of deregulation. Dismantling the Glass-Steagall Act was worth the effort and proved correct, according to those who had pushed hard for its effective repeal.

The record comparing commercial banks before and after 1999 did not prove the argument, however. Most indicators that banks used to measure their success remained the same and their operating results actually declined between 1996 and 2001.[37] If they were successfully offering expanded services to customers at lower rates, the economies of scale argument employed at the time did not seem to be panning out. Many bankers argued that the drop in the stock market indices and a slowing economy made performance more difficult and that without the mergers their results would have been substantially better. But the fact remained that over $310 billion had been spent on mergers between the larger banks during the 1990s and that better results had not been achieved. Only shareholders of the target banks and executives involved in the deals appeared to have benefited.

Consolidation in the securities industry produced similar results. When the underwriting, merger, and trading boom of the decade was strong, the securities houses produced record profits. By 2001, underwriting of new issues of stocks and bonds was almost 20 times the figure recorded in 1985 and trading on the exchanges and NASDAQ increased 12-fold. The activity, gaining momentum throughout the 1990s, prompted commercial banks and other finance companies to purchase securities firms. While smaller in size, many of the deals were notable since they involved very well-known securities industry names. The top 21 deals of the decade cost the buyers $122 billion. While well below the amount spent on bank mergers, it still represented a premium over many of the securities firms' values

308

at the time since many had much less capital than banks. When the market declined significantly in 2000, many of the deals proved less than successful and had a serious impact on the newly constructed banking companies' bottom lines, a problem caused by the demise of the Glass-Steagall Act.

The phenomenal explosion of mergers recorded in the closing years of the century proved again that the boom relied to a heavy extent on the boom in retail trading. Without the small investor, the 1990s version of the merger boom would not have succeeded as it did. Since the days when Pierpont Morgan relied on small investors to partially help fuel his deals beginning with U.S. Steel, corporate America has been restructured time and again, with investors giving their tacit approval by speculating in stocks that have been the targets of the buyer's eye. Sometimes they voted for the tactics of the acquiring company or simply were beguiled by the Nickel Plate strategy.

DEATH OF SYNERGY?

When Pierpont Morgan originally brought U.S. Steel to market, the extra $700 million he exacted from investors was classified by his detractors as pure "water." A century later it would have been called a premium. In order to achieve synergy from the deal, future earnings of the company would have had to compensate for the premium. Despite its large market share and dominant position in the industry, U.S. Steel did not perform well enough to cover the premium. Synergy was not an issue for the original deal of the century. The term *water* still applied, much as it had when Daniel Drew used to feed water to his cows to give them bloat, the illusion of weight in M&A terms.

Times changed and deals got bigger and more sophisticated, but the original terms still have relevance. Unfortunately, many deals at the end of the century were in the same position. The emergence of FAS 141 means that many of them probably will not be able to produce synergies because of the goodwill that looms over future earnings. But the emergence of a new, tougher accounting standard does not obscure the fact that many deals were done for their own sake—they produced wonderful results for the target company shareholders and executives involved as well as the investment bankers. Shareholders in the new companies created by mergers were less than thrilled by many of the subsequent results, however. The historical record of the deals discussed here supports the conclusion that "most major acquisitions are predictably dead on arrival—no matter how well they are managed after the deal is done."[38] Even a kinder interpretation suggests that synergy will be more difficult to achieve, especially in an economic slowdown, since the downstream revenues needed to offset the charges for goodwill are subject to fluctuation.

That the twentieth century ended on a note similar to the one on which it began is ironic, especially in light of the securities and banking laws passed to regulate the financial system. Throughout its history, mergers and acquisitions have been the major game played on Wall Street—the grand chess game that dominates all others. The by-products have had far-reaching effects, more than most commentators or financiers are publicly willing to admit. Industries have been built, dismantled, and reorganized by nonelected executives driven mostly by the profits extracted by deals more than by their long-term effects. On the balance, most of the large mergers of the century were nothing more than a way of allowing shareholders and executives to cash out their existing holdings at a profit while often containing costs at the same time by downsizing operations, firing staff, and cutting services.

NOTES

1. Universal banking meant that one financial institution was able to provide all of the traditional banking functions, ranging from commercial and investment banking to life insurance, under one roof. In American terms, this means under the protection of a holding company.
2. "Statement to the Senate Committee on Banking, Housing, and Urban Affairs," June 17, 1998. Reprinted in the *Federal Reserve Bulletin*, August 1998.
3. The Glass-Steagall Act was pure banking legislation, but its effect was to prevent the expansion of banks. For that reason it is referred to here as de facto antitrust legislation.
4. The deregulation of London's financial markets in 1985, referred to as

the "Big Bang," was also known to be relatively unsuccessful since it deregulated the U.K. financial markets immediately and many institutions were unprepared for the new environment that was created as a result.

5. *New York Times,* November 18, 1973.
6. Ibid., February 8, 1979.
7. *FDIC Quarterly Banking Profile,* 2nd Quarter 1999.
8. *Investment Dealers' Digest,* September 25, 1995.
9. *New York Times,* April 29, 1995.
10. Constricted by the McFadden Act, some banks used the Edge Act of 1919 to expand their influence across state lines by opening an "Edge Act subsidiary" in another state. The subsidiary had to be devoted solely to international business.
11. *Business Wire,* April 30, 1998.
12. Estimates of the California Reinvestment Committee, April 1998.
13. *PR Newswire,* November 30, 1998.
14. *New York Times,* July 29, 2000.
15. *Investment Dealers' Digest,* July 7, 1997.
16. *New York Times,* August 29, 1995.
17. *Washington Post,* February 6, 1997.
18. *Financial Times,* January 29, 1999.
19. *New York Times,* April 7, 2002.
20. Interview in the *Indianapolis Business Journal,* November 5, 1990.
21. *National Mortgage News,* November 16, 1998.
22. *Institutional Investor,* September 1998.
23. *San Diego Tribune,* December 19, 2002.
24. *New York Times,* April 8, 1998.
25. *American Banker,* June 25, 1998.
26. *Journal of Commerce,* September 1998.
27. Associated Press, March 3, 1999.
28. *Washington Post,* October 16, 1998.
29. *Multinational Monitor,* November 1998.
30. Amey Stone and Mike Brewster, *King of Capital* (New York: John Wiley & Sons, 2002), p. 230.
31. Federal Reserve Press Release, September 23, 1998.
32. Robert Reno, "Will We Want to Buy at Citigroup?" *Newsday,* April 12, 1998.
33. Stone, p. 13.
34. *American Banker,* December 28, 2000.
35. *New York Times,* November 12, 1999.

36. Alan T. Saracevic, "So Much for Wall Street Cleaning up Its Act," *San Francisco Chronicle*, October 13, 2002.
37. According to the FDIC, in the period from 1996 to 2001, bank ratios for return on assets, return on equity, and core capital remained about the same while net interest margins, net operating income, problem assets, and asset growth rates actually declined. See *FDIC Quarterly Banking Profile*, 3rd Quarter 2001.
38. Mark L. Sirower, *The Synergy Trap* (New York: The Free Press, 1997), p. 5.

BIBLIOGRAPHY

Anders, George. *Merchants of Debt: KKR and the Mortgaging of American Business.* New York: Basic Books, 1992.

Araskog, Rand V. *The ITT Wars.* New York: Henry Holt & Co., 1989.

Ashby, Leroy. *The Spearless Leader: Senator Borah and the Progressive Movement in the 1920s.* Chicago: University of Illinois Press, 1972.

Auerbach, Joseph and Samuel L. Hayes III. *Investment Banking and Diligence: What Price Deregulation?* Boston: Harvard Business School Press, 1986.

Baker, George P. and George David Smith. *The New Financial Capitalists: Kohlberg Kravis Roberts & the Creation of Corporate Value.* New York: Cambridge University Press, 1998.

Baldwin, Neil. *Henry Ford & the Jews: The Mass Production of Hate.* New York: Public Affairs, 2001.

Baskin, Jonathan B. and Paul J. Miranti. *A History of Corporate Finance.* New York: Cambridge University Press, 1997.

Benston, George. *Conglomerate Mergers.* Washington, DC: American Enterprise Institute, 1980.

———. *The Separation of Commercial and Investment Banking.* New York: Oxford University Press, 1990.

Berglund, Abraham. *The United States Steel Corporation.* New York: Columbia University Press, 1907.

Boesky, Ivan. *Merger Mania.* New York: Holt, Rinehart & Winston, 1985.

313

BIBLIOGRAPHY

Bower, Joseph L. "Not All M&As are Alike—and That Matters." *Harvard Business Review,* March 2001.

Brief, Richard P. (ed.) *Corporate Financial Reporting and Analysis in the Early 1900s.* New York: Garland Publishing, 1986.

Brooks, John. *The Go-Go Years.* New York: Weybright & Talley, 1973.

———. *The Takeover Game.* New York: E.P. Dutton, 1987.

Brown, Stanley H. *Ling: The Rise, Fall, and Return of a Texas Titan.* New York: Atheneum, 1972.

Bruck, Connie. *The Predators' Ball: The Inside Story of Drexel Burnham and the Rise of the Junk Bond Raiders.* New York: Penguin Books, 1989.

Bunnell, David. *Making the Cisco Connection.* New York: John Wiley & Sons, 2000.

Carosso, Vincent. *Investment Banking in America: A History.* Cambridge, MA: Harvard University Press, 1970.

———. *More Than a Century of Investment Banking: The Kidder Peabody & Co. Story.* New York: McGraw-Hill, 1979.

Celler, Emanuel. *You Never Leave Brooklyn: The Autobiography of Emanuel Celler.* New York: John Day Co., 1953.

Chandler, Lester D. Jr. *The Visible Hand: The Managerial Revolution in American Business.* Cambridge, MA: Harvard University Press, 1977.

Chernow, Ron. *The House of Morgan: An American Banking Dynasty & the Rise of Modern Finance.* New York: Random House, 1990.

———. *Titan: The Life of John D. Rockefeller, Sr.* New York: Random House, 1998.

Coffee, John C., Louis Lowenstein, and Susan Rose-Ackerman. *Knights, Raiders, and Targets: The Impact of the Hostile Takeover.* New York: Oxford University Press, 1988.

Cowing, Cedric B. *Populists, Plungers, and Progressives: A Social History of Stock and Commodity Speculation 1890–1936.* Princeton, NJ: Princeton University Press, 1965.

DeBorchgrave, Alexandra Villard and John Cullen. *Villard: The Life & Times of an American Titan.* New York: Doubleday, 2001.

Endlich, Lisa. *Goldman Sachs: The Culture of Success.* New York: Random House, 1999.

Faludi, Susan C. "The Reckoning: Safeway LBO Yields Vast Profits but Exacts a Heavy Human Toll—The '80s-Style Buy-Out Left Some Employees Jobless, Stress-Ridden, Distraught—Owner KKR Hails Efficiency." *Wall Street Journal,* May 16, 1990.

Foster, W.T. and Catchings, Waddill. *Business Without a Buyer.* Boston: Houghton Mifflin, 1927.

Geisst, Charles R. *Investment Banking in the Financial System*. Englewood Cliffs, NJ: Prentice Hall, 1995.

———. *Wall Street: A History*. New York: Oxford University Press, 1997.

———. *Monopolies in America: Empire Builders & Their Enemies from Jay Gould to Bill Gates*. New York: Oxford University Press, 2000.

———. *The Last Partnerships: Inside the Great Wall Street Money Dynasties*. New York: McGraw-Hill, 2001.

Gleisser, Marcus. *The World of Cyrus Eaton*. New York: A.S. Barnes, 1965.

Harris, Leon. *Merchant Princes*. New York: Berkley Books, 1980.

Hart, Robert A. *The Great White Fleet: Its Voyage Around the World 1907–1909*. Boston: Little, Brown, 1965.

Hendrickson, Robert. *The Grand Emporiums: An Illustrated History of America's Great Department Stores*. New York: Stein & Day, 1979.

Henriques, Diana B. *The White Sharks of Wall Street: Thomas Mellon Evans & the Original Corporate Raiders*. New York: Scribners, 2000.

Ickes, Harold. *The Inside Struggle 1936–39*. New York: Simon & Schuster, 1953.

James, Marquis and Bessie Rowland James, *Biography of a Bank: The Story of the Bank of America*. New York: Harper & Row, 1954.

Johnston, Moira. *Takeover: The New Wall Street Warriors*. New York: Arbor House, 1986.

Kennedy, David M. *Freedom From Fear: The American People in Depression & War, 1929–1945*. New York: Oxford University Press, 1999.

Kolko, Gabriel. *The Triumph of Conservatism*. New York: Free Press, 1963.

Lacey, Robert. *Ford: The Men and the Machine*. Boston: Little, Brown, 1986.

Lundberg, Ferdinand. *America's 60 Families*. New York: Citadel Press, 1937.

Mackay, Charles. *Extraordinary Popular Delusions & the Madness of Crowds*. London, 1841. Reprint, New York: Three Rivers Press, 1980.

Madrick, Jeff. *Taking America*. New York: Bantam, 1987.

Madsen, Axel. *The Deal Maker: How William C. Durant Made General Motors*. New York: John Wiley & Sons, 1999.

Mahoney, Tom and Leonard Sloane. *The Great Merchants*. New York: Harper & Row, 1966.

Malkiel, Burton G. *A Random Walk Down Wall Street*. New York: W.W. Norton, 1996.

Markowitz, Harry. "Portfolio Selection." *Journal of Finance*, March 1952, pp. 77–91.

Marsh, Barbara. *A Corporate Tragedy: The Agony of International Harvester Company*. Garden City, NY: Doubleday, 1985.

Mason, Alpheus T. *Brandeis: A Free Man's Life*. New York: Viking Press, 1946.

McCraw, Thomas K. *Prophets of Regulation*. Cambridge, MA: Harvard University Press, 1984.

McDonald, Forrest. *Insull*. Chicago: University of Chicago Press, 1962.

McFadden, Louis T. *Collective Speeches of Congressman Louis T. McFadden*. Hawthorne, CA: Omni Publications, 1970.

Millis, Walter. *The Road to War: America 1914–1917*. Boston: Houghton Mifflin, 1935.

Modigliani, Franco and Merton H. Miller, "The Cost of Capital, Corporation Finance, and the Theory of Investment," *American Economic Review* (June 1958), pp. 261–297.

Myers, Gustavus. *History of the Great American Fortunes*. 3 volumes. Chicago: Charles H. Kerr & Co., 1911.

Nader, Ralph and William Taylor. *The Big Boys: Position and Power in American Business*. New York: Pantheon, 1986.

Norris, George W. *Fighting Liberal: The Autobiography of George W. Norris*. New York: Macmillan, 1945.

O'Connor, Harvey. *Mellon's Millions: The Biography of a Fortune*. New York: John Day, 1933.

Patman, Wright. *Complete Guide to the Robinson-Patman Act*. Englewood Cliffs, NJ: Prentice Hall, 1938.

Perez, Robert C. and Edward F. Willett. *Clarence Dillon: Wall Street Enigma*. Lanham, MD: Madison Books, 1995.

Phalon, Richard. *The Takeover Barons of Wall Street*. New York: G.P. Putnam's Sons, 1981.

Porter, Michael. "From Competitive Advantage to Corporate Strategy." *Harvard Business Review*, May-June 1987.

Pickens, T. Boone Jr. *Boone*. Boston: Houghton Mifflin, 1987.

Ramsay, M.L. *Pyramids of Power: The Story of Roosevelt, Insull and the Utility Wars*. Indianapolis: Bobbs-Merrill, 1937.

Rappaport, Armin. *The Navy League of the United States*. Detroit: Wayne State University Press, 1962.

Reich, Cary. *Financier: The Life of Andre Meyer*. New York: William Morrow, 1983.

Ripley, William Z. *Main Street & Wall Street*. Boston: Little, Brown, 1927.

Rochester, Anna. *Rulers of America: A Study in Finance Capital*. New York: International Publishers, 1936.

Rossi, Jim. "The Common Law 'Duty to Serve' and Protection of Consumers in an Age of Competitive Retail Public Utility Restructuring." *Vanderbilt Law Review*, October 1998.

Sampson, Anthony. *The Sovereign State of ITT*. New York: Stein & Day, 1973.

Seligman, Joel. *The Transformation of Wall Street: A History of the Securities and Exchange Commission and Modern Corporate Finance.* Boston: Houghton Mifflin, 1982.

Seltzer, Lawrence H. *A Financial History of the American Automobile Industry.* Boston: Houghton Mifflin, 1928.

Sirower, Mark L. *The Synergy Trap.* New York: Free Press, 1997.

Slater, Robert. *The New GE.* New York: McGraw-Hill, 1993.

Smith, Roy C. *The Money Wars: The Rise & Fall of the Great Buyout Boom of the 1980s.* New York: Dutton, 1990.

Sobel, Robert. *NYSE: A History of the New York Stock Exchange, 1935–1975.* New York: Weybright & Talley, 1975.

———. *The Rise and Fall of the Conglomerate Kings.* New York: Stein & Day, 1984.

Sparling, Earl. *Mystery Men of Wall Street: The Powers Behind the Market.* New York: Blue Ribbon, 1930.

Stevens, William S. (ed.) *Industrial Combinations & Trusts.* New York: Macmillan, 1913.

Stone, Amey and Mike Brewster. *King of Capital: Sandy Weill and the Making of Citigroup.* New York: John Wiley & Sons, 2002.

Strouse, Jean. *Morgan: American Financier.* New York: Random House, 1999.

Thatcher, Margaret. *The Downing Street Years.* New York: HarperCollins, 1993.

Tucker, Ray and Frederick R. Barkley. *Sons of the Wild Jackass.* Boston: L.C. Page, 1932.

United States Department of Commerce. *Historical Statistics of the United States: Colonial Times to 1957.* Washington, DC: U.S. Government Printing Office, 1957.

United States Senate. "Stock Exchange Practices: Report of the Committee on Banking and Currency, pursuant to S. Res. 84 and S. Res. 56 & S. res. 97." June 16, 1934.

Urofsky, Melvin I. *Big Steel & the Wilson Administration.* Columbus, OH: Ohio State University Press, 1969.

Vlasic, Bill and Bradley A. Stertz. *Taken for a Ride: How DaimlerChrysler Drove Off with Chrysler.* New York: William Morrow, 2000.

Warren, Kenneth. *Big Steel: The First Century of the United States Steel Corporation, 1901–2001.* Pittsburgh: University of Pittsburgh Press, 2001.

Wasserstein, Bruce. *Big Deal: The Battle for Control of America's Leading Corporations.* New York: Warner Books, 1998.

Wechsberg, Joseph. *The Merchant Bankers.* New York: Simon & Schuster, 1966.

Weisberger, Bernard A. *The Dream Maker: William C. Durant, Founder of General Motors.* Boston: Little, Brown, 1979.

BIBLIOGRAPHY

Wheeler, George. *Pierpont Morgan & Friends: The Anatomy of a Myth.* Englewood Cliffs, NJ: Prentice Hall, 1973.

White, Lawrence. *The S and L Debacle.* New York: Oxford University Press, 1991.

Wigmore, Barrie A. *Securities Markets in the 1980s: The New Regime, 1979–1984.* New York: Oxford University Press, 1997.

Zweig, Phillip L. "The Case Against Mergers." *Business Week,* October 30, 1995.

INDEX

INDEX

INDEX

INDEX

INDEX

326